Welsh Periodicals in English

Editors:
Meic Stephens
Jane Aaron
M. Wynn Thomas

Honorary Series Editor:
R. Brinley Jones

Other titles in the Writers of Wales series:
Ruth Bidgood (2012), Matthew Jarvis
Dorothy Edwards (2011), Claire Flay
Kate Roberts (2011), Katie Gramich
Geoffrey of Monmouth (2010), Karen Jankulak
Herbert Williams (2010), Phil Carradice
Rhys Davies (2009), Huw Osborne
R. S. Thomas (2006), Tony Brown
Ben Bowen (2003), T. Robin Chapman
James Kitchener Davies (2002), M. Wynn Thomas

Writers of Wales

Welsh Periodicals in English 1882–2012

Malcolm Ballin

University of Wales Press

Cardiff 2013

© Malcolm Ballin, 2013

All rights reserved. No part of this book may be reproduced in any material form (including photocopying or storing it in any medium by electronic means and whether or not transiently or incidentally to some other use of this publication) without the written permission of the copyright owner except in accordance with the provisions of the Copyright, Designs and Patents Act 1988. Applications for the copyright owner's written permission to reproduce any part of this publication should be addressed to the University of Wales Press, 10 Columbus Walk, Brigantine Place, Cardiff CF10 4UP.

www.uwp.co.uk

British Library Cataloguing-in-Publication Data
A catalogue record for this book is available from the British Library.

ISBN 978-0-7083-2614-5
e-ISBN 978-0-7083-2615-2

The right of Malcolm Ballin to be identified as author of this work has been asserted by him in accordance with sections 77, 78 and 79 of the Copyright, Designs and Patents Act 1988.

The publisher acknowledges the financial support of the Welsh Books Council.

Printed by CPI Antony Rowe, Chippenham, Wiltshire.

This book is dedicated to all the editors of and contributors to Welsh periodicals in English, past, present and future

Contents

List of Illustrations	ix
Acknowledgements and Permissions	xv
Introduction: 'The New Old; Old New'	1
1 The Liberal Miscellanies: 1882–1914	10
2 The Independent Periodicals: 1914–1969	59
3 The Late Twentieth Century: 1969–2012	106
4 Conclusion	174
Notes	184
Bibliography	196
Index	201

List of Illustrations

Wales: ed. Owen M. Edwards, first issue, May 1894	34
The Welsh Outlook: ed. Thomas Jones, first issue, January 1914	65
Wales: ed. Keidrych Rhys, first issue, Summer 1937	76
Poetry Wales: ed. Meic Stephens, first issue, Spring 1965	114
Mabon: ed. Gwyn Thomas and Alun R. Jones, issue 2	134
Planet 1: ed. Ned Thomas, first issue, August 1970	136

Colour illustrations

Wales: *The National Magazine for the Welsh People*,
    ed. J. Hugh Edwards, first issue, May 1911
Wales: ed. Keidrych Rhys, first issue, October 1959
Second Aeon: ed. Peter Finch, issue 14, 1972
The New Welsh Review: ed. Belinda Humfrey,
    second issue, Autumn 1988
Dock Leaves: ed. Raymond Garlick, first issue, Xmas 1949
The Anglo-Welsh Review (incorporating *Dock Leaves*):
    first issue, Spring 1958

Acknowledgements and Permissions

I have acknowledged in the endnotes the help I have received from a great many people in the production of this study. I list below all those who have given formal permission for work to be quoted.

I wish further to record my special thanks to Meic Stephens, whose original idea this was, and to Sarah Lewis, my commissioning editor at the University of Wales Press for their patience and valuable suggestions. Meic Stephens regularly commented on earlier drafts and generously made available personal papers and copies of periodicals. I thank the Chief Executive, The Arts Council of Wales for permission to quote from Council papers. I also thank all those who gave their time to discuss the project with me at various times, including: Cary Archard, Tony Bianchi, Kirsti Bohata, Tony Brown, Gwen Davies, Jasmine Donahaye, Peter Finch, Peter Foss; Katie Gramich, Kathryn Gray; Belinda Humfrey; Matthew Jarvis, Robert Minhinnick, Tomos Owen, Roseanne Reeves, Francesca Rhydderch; Eva Rhys, Zoë Skoulding, Lucy Thomas, Emily Trahair; Alyce von Rothkirch. All errors surviving, despite this help, remain my own.

Every effort has been made to seek permission for quotations from original work. I acknowledge positive responses from or on behalf of the following editors of periodicals:

> From *Wales* [1937–59]: Eva Rhys on behalf of Keidrych Rhys.
>
> From *Dock Leaves* and *The Anglo-Welsh Review*: Iestyn and Angharad Garlick on behalf of Raymond Garlick.
>
> From *The Anglo-Welsh Review*: Glyn Mathias on behalf of Roland Mathias.

Acknowledgements and Permissions

From *Poetry Wales*: Meic Stephens; Sam Adams; John Powell Ward; Cary Archard; Mike Jenkins; Richard Poole; Paul Henry; Robert Minhinnick; Zoë Skoulding.

From *Planet*: Jasmine Donahaye, after consultation with all living editors.

From *New Welsh Review*: Gwen Davies on behalf of living editors; Roseanne Reeves on behalf of Robin Reeves.

I also acknowledge permissions from the following contributors in respect of original work:

From *Wales* (1937–59): Literature Wales on behalf of Glyn Jones; Carcanet on behalf of Hugh MacDiarmid; Gwyn Morris on behalf of Idris Davies; Eva Rhys on behalf of Keidrych Rhys; Gwen Watkins on behalf of Vernon Watkins; Helen Richards on behalf of Alun Richards.

From *Life and Letters To-Day*: Gwydion Thomas on behalf of R. S. Thomas (*Stones of the Field* 1946: copyright: Kajuna Thomas 2001).

From *The Welsh Review*: Gwyn Morris on behalf of Idris Davies.

From *Dock Leaves*: Bobi Jones.

From *Poetry Wales*: Alison Bielski; Peter Gruffydd; Meic Stephens; Christopher Mills.

From *Planet:* Iestyn and Angharad Garlick on behalf of Raymond Garlick; Brian Davies.

From *The New Welsh Review*: Duncan Bush; Gareth Calway.

Introduction: 'The New Old; Old New'

Tensions between older ideas of Wales and newer conceptions of the nation, together with contradictions between overlapping traditions of Welshness, Britishness and Englishness, frequently surface in the history of Welsh periodicals written in English. The calls of older traditions compete with the seductions of innovation. Such pressures demonstrate that play of cultural forces which Raymond Williams saw as operating between 'residual' elements that, while belonging to the past, are still active, and those 'emergent' meanings which are in the process of being created.[1]

A sense of stirring unease can be creative and challenging; it survives into the present of literary journalism in Wales. For example, in the closing paragraph of her editorial, 'Redux', for Summer 2010, Kathryn Gray puzzles (while considering the nature of the significantly titled *New Welsh Review*) over the teasing relations between the new, the old, the recycled and the recovered:

> As it happens, the new is very often the New Old. Admittedly, the New Old is a hard sell . . . That said, new plays a very big part in my thinking . . . But what puts the new in *New Welsh Review* is, I believe, a strong commitment to the preoccupations of our writers now, above all. A belief that where the writers lead – or wherever they choose to return – a readership and a criticism will follow or, in the process, even, be created. Hybridity, slant approach, collage . . . Freedom of direction, and openness. Return. It's not *exactly* new, that's true. It's the New Old. Old New. You'll find it here. (4–5)

This deliberation about tradition and the challenges to it is often found throughout the story of Welsh periodicals written in English. The continual interplay almost constitutes a separate kind of tradition. Editors worry about whether a new paradigm may be emerging and consider whether their readers are indeed, as Kathryn Gray hopes, 'following' or 'returning' wherever the journal's writers are leading. The intimate public sphere which they are addressing – the Anglophone intelligentsia within Wales and aspirants to membership of it – harbours long-held conditioned responses and needs to be gently and persuasively coaxed into absorbing new approaches. M. Wynn Thomas records a structural opposition between 'the rural and nonconformist' world of the Welsh-speaker, based in tradition ('The Old' or the 'residual') and the 'new industrial south Wales where the hegemonic power of English was very apparent' ('The New' or the 'emergent'). He observes that the beginnings of Welsh writing in English were marked by conflict and rivalry, and argues that there is a need to develop 'new subtle ways' to explore the relations between the resulting 'liminal or boundary states'.[2] The concept of interlocking 'counter public spheres' may illuminate these areas of contention.

The earliest Welsh periodicals in English experienced similar dilemmas when they needed to negotiate stresses with the traditions created by the more prolific and longer-established Welsh-language periodicals. Gwyn A Williams traces the history of periodicals in Welsh back to *Y Cylchgrawn Cymraeg*, published in Pontypool by Morgan John Rhys, a Baptist Minister, in 1793.[3] But by 1850, 'dozens of Welsh periodicals had appeared and the language had become the medium of a wealth of cultural activities.' Moreover the circulation of some of these journals was measured in 'tens of thousands'.[4] Within these Welsh-language periodicals the bibliographer Huw Walters discerns at least two competing strands, 'one rooted in the Welsh societies of London and the other in the Methodist and Nonconformist movements in Wales itself'.[5] Denominational magazines like *Y Drysorfa* (The Treasury), founded in 1830, became 'legion', according to Walters, as religious revivals swept the nation. Early London-based Welsh magazines included antiquarian and literary productions like the *Cambrian Register* (1795–1818). An example of the way influences were imported from outside Wales into the secular periodicals would be the 1845 Denbigh-based *Y Traethodydd* (The Essayist), edited by Lewis Edwards. Edwards was a pupil of 'Christopher North', the pseudonym of John Wilson, an influential contributor to *Blackwood's Magazine*. Lewis Edwards modelled *Y Traethodydd* on *Blackwood's* and in doing so extended the traditional religious content of Welsh-language periodicals to include philosophy, education and history.[6] Early English-language periodicals based in Wales, such as *The Cambrian Visitor* (Swansea 1813), aimed 'to educate the English with regard to the history and people of Wales'.[7] Such Anglophone Welsh productions were often directed primarily towards readers in England. It was not until the production of *The Red Dragon*, edited by Charles Wilkins in 1882, that an English-language periodical was specifically directed towards 'a cultured Welsh audience'.[8]

The theory of an influential bourgeois public sphere in Britain, developed by Jürgen Habermas in the 1960s, ascribed special significance to the development of independent periodical journalism in London during the seventeenth and eighteenth centuries.[9] This thinking has recently been challenged or further developed by Habermas's later critics who propose a broader concept of 'a host of competing counter publics', embracing separate discursive communities such as nationalist or feminist groups.[10] Nancy Fraser suggests that such 'subaltern counter-publics' are created by 'subordinated social groups' in order to formulate 'oppositional interpretations of their identities, interests and needs'.[11] The English-speaking community in Wales can be regarded as constituting a 'counter public' of this kind. Indeed this Anglophone 'counter public' in Wales can be seen as twice distanced from cultural power centres: in the first place in its reaction against the centralising influence of a London-based English culture; second, in its distinction from the Welsh-speaking centre of the artistic and social life of Wales itself. The insecurities, hybridities and tensions within this cultural 'counter public' are reflected in the history and content of the periodical literature that exists to serve it. The space that periodical literature in Wales affords for intellectual debate and the prestige afforded such activity also differ from English stereotypes. Wynn Thomas believes that, while both the languages are 'competing for *Lebensraum*, the study and practice of Welsh "internal difference" is important work, that has to be started somewhere'.[12]

In his study of English intellectuals, Stefan Collini discusses the aversion of English society to recognition of 'the intellectual' as a significant force in society, a resistance that generates 'paradoxes of denial' even among self-confessed intellectuals themselves. He suggests that this phenomenon is, however, less prevalent in Wales, Scotland and Ireland.[13] Collini also highlights the significance of the periodical in providing a route to the regular validation of the opinions of those seeking cultural authority. He goes on to describe the extensive role of the 'literary journal' in British culture and concludes that 'periodical journalism in the broadest sense is not just the intellectual's natural habitat; it is also the noise made by a culture speaking to itself'.[14] Anglophone literary journals in Wales provide a space for such internal debate, and it will be helpful to consider to what extent their role in Welsh society justifies Collini's view that the reception of intellectuals in Wales may be more positive than the pattern set in England. Elsewhere Collini suggests that 'the true little review . . . exists to serve the needs of writers more than of readers.'[15] This mirrors the openly declared motivation of some Welsh periodicals in English, such as *Dock Leaves*, which aim primarily at providing a platform for Welsh writers. But, as I have shown elsewhere, most Welsh periodicals in English do not concentrate on poetry or fiction alone, but adopt the miscellany form, combining creative writing with social and political comment.

In earlier work on Welsh periodicals in English I have discussed the generic origins of the 'national' magazines of the nineteenth and early twentieth centuries. My research suggested that the serious Liberal miscellanies of that time, periodicals like *Cymru Fydd*, Owen Morgan Edwards's *Wales* or *The Welsh Outlook*, set an influential pattern. Many later magazines seemed to migrate towards this traditional periodical template under the cultural and economic pressures that beset them.[16] As an example of this process, the sparky little magazine *Wales* (first edited by Keidrych Rhys in 1937) turns into a serious miscellany by the time of its final series in 1958. Similarly Raymond Garlick's Pembrokeshire-based *Dock Leaves* (1949–58) migrates at the end of its life into *The Anglo-Welsh Review*, another sober miscellany, also resembling nineteenth-century predecessors. This repeated patterning in their literary history marks a difference in the generic behaviour of Welsh periodicals in English from that demonstrated by equivalent productions in England or Ireland. However, while still bearing in mind these behaviours, I want to concentrate in this study on a discussion of their contents rather than their forms.

Any serious analysis of periodical production demands close attention to a wide range of cultural signifiers, including para-textual factors – periodicity, design, advertisements – as well as their primary contents, such as editorials, and the mix of creative, non-fictional and critical materials. Regard needs to be paid to the choice of contributors, whether drawn from a wide range or confined to a coterie. A periodical's readership is crucial, but it is not always easy for the editor of the day, let alone the later critic, to identify it with confidence. Analysis of this kind can provide what the anthropologist Clifford Geertz, in his work on the interpretation of cultures, has characterised as 'thick description'.[17] Earlier scholars writing about periodicals have emphasised the difficulties created by the sheer volume of materials produced in periodical form and the resulting need to be selective in approaching them.[18] For each periodical, therefore, I have tried to look at a characteristic range of issues throughout its life, examining the work of different editors and contributors, while remaining alert to changes in periodicity, presumptions about audience, and influence from other contemporary productions. Valuable bibliographical work has been done in the field of Welsh periodicals, including work on the eighteenth and nineteenth centuries, produced for the National Library by Brynley F. Roberts and Huw Walters.[19] In addition, several 'Subject Indexes' have been produced, covering much of the twentieth century and dealing with both Welsh- and English-language journals.[20] These indexes are complex productions; they are not always easy to interpret but nevertheless some generalisations can be suggested, based on a subjective analysis of the numbers and types of articles listed. There is, for example, a sharp increase in the total number of articles recorded, from around one thousand articles a year in the 1930s and 1940s to as many as four thousand a year in the 1970s. This reflects a steady overall increase in the level of periodical activity in Wales over the century. If one examines further the listings of articles devoted to particular topics, it can be seen that serious attention is always given to 'Literature'. Indeed, attention to this topic increases with time, reaching over 300 articles a year in the early 1970s. The proportion of religious articles, however, though running at the same level as the literary articles at the beginning of the period, declines substantially by the end. There is a consistently high level of interest in educational topics in Welsh journals and a similar emphasis on articles about politics and economics. International subjects attract a smaller number of articles, but the level of interest appears consistent and regular, and the number of articles increases towards the end of the period. Although the overall proportion of 'International' articles is relatively low it can be shown that the range is wide.[21] Articles specifically written about Wales and about local interests, such as folklore and place-names, appear more frequently at the beginning of the period, but their number falls off considerably by the 1980s. There appears to be, overall, a surprisingly small coverage of the arts and music, even taking account of the regular reports on eisteddfodau.

This kind of research should become easier to undertake with the future development of digitisation projects in respect of periodicals. It has recently become possible to subject some English periodicals to formal 'content analysis'. Unfortunately these projects are at a very early stage in respect of Welsh periodicals, and such sophisticated methodologies are therefore not yet available to researchers in this field.[22] However, this may not be too serious a disadvantage. The leading theorist of 'content analysis', Klaus Krippendorf, warns against over-mechanical methodologies that resort to what he calls 'a shallow counting game', and insists on the continuing importance of open-ended readings which are closely linked to the researcher's 'research questions'.[23] In her recent detailed work on the magazine *The Welsh Outlook* Alyce von Rothkirch has shown how much close analysis can be achieved without access to digitised texts.[24]

In this spirit, I will aim to show how Welsh periodicals in English behave in the context of their histories and the cultural climate that produces them, and how they differ from other periodicals within Wales and outside. The Anglophone 'counter public sphere' addressed by *The Red Dragon* in 1882 in the heyday of nineteenth-century Welsh Liberalism was of course different in many respects from that perceived by the editors of *Planet* or *New Welsh Review* today. But it had some things in common as well. All these magazines address a relatively intimate group among a self-selected intelligentsia presumed to have common interests in contemporary Wales. All of them at some level refer to the Welsh national project. Welsh national feeling often invokes issues centred about the Welsh language, and, by their very existence, these Anglophone periodicals perform variants on this theme. Benedict Anderson does not specifically deal with Wales in his authoritative study of the nation-building process, but he does suggest that language is a vital element in building the 'deep horizontal comradeship' that is created in the processes of nation formation. He asserts that 'through that language, encountered at mother's knee and parted with only at the grave, pasts are restored, fellowships are imagined, and futures dreamed.'[25] Using English as a medium is inherently problematic for some nationalist thinkers in Wales. Ned Thomas, the first editor of the English-language magazine *Planet*, suggests that for the Welsh-speaker 'his language is still for him the language of his self-respect, while English is often the language of his servility.'[26] This suggests a potent emotional blockage to Anglophone materials. However, Welsh periodicals written in English can be envisaged as inviting a significant part of the substantial English-speaking population within Wales to participate in a celebration of Welsh culture and a discussion of Welsh society, while establishing recognition for the linguistic community of which they are members.

In her study of twentieth-century women's writing in Wales, Katie Gramich identifies a category of 'creative journalism' in which the work of women writers appears. A trajectory can be traced in which regular involvement of women writers in these periodicals develops strongly from the nineteenth century onwards, from an era in which such contributions are relatively rare to a present where three of the major Welsh periodicals in English are edited by women and there is a strong flow of contributions by women writers and commentators. Participation in temperance issues and suffrage campaigns strengthens women's confidence, powerfully supported by Welsh-language publications such as *Y Gymraes* in the 1850s and *Y Frythones*, edited by Sarah Jane Rees ('Cranogwen') in the 1880s.[27] This process reflects, in Gramich's terms 'how Welsh women over this century are . . . united by a shared experience of migration, industrialisation, war, language loss and a post-war reconstruction of identity, all of which they express in their own, distinctive ways'.[28]

Many of the journals we are concerned with present their readers with a powerful mix of fiction, poetry and political and critical commentary in the classic miscellany style. They appeal to traditional Welsh themes, but many of them simultaneously seek to create novelty, exploiting the intriguing appeal of 'The New Old. The Old New' that Kathryn Gray identifies as the keynote of *New Welsh Review*. The 'emergent', in Raymond Williams's formulation, is striving to become the 'dominant'.

The accounts that follow will seek to illustrate these processes while showing how audiences for English-language periodicals are identified, gender patterns are developed and the role of the Anglophone public sphere is established. It is time to take a more detailed look at some of the nineteenth-century founders of this tradition.

1
The Liberal Miscellanies: 1882–1914

The Red Dragon: The National Magazine of Wales (1882–1887)

Some of the contradictions and key oppositions in the periodical literature of late nineteenth-century Wales are brought out by the opening paragraph of the very first contribution in *The Red Dragon*. A series of articles, 'Notable Men of Wales', begins in February 1882 with an account by the magazine's editor, Charles Wilkins, of the life of Thomas Stephens, citizen of Merthyr Tydfil, literary critic and author of *The Literature of the Kymry*:

> From Pontneddfechan to Merthyr. From fairyland to the furnaces. From scenes where nature revelled in pine woods and mountain streams to a vast hive of labour, where there was a Babel of nationalities and fullest scope for undisciplined physical vigour and unrestrained human passion, with only a valley constable and a justice of the peace to enforce the law – such was the transition of Thomas Stephens. (1)

Editing Welsh periodicals in English often involves intimate connections. Charles Wilkins, also a literary historian and a fellow citizen of Merthyr Tydfil, had lived next door to Thomas Stephens in his youth.[1] Here he immediately invokes his first-hand awareness of the challenge of nineteenth-century industrial development to the traditional culture of Wales, bringing with it the clash of different languages, the dilution of Nonconformist restraint, the dangers of lawlessness, indeed all the shock of the new. Gwyn A.Williams observes that, in the aftermath of the controversy about the 1847 'Blue Books', Welsh-language culture had 'broken decisively with its own past', and had adopted 'a largely middle-class-cum-populist culture' inflected by a particular emphasis on distinguishing Welsh from the English of business and success. Williams sees the 'Merthyr Circle' around Thomas Stephens and Charles Wilkins as a significant 'regional variation on English literature'.[2]

Crises of industrial development were not confined to Wales. The 1880s in Britain, leading up to Queen Victoria's Golden Jubilee in 1887, were marked by persistent concerns about the 'grinding degradation' of the poor. It was the era simultaneously of W. T. Stead's 'The Maiden Tribute of Modern Babylon' and of the influence of Marx on thinkers like Bernard Shaw and William Morris.[3] Kenneth Morgan notes that Wales in the 1880s was still thought of by many British people as 'a semi-civilised picturesque survival' while actually facing the upheavals of industrial development and the uncertainties of rural decline, together with the challenges of massive inward migration. At the same time the dominance of Anglicised Tory landowners was being challenged by electoral shifts to the Liberal Party, and education was becoming a national passion. The decade came to be characterised in retrospect as, more than elsewhere in Britain, 'a major turning-point' and 'an epoch of extraordinary achievement in politics'.[4]

Charles Wilkins would have been aware, as he planned his new magazine, of the development of 'articulate and powerful groups of business and professional Welshmen who congregated in London'.[5] An autodidact who left school at the age of fourteen, he had become 'the most learned literary figure in Merthyr – and indeed in Wales'.[6] He became a member of the Cymmrodorion and was currently in 1882 working on his *History of the Literature of Wales* (published in 1884).[7]

London Welshmen were an important part of the 'counter public sphere' that provided an audience for *The Red Dragon*. These potential metropolitan readers, as well as their equivalents throughout Wales itself, would have had access to the prolific periodical press available in England since the eighteenth century.

According to John Davies, 'London periodicals such as *The Spectator* and *The Gentleman's Magazine* were eagerly read; the most recent novels were bought and gossip from London was avidly discussed.'[8] In 1882, magazines like *The Cornhill*, *The Fortnightly* or *Blackwood's*, were all selling over ten thousand copies.[9] These miscellany periodicals were intent upon becoming ever more commercial. This process links with Habermas's perception that the role of literary periodicals was changing – not necessarily for the better – as 'the disintegration of the public sphere in the world of letters' created a new public made up of consumers who were more inclined to uncritical reception.[10]

The 1880s also saw the introduction of compulsory education and the mass printing of popular classics.[11] When William Blackwood became head of his firm at the end of 1879, he mounted a 'root and branch revaluation' of *Blackwood's*, leading eventually to more space being given to women's fiction and to colonial themes.[12] In retrospect, T. H. S. Escott, writing in *Blackwood's* in 1894, concluded that 'the province of Bohemia has no longer a place on the map of socio-literary London.' As a result, he declares, 'journalism of the Metropolis at this close of the nineteenth century is essentially of the bourgeois kind, and is in fact identical with that for which country editors have long found it advantageous to cater.'[13]

As a 'country editor' in Wales, Charles Wilkins provides an example of the kind of editorial practice that Escott describes. However, Wilkins also took up a particular stance derived from his unique position in south Welsh society at this juncture. As Roland Mathias suggests, *The Red Dragon* is a 'calculated attempt to reach out to a new public literate in English but unschooled in a knowledge of Wales'.[14] In a society where, throughout the 1880s three-quarters of the population spoke Welsh – though few of them exclusively so – this project carried a significant risk.

The first issue of *The Red Dragon* presents itself as a respectable quarterly journal, ninety-six pages long, published from Cardiff by Daniel Owen and Company. It bears the subtitle 'The National Magazine of Wales', with a crest showing two shields bound together and the royal motto 'Dieu-et-Mon-Droit', clearly signifying its unionist stance. There are a few pages of advertisements, for items such as gentlemen's hair oil, Quinine Bitters, Debrett's *Peerage* and the London-based magazine, *The Squire: A Monthly Magazine for Country Gentlemen*.[15] These paratextual indicators confirm its appeal to a prosperous readership, partly London-based, with a conventional range of middle-class interests. They reflect the desire of Welshmen in the nineteenth century to 'take advantage of the British context to construct a highly respectable Welsh identity that could nevertheless be contrasted to Englishness'.[16]

This impression is reinforced when Wilkins introduces the first episode of Frederick Talbot's *One of the Firm*, a serialised novel of manners. The opening scene is set in 'extreme quietude . . . a fine spacious dining room, blazing with light, a noble fire burning at either end' (19). It would be difficult to imagine a more bourgeois setting, though the novel later deals with intrigues about life and love below stairs as well as between members of the gentry. The next piece is John Foster's article about the Sunday Closing Act of 1881, contrasting the flashy 'beer-houses, long bars, buffets and gin palaces' of the developing towns of the day with more traditional rural ale houses; this is immediately followed by Cadwallader Griffiths, praising the noisy merriment of a seaside eisteddfod held in the Gauntlet and Scissors (49–56; 57–61). The divisive contemporary issue of Temperance meets a touch of national pride in the first Act of Parliament since the seventeenth century to provide separate legislation for Wales.[17]

Wilkins then brings in the first of a number of articles in *The Red Dragon* about science: Thomas Jones Dyke's account of infectious fevers, drawing on international sources in France, Italy, India and the USA (62–5). It is followed, a dozen pages on, by 'Half Hours with the Microscope', under the pseudonym of 'Our Artist', marvelling at the 'rainbow hue' of a butterfly's down (76–8). The didactic and political content of this first issue is substantial, embracing for example material about the Irish

Land Act, expressing frank doubts about whether the 'present notions of public honesty and morality' in Wales would allow similar benefits to be obtained (67–76). There are three articles about the possible siting of the Welsh University, one arguing for Merthyr's pure water, good drainage and 'bracing mountain air' while others praise the 'healthy and beautiful surroundings' of Swansea or the 'social *status*' of Cardiff (83–5; 85–9; 89–94).

But, in the manner of miscellanies, the first issue of *The Red Dragon* also provides lighter fare, including social observation: a 'Welsh Character Sketch', about an old huntsman – 'indescribably comic and grotesque were his attitudes and his utterances (79–82).' There is the first of a series of 'Draconigae' containing various 'notes and queries': anecdotes, after-dinner stories, brief obituaries, and antiquarian items (95–6). The only poetry in this first issue is titled 'Welsh Poetry in English Dress: The Shake of the Hand', a translation from Welsh, taken from a conventional piece of occasional verse:

> When I offer my hand to a friend,
> Should he take it with icy disdain,
> Our fellowship quickly should be at an end
> For he never should take it again.
> The touch of the cold-fingered few
> My friendship should never command
> But give me the man who is honest and true
> And I'll give you my heart with my hand. (66)

This series of translations becomes a regular feature, featuring a wide range of ballads and romantic verse, paying tribute to the tradition of writing in Welsh.

This first issue clearly aims at an educated readership, predominantly male – the sole exception is Amy Dillwyn, who writes the 'Marginal Notes on Library Books' – providing a mix of entertainment and instruction with a moderate political position. Roughly half the articles in *The Red Dragon* are either anonymous or pseudonymous, a rather higher proportion for the 1880s than in equivalent English and Scottish miscellanies such as *Blackwood's*. Laurel Brake points out how anonymity often gives a journal an 'illusion of unity', conferring additional authority on the editorial role.[18] Brynley Roberts places *The Red Dragon* in the context of Wilkins's need to overcome the resistance of 'the Welsh consciousness of English speakers' to exploring 'the Welsh dimension to society, politics and economics'.[19] The immediately subsequent issues follow a similar pattern to the first, continuing the series initiated at the outset, but also giving space to land issues, as in John Howell's 'The Land Question', emphasising the 'high social position, political and country influence conferred by possession of property' (August 1882, 76–86). *The Red Dragon* introduces weighty articles on education and regularly reports on the activities of Welsh members at Westminster.[20] Dillwyn's 'Marginal Notes on Library Books' provides reviews, for example, 'Journals and Letters of Caroline Fox' in April 1882, with its glimpses of John Stuart Mill, the Carlyles and Coleridge (475–7). Her successor as reviewer for the series, Arthur Hamilton, expatiates at length on Froude's controversial biography of Carlyle (19 November 1882, 377–82). But most reviews in *The Red Dragon* are of novels, such as Trollope's *The Fixed Period* (May 1882, 559),'an amusing satire on the folly of being too theoretical'.

By the March 1883 issue Wilkins has achieved his mature style, mixing social and political comment with substantial literary material. The issue makes some sharp points about recent Welsh economic history, from both extremes of the social scale. The 'Notable Men of Wales' article about Dr Oliphant, bishop of Llandaff (former Regius Professor of Divinity at Cambridge) reminds readers that, at the date of his inauguration in 1849, 'not a ton of coal had been exported from our harbour.' The population had doubled since then (193–211). Wilkins himself has an article on 'The Shipping of Wales', describing Cardiff's growth to pre-eminence over Swansea (242–5). The interest in science and technology continues with John Howell's reminiscences about the first locomotive in Dowlais, and a highly technical article on geological strata. 'Alpha' (a former School

Board Member) contributes 'The Massacre of the Innocents', a fierce denunciation of the 'forcing' system going on in elementary schools, said to impact especially harshly on the 'poorly nourished and ill clad'. However, the broadly conservative social stance of *The Red Dragon* is regularly reinforced. 'Hunting in Wales' is celebrated in an article about the two hundred years of the Llantarnam pack (252–6). In similar traditional vein, the series of 'Welsh Character Sketches' continues with 'Ap Adda's' account of 'The Old Welsh Gentleman: One of the Olden Time'. He traces his lineage back to the mingling of Danes, Saxons and Flemings in the 'British race' and displays not 'the slightest trace of la-de-dawdism' but instead a 'cheery heartiness' as he deals on the bench 'somewhat rigidly' with poaching and trespass. At his funeral there is 'not a bought tear or a purchased sadness in the whole crowd' (257–60). Throughout the issue, Wilkins takes care to preserve a balance between a range of constituencies: town and country, rich and poor. The parliamentary sketch, 'Our Dragons at Westminster', takes a sceptical tone about Westminster where 'Ministers are more exacting, Whips more tyrannical, the sittings more protracted, the discussions more dreary.' Meanwhile it is suggested that Welsh members appear 'satisfied to bear the yoke' and 'nothing but downright personal frailty or grave embarrassment of their affairs would cause them voluntarily to throw it off' (272–4).

The series 'Gossip from the Welsh Colleges' gives further clues to the potential readership of *The Red Dragon* (266–71). This issue has a note from Jesus College, Oxford including a complaint that the Oxford Union Society has preferred 'by a large majority' to take in the Unitarian magazine *Yr Ymofynydd* (The Inquirer) in preference to *The Red Dragon*. The Oxford correspondent is also disappointed by the proposed programme for the Cardiff Eisteddfod, particularly because 'so few subjects are not at all English in character ... in a *South Wales* meeting ... in fact the character of the syllabus is more clannish than national.' This hints at some growing assertiveness within the culture of the Anglophone Welsh community. Owen M. Edwards's contribution from Aberystwyth is pleased that 'the good people of Aberystwyth seem to be determined to keep [the College] here . . . despite the battle of the sites', while the note from Lampeter, on the other hand, recognises 'the current of Higher Education towards larger towns'. Working at these collegiate links is clearly important to *The Red Dragon*.

The literary content of this issue is substantial. It includes another episode of the serial novel *Of High Degree* and some etymological speculation about the Welsh origins of Latin place-names. The unsigned 'Marginal Notes on Library Books' has an attack on the self-importance of 'Journalistic London', claiming that 'while it thinks itself *en rapport* with St Petersburg, Berlin, Vienna, Paris and New York [it] is often as ignorant as the man in the moon of the state of feeling existing under its very nose' (277). The 'country editors' are asserting themselves against the centre.

The selections of poetry in this issue of *The Red Dragon* and the commentaries on it display some uncertainties of taste. There is an example of moralising Victorian verse:

> Though low my lot my wish is won
> My hopes are few and staid;
> All I thought life would do, is done,
> My last request is made.
> If I have foes, no foes I fear,
> To fate I live resigned
> I have a friend I value here
> And that's a quiet mind. (225)

It is tempting to dismiss poetry of this kind as merely a form of 'filler'. Joseph Bristow asserts that by the mid-century 'poetry as an art was visibly breaking up in Victorian Britain, just as the nation seemed to be polarised (both in terms of class and gender) in the face of industrialisation.' He argues that in the 1880s poetry was especially 'associated with a negative femininity' that made it more marginal and less influential in a society preoccupied with the ethos of 'manliness'.[21] Kathryn Ledbetter, however, in her study of poetry in Victorian women's periodicals, challenges judgements of this kind, describing them as stemming from 'an elite perspective that penetrated the academy' in the aftermath of modernism, causing readers to 'practise a dismissive critique'. She points out that the deliberate emotionalism and shunning of irony and sophistication in Victorian verse created 'a public space packaging private emotions', helping such work to cross social and gender boundaries.[22] Much of the poetry in *The Red Dragon* follows patterns of this kind, privileging an acceptable social, sentimental and patriotic agenda.

This issue of *The Red Dragon* also has the last appearance of 'Welsh Poetry in English Dress', an anonymous three-page translation from 'The Bard and His Shadow' by Dafydd ap Gwilym (246–8). Its literary articles display more critical interest in poetry than earlier issues, generally endorsing conservative values. Swinburne's verse 'is tainted with a fleshliness dangerous to the contact of any but a professional dissector' and his 'morals are only to be judged by a code which he seems to have invented for himself' (275–80). The accession of Tennyson to the Cymmrodorion is noted, together with that of the Marquis of Bute (281–6). J. Cynddylan Jones presents a detailed exegesis of *The Wanderer* by Lewis Morris, described here as 'one of the best contemporary poets, ranked with Tennyson and Browning' (236). In the next issue of *The Red Dragon*, however, the contributor of the 'Literary Notes' remarks that Jones's assertions that Lewis Morris is the equal of Browning or Tennyson 'are simply ridiculous' (May 1883, 474). Lewis Morris, despite being a prolific best-seller and a distinguished academic, was later to be disappointed in his hopes of succeeding to the Laureateship after Tennyson despite his frustrated attempt to recruit Oscar Wilde to his cause. He is, as will be seen, frequently quoted in the periodicals.[23] *The Red Dragon*'s level of interest in Morris suggests, however, that its editor had little time for the changes in aesthetic taste being brought about in the 1880s by writers like Wilde and Pater. Even more revolutionary, in his Jesuit seminary in north Wales, seven years earlier, Gerard Manley Hopkins had created 'sprung rhythm' and written 'The Wreck of the Deutschland'.[24] Meanwhile, the poetry in this first Welsh periodical in English adheres firmly to mid-Victorian convention.

Over the next two years, until Charles Wilkins hands over to James Harris in July 1885, *The Red Dragon* continues to strike a similar tone. The magazine's awareness of social difference continues as a regular theme. For example, in May 1883, the 'Notable Men of Wales' essay points out how David Owen, son of a shoemaker, better known as the writer and editor 'Brutus', had in his youth been expelled from the Baptists after being found out obtaining money by false pretences:

> Ah! little know such of the readers of *Red Dragon* as are comparatively rich of the sorry heart-aching shifts to which many worthy poor people are put in trying to make both ends meet . . . Hunger is deaf to reason, laughs at logic, and nothing but food can silence the clamours of an empty stomach. (393)

Sustained awareness of the pressures on the poor and a clear-sighted appreciation of the realities of working life are among the most attractive elements in *The Red Dragon*. In the same issue the sketch of 'The Old Puddler' recognises the 'quick-witted, resolute and hardy' character of the iron-making artisan' (447). The regular features of the magazine are consistently maintained over the period and a new 'Notes and Queries' section, devoted to literary and antiquarian curiosities, starts in July 1884, at the point where the 'Marginal Notes on Library Books' come to an end. One senses some loss of energy towards the end of Wilkins's editorship.

For his last number in June 1885 Wilkins opts to return to the key themes of the first. His account of John Griffith, rector of Merthyr Tydfil, again opens with the contrast between town and country, comparing Griffiths's home in Aberystwyth with the squalor of Merthyr:

> Then to Merthyr. The great village was known then as the metropolis of the iron trade. King Coal, with his dusky hue, had not risen to

contend for Empire. There were the ring of iron and the flash of metal everywhere. Merthyr was cloudy and dirty and the roar of wheels haunted you at every turning. (483)

At eighty-five pages the issue is shorter and there is heavier reliance on personal memoirs such as 'Cramming for an Exam' or 'The Pic-Nic at the Pass of Llanberis'. 'Notes and Queries' now runs to nearly ten pages and the issue ends with a comic 'Welsh Rare Bits' piece.

James Harris, a competent Welsh scholar and experienced editor, who had been associated with *The Red Dragon* almost from its inception, took over from its July 1885 issue.[25] Initially Harris continues the 'Notable Men of Wales' series, the serialised fiction and the reliance on personal memoirs. However, he reverses the 'Original and Translated Poetry' idea to include a translation of Tennyson into Welsh, and sharply reduces the social and political content. In January 1886 Harris resorts to including the Irish patriot Thomas Davis in the 'Notable Men of Wales', on account of his Welsh descent. However, he adds a footnote criticising Davis's poem 'Cymric Rule and Cymric Rulers', saying that 'the sentiment of this song is hardly Welsh, neither is the measure at all points' (114).

Within a year, *The Red Dragon* has changed substantially. In July 1886, Harris drops the keynote 'Notable Men of Wales' series, and becomes more reliant on short fiction, poetry and personal memoirs, including his own fourteen-page account of a day out exploring the caves at Ystradfellte (102–16). The poems continue to follow Victorian stereotypes, as in John Walker's 'Apple Bloom':

> O apple bloom, throughout the years
> A faithful friend thou art to me:
> God's messenger in sweet Maytime;
> The soul of every simple rhyme
> With which I ease captivity;
> And dear dispeller of my fears. (40)

Harris adds more formal reviews, including, for example, a moralistic condemnation of a version of Flaubert's *Salammbô*:

> We cannot recommend even the least squeamish of our readers to take a turn at this book. Realism and the realistic may be all very well but the line must be drawn somewhere. Even the unhappy reviewer, who in the course of his professional career has to stand Balzac, Zola and Daudet, may reasonably object to descriptions of bacchanalian orgies . . . of leprosies down to the most disgusting details. (73)

In its final years *The Red Dragon* displays some problems in coping with the challenges of the new in the social and literary fields. Harris's personal interests seem to lie in the minutiae of literary history: there are four closely printed pages of corrections of errors in the Brontë sisters' biographies (73–7). The fifteen pages of 'Notes and Queries', now combining antiquarian and topographical items with family history and literary curiosities, deal with such matters as 'Why are Welshmen called Taffy?' or 'Extraordinary Longevity in a Welshman' (80–95). There are no articles bearing on political, social or scientific subjects. Eventually the magazine loses its audience and comes to an end. Harris's valedictory letter, introducing the last 1887 volume, claims:

> My one great aim has been to raise the standard of its literary excellence. Gradually eliminating the amateurs, while at the same time extending a critical reception to the beginners of talent and promise . . . [Critics have helped] in the furtherance of our primary object, namely, that of making known to the great English world the manifold beauties innate in the language, literature, music and folk-lore of its little Welsh neighbour.

This emphasis on the audience for the magazine in 'the great English world' may have been excessive.

During *The Red Dragon*'s mature phase Charles Wilkins successfully mixed social and political commentary with scientific and technical reporting, together with critical literary comment, well leavened with varied creative inputs and topical and antiquarian material. *The Red Dragon*'s essentially conservative and traditional ethos still encompassed a sense of admiration and affection for working people in Wales, whose lives were treated respectfully and with real interest. Admiration for such 'residual' elements in the culture was an important feature of the journal's appeal. It also provided an outlet for a scatter of women writers, including serial novels by Amy Dillwyn and Kate Dodd and poems by Jeanette Forsyth and Ella Egerton. At its peak it commanded for the first time the attention of a newly recognised audience for a Welsh periodical in English. The new counter public sphere that *The Red Dragon* created was next addressed by the bilingual magazine *Cymru Fydd*, one year later, in 1888.

Cymru Fydd (1888–1891)

The opening editorial by 'Adfyfyr' (Thomas John Hughes) in January 1888 immediately makes clear the periodical's politics:

> In issuing the first number of a Nationalist publication for Wales, we feel no apology is necessary. Welsh mind and aim having been during the past two years [i.e. since the founding of the Cymru Fydd organisation] unceasingly and decisively directed towards the remedy of home grievances, social and political. The irredeemable constraint of external conditions has made political quietism no longer possible among us. State Churchism, educational monopoly and jobbing, a landed system which has degenerated into rude despotism . . . The clergyman is frequently a more bitter foe of popular rights than the priest . . . The State Church of England in Wales, by its icy indifference towards the suffering Welsh tenantry has decreed its own speedy dissolution as a State Church . . . CYMRU FYDD is intended to serve in this epoch of transition as an outlet for the national feeling in its protest against wrong. (1–2)

The magazine adopts a practice of alternating articles in Welsh and English, charges a modest one penny for its monthly productions and carries a few advertisements, typically for books, university colleges, and for teas and coffees. It takes its stance on the radical wing of the Liberal Party, pronouncing the death of 'political quietism' while demanding changes in respect of disestablishment, educational provision and land reform. The magazine makes very few concessions to pressures for commercial viability, and seems to be largely addressed to the already converted. Brynley Roberts observes that, in any case, bilingual magazines in Wales are mostly commercial failures.[26] They tend to split their prime audience, identified by Glanmor Williams as a 'strategic core readership among ministers and church elders', largely centred about a deeply ingrained respect and affection for the Welsh language.[27] The very fact, however, that the editors of *Cymru Fydd* feel it necessary to appeal to an English-reading audience betrays their awareness of a new readership that now needs to be included in the process of mobilising public opinion and national awareness in late nineteenth-century Wales.

Thus, in the first issue, there are articles in English by the editor and by Stuart Rendel, that together make the link between Irish Home Rule and Welsh disestablishment, together with a contribution from Tom Ellis arguing for 'the rapid dethronement of the Welsh squirearchy from the leadership and the confidence of the people' (20–8; 33–5; 41–3). The reports of Liberal Federations are also provided in English. In Welsh, there is an alternative editorial, a substantial article by Owen M. Edwards about Geneva and, reminiscent of *The Red Dragon*, a note about the activities of Welshmen in the colleges (28–32; 59–62).

Cymru Fydd continues in this manner throughout Thomas John Hughes's editorship and indeed into the early issues of the period (1889 – 91) under Owen Morgan Edwards and Richard Humphreys Morgan. In his first English editorial, however, Morgan, while paying due tribute to 'Adfyfyr', comments that 'the readers of *Cymru Fydd* have long felt that its scope is too narrow', and that while 'occasional Jeremiads and Philippics are exceedingly useful' they become 'monotonous and ineffective' if overused. Therefore, 'We hope to extend the scope of the magazine . . . and to introduce into it all matters, literary, scientific, linguistic, social and religious, which are of interest to Wales generally.' *Cymru Fydd* will still campaign for disestablishment and will continue to 'resist the leprosy of sacerdotalism now creeping into the church in Wales (273–5).' By the January 1890 issue the periodical has, indeed, changed substantially, becoming much more of a cultural miscellany, with far less political content. It now includes poems, book reviews and a reasoned critique of the organisation of the National Eisteddfod in Brecon (7–9; 22–3; 31–5). There is a significant increase in the proportion of Welsh-language content. The editors include a letter from an 'indignant correspondent', protesting about the fall-off in coverage of 'Welsh National Life' (36–41). The dilution of political campaigning clearly has its critics.

However, the editors persist with introducing more fiction and religious writing. The June 1890 number opens with a lengthy diatribe about the 'scandalous abuses' revealed by a statistical analysis of the revenues of the Church of England in Wales (321–8). But there is also the first instalment of an anonymous romantic serial, *Lady Gwen: or the Days That Are to Be*, imagining the triumph in the year 2000 of Lady Gwen Tudor, the new ruler of an independent Wales, 'a loyal Province of the great Empire' (331–4). This is a new departure for *Cymru Fydd*, and it is part of its revised project, aiming to convey a nationalist political message in a more popular form. Kirsti Bohata, in her essay about *Lady Gwen*, remarks on the way that 'its political messages dominate the narrative and the emphasis is on historical and social comment rather than depth of character or plot.'[28] Bohata sees the role of Lady Gwen here as part of the reaction against the Blue Books' portrayal of Welsh women as immoral and also as 'undermining the criticism of those who saw professionally active women as desexed and dangerous'.[29] Lady Gwen tries to look into the future, maybe in reaction against the backward-looking tendency in *Cymru Fydd*, well illustrated by another article in this issue about old Welsh saints, which specifically adopts the refrain: 'look to the past for the necessary guidance' (352–63, 356). The tensions between tradition and modernity surface again. The English poetry is in much the same vein as that in *The Red Dragon*. 'Watching the Golden Grain' by Arthur Jones reads:

> I am a foolish dreaming lad
> An idle fancy keeping.
> 'Tis I who watch the golden grain
> Another will come reaping;
> Why wilt thou not come after me?
> Day after day is going
> And thou each day, my little maid,
> Art fairer, fairer, growing. (382)

This conventional elegiac tone appeals to a more popular Victorian taste than the forceful nationalist rhetoric of the earlier issues.

The editors become aware of the need to defend their record. In July 1890 they declare a broad liberal position:

> There are many articles with which our readers do not agree; there are many articles with which the editors do not agree. But these articles are about the future of Wales, and written by men who, however mistaken, are inspired by a love for their country. (427–8)

However, by the last issue in April 1891, *Cymru Fydd* has shrunk to around forty pages, including another instalment of *Lady Gwen* (never to be finished) and a farewell editorial by R. H. Morgan that exudes a palpable air of relief:

> The transfer of *Cymru Fydd*, and its appearance in another form and under another name, has given me a much desired opportunity of severing my connection with the magazine as joint editor . . . The reader may be astonished to understand that the semi political character of the magazine was a feature quite foreign to my taste. I have never believed that politics are the principal thing. (230–1)

The tensions that were evident in *The Red Dragon* – between nostalgia for the past and hopes for the future, between respect for the old and desire for the new, between cultural nationalism and political activism – appear again in *Cymru Fydd*. Tom Nairn identifies significant differences between a more lenitive 'ethno-linguistic' Welsh nationalism and its more violent Irish equivalent, and comments on the common interest in 'the backwards glance', displayed both by city intellectuals and rural emigrants.[30] The story of *Cymru Fydd* echoes these perplexities; indeed an inability to resolve them may have contributed to its failure to command a regular audience within the divided public sphere it addressed. Recognising these dangers, Owen M. Edwards immediately launched his non-political and non-sectarian periodical *Cymru* in August 1891, as a separate magazine for the Welsh-speaking community. Huw Walters describes this publication as 'the most notable product of the Welsh periodical press at the end of the nineteenth century'.[31] Shortly afterwards, in November 1891, Ernest Bowen-Rowlands produced for an Anglophone audience a short-lived, new and highly political Liberal journal, *The Welsh Review*.

The Welsh Review (1891–1892)

Bowen-Rowlands was a lawyer and a Liberal MP. *The Welsh Review* was published from London. His lengthy first editorial in November 1891 (four closely printed pages followed by some dozen pages of supportive signatures) has some critical (and sometimes inaccurate) things to say about earlier Welsh periodicals in English:

> . . . until the WELSH REVIEW appeared Wales never possessed a magazine which was not purely and entirely a Welsh production, having for its end a circulation in Wales.
> True, there have been magazines which, conducted in the most able manner and characterised by noble resolves and high literary worth have circulated in Wales, but failed to secure a sufficiently strong hold on the reading public, because – it is my opinion – they did not aim at a circulation outside Wales. (I do not now allude to magazines published in the vernacular, of which Mr. Owen Edwards' *Cymru* is a brilliant example). (2)

The editor goes on to announce ambitious international aims:

> Its purpose is to make known the cause of Wales, to afford an outlet to Welsh genius and to act as a medium of communication between Wales and other countries, as a means of bringing into closer association the minds of Welshmen living in all parts of the world . . . Now in every part of the habitable globe the sons of Wales are to be found treading the road to success. In every important town in the United Kingdom are to be found prominent citizens who boast the heritage of a Welsh descent. In the Antipodes, the Americas, and the Continent have been carried the characteristics of the Brythonic race; and with social eminence, the desire and the capacity to develop literary and artistic tastes have arisen, and find expression in the daily life of the people. (4)

This proposes a particular view of the audience available to Welsh periodicals in English. It adopts a more ambitious perspective than that taken by *The Red Dragon* or *Cymru Fydd,* more centred on the metropolis and the diaspora, concerned with 'social eminence'. *The Welsh Review* will treat 'contemporary literature' seriously and will avoid political partisanship (4).

The contents of the first issue do not, however, immediately encourage confidence in these assurances. The six verses of Lewis Morris's introductory poem, 'Proemium' open and close on a somewhat world-weary note:

> Another venture on Thought's trackless sea,
> Another bark launched from our Cambrian shore,
> And once again the summon comes to me
> For word of welcome oft times said before . . .
>
> Sail with Imperial England, round the earth,
> Using the lordly tongue which sways the Race,
> But oh! Forget thou not the Cymric grace,
> The snows, the heaven kissed summits of thy birth. (14)

Reliance on the 'lordly tongue that sways the Race' may well have irritated as many Welshmen as it 'swayed'. Despite claims to impartiality, *The Welsh Review*'s devotion to the Liberal cause is confirmed by the next article, giving space to Tom Ellis's attack on the Tory government's policy of excluding Nonconformists from the new 'Free Schools' (15–21). The next article tries to moderate the extreme views of the Welsh Temperance movement, seen as risking 'injustice that may be done to the sober many for the sake of the drunken few' (22–7). The magazine then introduces the fictional new 'Member for Treorky' (who is to become a regular pseudo-contributor), declaring that, although 'of an extremely retiring and sober disposition' he has immediately been elected the leader of 'a new United National Welsh party . . . making the thirty-first since 18—'. Political satire and gossip is near the heart of *The Welsh Review:* this article is accompanied by several cartoon representations, including drawings of 'Mabon' and of Bowen-Rowlands himself (28–40).[32]

The five unsigned pages of 'Welsh Notes'(64–8) take pleasure in Gladstone's visit to the resuscitated National Eisteddfod and his 'glowing eulogium on Mr. Henry Richard'. However, other achievements are less well received. The appointment of the first Welsh Lord Mayor in London is said to have been 'secured largely by the simple rules of priority and a long purse. It is not a matter which need have raised such general feelings of rejoicing.' The success of the Welsh in music is described as 'almost entirely due to outside instruction'. Any prospect of a 'presentable appearance' by Wales in the World Fair due in 1893 will be caused by the presence of 'the American migrants who are still Welsh in sympathy'. Milford Haven is criticised for its 'supineness' due to its dependence on south Wales goods traffic. These notes interpret Wales from the Westminster perspective of a political professional.

The magazine's claim to serious literary content relies on material directed to a predominantly middlebrow audience. Stephen Coleridge's first article on literature deals with 'Love as the Begetter of Poetry', remarking that 'in this century men have perceived the awful sacredness of little children more than at any period,' citing Wordsworth, Elizabeth Barrett Browning and Coleridge as exemplars (44–52). W. Hamilton Johnstone deplores the vanity of modern literary critics, judged as more concerned to display their erudition than to help the reader' (69–73). A 'Books of the Month' column contains a few reviews, and there is the first episode of *Owen Sethenyn*, a serialised novel, imagined as a translation of an old Welsh manuscript, set in Breconshire (78–81; 82–96). D. Tudor Evans contributes a study of 'Welsh Periodical Literature' (to be completed the next month) describing earlier periodicals as 'repeated patriotic and self-denying efforts by educated Welshmen to elevate their countrymen'. Neither *The Red Dragon* nor *Cymru Fydd* is mentioned. The writer concentrates on Welsh-language magazines, either antiquarian or sectarian in character (74–7). The second part of the article (in December) reaches the conclusion:

> It is evident from a careful study of the subject that the first impulse on behalf of Periodical Literature came from the bards and arose from a desire to furnish Welsh-speaking persons with useful information, and make them familiar with the literature and the prowess of their ancestors. (179–83, 183)

This desire to create an association with bardic predecessors and to claim a primarily educational role for periodical production, especially one aimed at 'Welsh-speaking persons', fits in well with the didactic ambitions of the earlier editorial.

Later issues take a similar shape, engaging with contemporary issues such as women's suffrage. In February 1892 Nora Philipps advocates Liberal support, arguing that 'woman is the problem of the nineteenth century as man was the problem of the eighteenth century.' The article leads to a sharp exchange of views with Eliza Orme over the next few months.[33] The decision to highlight the nascent suffragette movement and to deploy women correspondents in pursuit of it must represent a conscious editorial stance. In May, James Duncan advocates payment for Members of Parliament, facilitating direct representation of the working class (701–8). Some twenty pages are allocated to 'The Duchess of Treorky', who writes light-hearted, knowing political skits (rather in the manner of today's *Private Eye*) using the names of real politicians, such as Joseph Chamberlain or Randolph Churchill (681–700).

By the last issue in August 1892 the 'Duchess' is describing her holiday experiences on the beach, at the Bowen-Rowlands' holiday home, 'a small house with a large garden and a stable in which my ponies are quartered', near Broadhaven in Pembrokeshire. At a picnic on Newgale beach, political interchanges about Home Rule and disestablishment involve figures such as 'the Stuart Rendels', Mr and Mrs Gladstone and Mr Tom Ellis. A typical conversation reads:

> 'You would make Hodge as good as his master, then?'
> 'Better! Better!'
> 'Yes, if by his master you mean the drowsy parson or the illiterate squireen.' (977–1003)

It is difficult to be sure how much of this gossip and discussion is intended to be read as fictional and how much is reportage. By now, the magazine's class bias and London focus are irredeemable. 'Studies of the Stage' by 'Liknon' ends thus:

> I shouldn't be surprised if I went down to the Rhondda Valley on a voyage of search. Surely among the teeming thousands of that industrial neighbourhood a greater than Ibsen can be brought to light. (1050)

The *bien-pensant* tone is dominant in this terminal stage of *The Welsh Review*'s existence. 'Welsh Notes' has another couple of pages of mockery of the unfortunate Welsh Lord Mayor of London, together with accusations that the Cardiff Music Festival's 'No-Welsh Committee' is engaged in 'sneering at, boycotting, and attempting to cheat Welshmen'. (1051–9). This last issue has no reviews or literary articles and actually contains very little material about Wales. But, ironically, the Duchess of Treorky's opening article takes pleasure in the claim that

> During the ten months that I or my husband have written on political affairs the WELSH REVIEW . . . has secured a position as secure as it is satisfactory . . . and no longer can it be hurled as a

reproach at Wales that it possesses no medium whereby to communicate its needs and genius to the civilised world. In Australia, America, Turkey, and in most European countries, the WELSH REVIEW reckons its subscribers. (977–1003, 1002)

Despite these confident assertions the magazine produces no further issues. The end is sudden and apparently unforeseen: the last issue has the start of a new serialised novel, never to be continued. *The Welsh Review* has not been a commercial success but it has edged open a door into a different section of the potential audience for Welsh periodicals in English. Its London base may have been too narrow and the privileged circle around the Liberal elite in Parliament too introverted to provide it with a sufficient scope. A few years after its demise, however, Owen M. Edwards decides that there is room for another attempt to command an English-speaking audience within Wales.

Wales (1894–1897)

Owen M. Edwards was the leading Welsh intellectual of his day. A founder of the Dafydd ap Gwilym Society in Oxford, aiming at 'the reawakening of Wales', he published the outcome of the society's work on the Welsh language in *Cymru Fydd* in July 1888.[34] By 1894 he had already been a contributor to *The Red Dragon*, the joint editor of *Cymru Fydd* and founder-editor of the long-lasting Welsh-language journal *Cymru*. By 1894 this magazine had over three thousand subscribers, seeking 'to bridge the gap between the unsophisticated and the literati', and he had established his preferred editorial practice, according to his biographer Hazel Davies, in tune with the classic miscellany. 'I like to be able to put an occasional amusing, soothing tale . . . between things whose enjoyment depends on more vigorous mental effort.'[35] Then in his thirties, a fellow of Lincoln College, Oxford, O. M. Edwards travelled weekly between Oxford and Wales and worked across an enormous range of potential audiences. He founded the children's magazine *Cymru'r Plant* in 1892 and the literary magazine *Y Llenor* (The Man of Letters) in

1895, as well as producing two short-lived ventures: a local newspaper for his home village of Llanuwchllyn, *Seren y Mynydd* (The Mountain Star) and a controversial current affairs journal, *Heddyw* (Today). These activities, together with the demands of his subsequent career in academia, education and politics took their toll on his private life.[36]

The first issue of *Wales* appeared in May 1894, forty-eight pages long, offering a dense textual presence with two columns a page, price 6d. It is well supported by nine pages of advertising: books, 'national songs,' proprietary medicines. The olive-green cover depicts statues of eminent Welshmen (Glyndŵr, Thomas Charles of Bala, Hugh Owen) together with pictures of rural scenes, castles, waterfalls, and representations of the three colleges of the University of Wales. In his 'Introduction', Edwards quotes the democratic experience he has had in recruiting new writers for *Cymru*: 'Quarrymen write for me, as do agricultural labourers.' He goes on:

> According to the census of 1891, nearly one half of the inhabitants of Wales cannot speak Welsh and more than three in four can understand English. My aim is now to help English-speaking Welshmen as I have tried to help their Welsh-speaking brothers. I want to tell you the history of your forefathers . . . I want you to know what Llewelyn suffered, and what Glendower had hoped for . . . It will be one of the aims of the magazine to lay before the English-speaking Welshman the treasures of his ancestors' thoughts. (1–2)

The aim is unashamedly didactic. Edwards, signing himself from his base in Lincoln College, identifies the cultural needs of the English-speaking Welsh, seen as new potential members of *y werin*. He makes the class basis of this comparison explicit in the introduction to the first volume (written retrospectively in January 1895):

> There is, undoubtedly, something like a literary awakening among English-speaking Welshmen . . . If this desire can be fostered and rightly led, Wales will be a benefactor to the English-speaking world . . . and Welshmen will become a thoughtful people, tempering their

religious creeds and political opinions by a love for literature and a sound knowledge of history. The absorbing question in Wales at the present time is education. The Welsh people may be divided into two classes, – those who are striving to give their countrymen the best education and those who are striving to get it . . . To [the first class] belong the enlightened aristocracy and squirearchy, clergymen and ministers of religion, doctors, bankers, the leaders of the various industries, tradesmen who travel . . . The other class is composed of Welshmen who are confined by their occupations to one place and see little of the world, – farmers, farm labourers, quarrymen, tin-platemen, small tradesmen and artisans, colliers . . . As far as this class is concerned . . . it is not too much to say that English Wales is at least a century behind Welsh Wales.

However, the aim of *Wales* is to ensure that the members of this group 'will be as intelligent as the working man of Cardigan or Merioneth, that the peasant of eastern Monmouth will be as intelligent as the peasant of Arvon or the Vale of Towy'.

Wales therefore addresses itself to a wider public sphere than the bourgeois audience in England identified by Habermas – or, indeed, the readerships that are sought by Charles Wilkins or Ernest Bowen-Rowlands. The references to the 'peasants' recall the idealisation of this group by contemporary Irish writers such as Yeats or Synge. The 'notion of a rural peasantry which embodies an essential national identity' – and the related elaboration of the myth of *y werin* by Owen Edwards and his supporters – is seen by Katie Gramich as an expression of cultural nationalism that is 'problematic for cultural projects identified with modernity'.[37] A strong emphasis on this tradition, linked with expressions of resistance to modernity, regularly appears in the pages of *Wales*.

In the first issue (May 1894) Ernest Rhys writes a highly allusive account of 'The House of Hendra' in ballad form, ending on a traditional funereal note:

> There with Arthur and with Merlin
> To his Peace
> From this torn world passes Brechva
> In the soul's most high increase. (4)

Welsh Periodicals in English

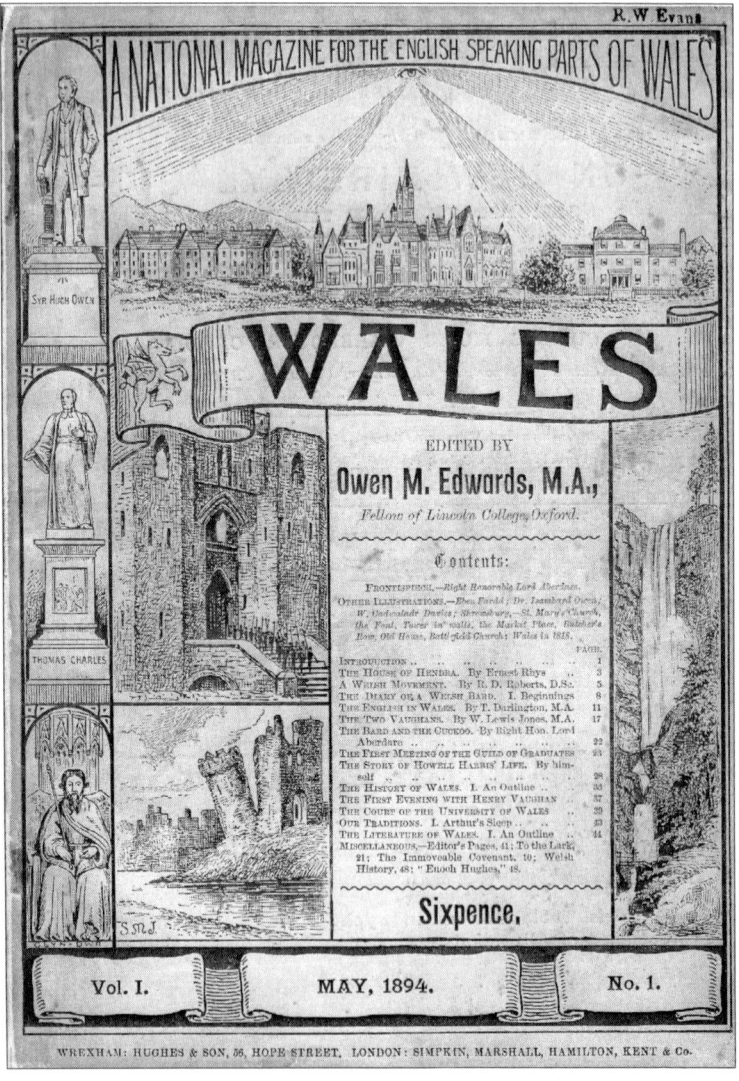

Wales: ed. Owen M. Edwards, first issue, May 1894

R. D. Roberts's article 'A Welsh Movement' argues that 'in certain matters Welsh public opinion is riper than in England', especially on educational issues, if not on artistic topics. He advocates a national gathering along the lines of the Chautauqa Assembly in the United States (5–8, 5). More poems follow, including Ebenezer Thomas's 'The Diary of a Bard' reprinted 'from a transcript made for John Jones ("Myrddin Fardd"), the blacksmith antiquary of Chwilog' (8–10). Then T. Darlington discusses the rapid growth of the English-speaking population in Wales but argues that there is no Ulster in Wales: 'There are not even the materials for a Welsh Ulster' (16). Next, W. Lewis Jones, writing from University College, Bangor, compares the poetry of the brothers, Thomas and Henry Vaughan, tilting at the opinions of the academic, George Saintsbury and the prevailing decadence of London's literary world:

> Those who delight in the simpering refinement of the so-called aesthetic poetry of these latter days or in the wild vagaries of what has been well styled 'the Fleshly School' of poetry, will not find much to their taste in Henry Vaughan. (17–21, 19)

The tastes associated by Edwards with Welsh-speaking members of *y werin* are well represented and *Wales* shows itself scornful of London's opinions and values. There are very few signs of 'talking down' to the chosen 'peasant' audience.

This first issue also has a number of articles that chime with the editor's preoccupation with education. There is a full account of the first meeting of the Guild of Graduates from the new University: it is critical of the meeting's tone ('not inspiring') but welcomes an organisation which could maintain lifelong links between Welsh graduates (23–7). Edwards sees institutions like the Guild as providing opportunities to access and influence newly educated opinion in Wales. The magazine's record of the first meeting of the Court of the University of Wales, held (perhaps significantly) in Whitehall, quotes without comment the new Liberal Prime Minister, Lord Rosebery, who sees the Welsh University as 'The place where the son of a peasant or a farmer or a mechanic may come and grasp with a hard and even a horny hand, the weapons with which he means to carve out his career' (39–40, 39). In a possible gesture towards the sensitivity of these issues the 'Editor's Pages' contain a promise that *Wales* will pay much attention to industry and to history – and that it will deal with religion and politics 'from their non-contentious sides' (41–2).

The 'Editor's Notes' in October 1894 report the arrival of a packet of magazines from America, prompting the comment that

> The danger of most Welsh magazines is dullness. Bright, chatty descriptions of existing conditions are regarded as shallow and superficial; whole articles on theology and philosophy – often as dull as they are uncritical and devoid of originality – are welcomed . . . The 'new journalism' strikes many as being too personal and too shallow. (280–3, 280)

Satisfying his preference for mixing 'soothing materials' with sterner topics, Edwards has already introduced more entertainment into the magazine. Two episodes of serial fiction appear in this issue. The eighth chapter of *Enoc Hughes* is translated from the Welsh of Daniel Owen (273–7). In June 1894, he publishes the first of nineteen episodes of *Gabriel Yorath*, a novel by E. Cynffig Davies about a virtuous young miner who is unjustly deported to Van Diemen's Land but eventually triumphs over adversity and becomes a wise, socialist mine owner (94–6)). Edwards produces a broad miscellany of topics, including in this one issue historical materials (accounts of the Romans in Wales and of eighteenth-century Bangor), original poems including a ballad taken from a collection by Charles Wilkins (245–6), topographical articles about Radnorshire (251–4) and Monmouthshire (257–61) and some literary pieces, such as a discussion of Celtic women in Shakespeare (261–4). Edwards maintains this eclectic style well into 1895.

An attractive eight-page supplement 'Among the Mountains', profusely illustrated with photographs and poems, appears in

August 1895. However, after almost two years, circulation is beginning to decline and, probably consequentially, advertisements are now sparse, confined to the magazine's covers. In his Introduction to Volume II, Edwards says that, while he believes that *Wales* has 'succeeded in bringing into communication with each other a number of Welshmen, of all shades of political opinions and religious creeds', nevertheless he recognises that

> The farmers, the artisans, and the labourers of the English-speaking parts of Wales have not welcomed it with the enthusiasm that their Welsh brethren showed when *Cymru* and the *Llenor* were offered them. *Wales* is gradually, but very slowly, making its way to the peasant homes of the Severn valley, and to the cottages of the great industrial centres of South Wales. I desire, above all things to see the peasants of eastern and southern Wales becoming readers . . . For this purpose the third volume will be of a more popular character; while at the same time its interest to scholars will be kept up. (i–iv, iii)

Despite this promise of concessions to 'popular' taste, the contents of the February 1896 issue do not appear very much changed. There is the usual emphasis on higher education. The editor congratulates the University College of North Wales on securing a new distinguished Professor of Philosophy (50) and reprints a solemn address by J. Viriamu Jones, Vice-Chancellor, on the relations between the University of Wales and the community generally (57–63).

The 'Editor's Notes' record his decision to reject a 'well written article' about Young Italy because it is 'glaringly unjust to modern Welsh politicians when comparing them to Mazzini and Cavour and Garibaldi' (90). A narrative poem by J. Craven Thomas about a mysterious voyage echoes Coleridge's 'Rhyme of the Ancient Mariner':

> At intervals from every part
> The oars fell with a thud;
> The ship tacked round and drifting brought
> Her quickly to the flood.

> My King, it was a fearful sight
> For every spirit fled
> Before our eyes in shapes of light
> From all the luckless dead. (87)

Much of the poetry in *Wales* is in this vein: romantic in style, derivative, frequently written in ballad form, often translated from Welsh.

Minor changes in style fail to bring about the necessary improvements in circulation: in the Introduction to Volume III, Edwards confesses ruefully that 'the truth goes straight to a publisher's or editor's pocket.' However, the editorial task has given him 'unalloyed pleasure' and he has been much complimented on the quality of the magazine. Edwards is therefore determined to persevere with *Wales,* but the price is to be lowered and the size diminished. The motivation remains unchanged: 'this *is* done in deference to a very general desire to bring it within reach of the farmer, the artisan and the labourer.' In a gesture resembling the socialist aesthetic of William Morris, *Wales* will make it a priority 'to teach the Welsh people to make their homes and their surroundings more beautiful'.

The first of the new series appears in January 1897, again ostensibly 'on a more popular plan', halving the price (to 3d) and the length (to twenty-four pages). The miscellany form and the didactic imperatives are maintained. There is another ballad – this time translated by Allen Raine from the Welsh of Ceiriog (3–4), and a new serial story *The House of the Twisted Sapling* by Owen Rhoscomyl, together with anonymous excerpts from *The Philosophers of Today* and Annie Foulkes's brisk account of her holiday in the Pyrenees (9–10). An interview with 'The Vicar of Llanidloes' (once Captain of Boats at Merton College, Oxford) declares that 'Welsh nationality and Welsh provincialism are two different things, one is good and the other bad' (23). This material hardly seems to accord with the idea of 'a popular plan'; according to Hazel Davies the circulation falls from 3,700 in the early days to 1,100 by the end of 1897.[38]

It is unsurprising then that the 'Introduction to Volume IV', dated from Lincoln College on 18 November 1897, marks 'the editor's farewell'. It records the end of this attempt to inculcate in 'the peasants of the English-speaking parts of Wales' development 'in love of reading, enlightened patriotism, in love of flowers, in a higher conception of duty'. Edwards has resisted many offers to continue the magazine without him, 'in justice to the contributors who wrote for me'. The central core of these contributors comprised a selective group of seventeen writers, largely composed of academics, men of letters and clergymen, all of them male.[39] *Wales* also includes a sprinkling of women writers, including Winnie Parry, 'Y Ddau Wynne', Allen Raine and Sioned Pryce.[40]

Wales, unlike its predecessors, has been a periodical that has appealed to a new if relatively narrow public sphere. It has, however, failed to arouse the intellectual excitement it hoped for or to create a new readership of any substance among working people. The enthusiasm of its founder-editor and his cohort of loyal writers has however reinforced a generic pattern of liberal sentiment, middle-class values, educational intent and miscellaneous content that has been typical of his predecessors and is to be reproduced repeatedly in the future of Welsh periodicals written in English. These characteristics appear again in *Young Wales*.

Young Wales: A National Periodical (1895–1904)

John Hugh Edwards, Liberal MP for Mid-Glamorgan from 1910 to 1922, was the editor of *Young Wales*, originally addressed to the youth section of Cymru Fydd. The title pays homage to the nineteenth-century movements associated with Mazzini's Young Italy, Young Austria, and, of course, Thomas Davis and Young Ireland.[41] *Young Wales* appears as a slim production, around twenty-five pages, having a high-minded motto at its masthead:

> Be Just and fear Not
> Let all the ends thou aimest at be thy Country's,
> Thy God's and Truth's

It differs from its predecessors, *The Red Dragon*, *The Welsh Review* or *Wales* in having a more precise target audience, and it bears, understandably, some strong resemblances to the earlier *Cymru Fydd*. A typical early issue in January 1896 is priced 3d, quite densely printed in two columns per page, and carries a colour portrait of J. Herbert Lewis MP on the cover. Its presentation signifies nationalist intentions. *Young Wales* deals with serious subjects but usually tries to avoid solemnity, thus making an appeal to the critical sense of the young people it sees as its primary audience and to their desire for political and cultural change.

In the same issue, The Revd Elvet Lewis writes about the National Eisteddfod in unusually critical terms: 'up to a certain point [it] is an ally of progressive national life,' but it is not the site of the nation's best artistic achievements. It ought to suffice if work is 'creditably done' but its 'competitive mania' is to be deprecated (1). Llewelyn Williams deploys an ironical tone when writing of ambivalent relations with the English:

> I confess that, with all his faults, I have a tender spot in my heart for John Bull. He is so solemn, so stolid, so wrapped up in his own conceit, so unlike a Celt in every way, that one cannot help being attracted to him . . . 'Nationalism', he would say 'is so very un-English' – his very denial betraying the truth . . . But have we not been taught by Christian England that Commerce is greater than morality, and have we not an Archbishop's word for it that no country can be run on the lines of the Sermon on the Mount? (8)

This satirical tone is repeated when J. Young Evans proclaims that the new University is 'the embodiment of nineteenth-century progress' providing for women to exercise influence. 'To the taste of Lady Verney, the University will be indebted for the use of the delicate shades of shot silk for the lining of the hoods of the various faculties' (17).

This light-hearted note is not, however, sustained very long. 'Our Sunday Notebook' by William George resists any suggestion that Cymru Fydd is an irreligious movement and asserts that readers will be 'interested in the various moral, ethical and religious questions affecting Welsh life' (17–18, 17). There is an article by T. W. Phillips BA about the new Welsh Intermediate Schools, arguing that preference for appointments should be given to those trained in the Welsh University Colleges (19–20). An unsigned contribution gives a detailed account of Tom Ellis's role as Liberal Chief Whip (21–2). The 'Notes and Comments' section announces a new feature, 'Beyond Offa's Dyke', intended to create 'a bond of union' with readers in England. This section criticises the Liberal government's failure to appoint Lewis Morris as poet laureate; the disastrously divisive Newport meeting of the South Wales Liberal Federation in Newport is reported, deploring the 'blatant glee' of those who refused to allow Lloyd George to speak (22–4).

Any tendency to cater for youthful rebellion is suspended in a special, heavily illustrated issue in June 1896, celebrating the installation of the Prince of Wales as Chancellor of the University of Wales. This opens with a three-page Ceremonial Ode, by Sir Lewis Morris, beginning:

> This is our joyous hour
> The Dawn expected long
> Break 'Sea of Music' in a surge of Song!
> The long, long night of ignorance is done,
> Triumphant o'er our land the Orient Sun
> Shines with renascent power.
> Our little Wales that lay asleep
> In secular slumbers deep
> Awakes for whatsoe'er of nobler fates,
> What ampler happier futures fair
> The hidden years prepare. (121)

Cymru Fydd's difficulties in reconciling nationalism with unionism, patriotism with imperial involvement, become more evident throughout this issue. For instance, J. Young Evans's article about 'Wales and the Empire' exhorts the Welsh people to 'a greater pride in British citizenship'. He asks 'what will be done by the University of Wales towards making the Welsh national life, while jealously retaining its individual characteristics, more potent in the life of the Empire?' Evans urges young people to take advantage of increased opportunities for careers overseas, declaring that 'It is but a clap-trap and vapid patriotism that attempts to isolate and alienate the life and thought of Wales, thus causing Welshmen to fail in their duty both to themselves and to the world' (150–2). The rhetoric of *Young Wales* frequently attempts to resolve tensions between the preservation of traditional Welsh culture, the distracting opportunities for individuals in the rest of Britain and the Empire, and the growing ambitions of women to contribute to political and social activities.

In March 1896 Nora Phillips (Mrs Wynford Philips) and Mrs Elsbeth Phillips announce that the editor has allocated a space every other month, to be known as the 'Progress of Women Page' devoted to 'the opinions, work and history of the Welsh woman-workers' (64). They suggest a historical perspective, citing Mary Wollstencroft and reporting the support of the Women's [Liberal] Federation for a progressive approach to women's suffrage. Over the next year, regular entries deal with topics such as 'Women as Poor Law Guardians' (May 1896) and 'News of the Suffrage Movement' (December 1896). Gwyneth Vaughan writes about 'Women and their Questions' in January 1897 (210–12), claiming that 'the air is thick with women's questions', especially in the United States and in France, though 'John Bull as usual is lagging behind in his own thick-headed fashion.' Such contributions become more sporadic in the period 1898–1903, though 'Un o'r Dddau Wynne' (Alis Mallt Williams) writes of 'Patriotism and the Women of Cymru' (May 1898, 115) and Ellen Hughes of Bedford celebrates the passion of Wales for education in April 1900 (86–7). The original bi-monthly series is revived in March 1903 but is short-lived, lapsing after the May 1903 issue's account of student life in Alexandra Hall,

Aberystwyth.[42] There are also regular pieces of fiction contributed by women, such as Annie Pierce's serial, *The Daughter of the Mill: A Welsh Idyll* (May and June 1899) or 'The Tyranny of Tabitha' by Mrs M. D. Evans of Cantref Rectory, Brecon (April 1903).

The magazine characteristically mixes the irreverent and the solemn, for example in December 1901, when the public image of Welsh MPs is under attack. T. Artemus Jones remarks on

> The collective inaction of the Welsh members throughout the last session . . . The influence of the halfpenny and penny press has done much to sharpen popular interest in Imperial politics . . . the Welsh members as a body have failed to show that organisation and those powers of concerted attack which they revealed in previous sessions or to display that vigilant and unceasing interest in Welsh affairs which should be one of the primary functions of all members from the Principality. (265–7)

On a vital amendment to the Education Act only five out of twenty-six Liberal members from Wales were present: 'Where were the Welsh Whips?' By way of contrast, 'The Incorporation of London Welsh Freemasons' is marked as 'a red letter day in the history of London Welshmen', listing twenty-seven names, including Conservatives, Liberals and Unionists 'but, apparently, no Socialists, or even followers of the Independent Labour Party' (268–9).

There is a considerable amount of serial fiction, making up almost half the December 1901 issue. Ernest Rhys supplies the concluding episode of a serial, *The Disillusions of John Probert*, about the life of an aspiring Welsh writer in London (270–2). 'Y Ddau Wynne' (the pseudonym of the sisters Mallt and Gwenfreda Williams) contribute two chapters of *A Maid of Cymru*, a flamboyant historical romance about the beautiful Tangwystyl Hywel and the brave Cadwgan (272–5). The unsigned 'Uchmor Lloyd' is about a courageous young collier who refuses to bow to the parson's son, is expelled from school, leads a strike, attacks the mine manager and is killed by English soldiers (281–4). Romantic images of young Welsh lives are clearly aimed at the target readership. There is also in the same issue a long biographical article about Dr Abraham Emrys Jones, an authority on diseases of the eye and president of the Manchester Welsh National Society, written by F. E. Hamer of the *Manchester Guardian* (276–81). The article explores in some detail a wide range of contemporary political issues including disestablishment, evictions, the need for better education in both languages, support for unionism and a reduction in intolerance. The magazine also features in 1901 and 1902 a series of articles by D. Wynne Evans expatiating on the traditional consciousness of cultural, religious and political links between the Welsh and the Jews.[43] The range of attitudes – and some of the evident frustrations reflected in these accounts – are reminiscent of those in the earlier *Cymru Fydd* magazine.

In April 1903 W. George Roberts writes critically about the influence of Welsh Nonconformity:

> The mind of Wales was so hermetically sealed against anything 'new' . . . that to impress the nation with any doctrines savouring of what is called 'heresy' would have been an impossible task. The close personal relationship of the ministers and their congregation was so distinctly that of the teacher and the taught that the former's position became almost pontifical. [This led to] the tranquil relief of the bulk of the inhabitants from all intellectual and ethical difficulties. (86–94, 87)

Roberts asserts that between 1801 and 1851 the Church of England established 263 new churches and the Nonconformists 2,280 (87). Despite censoriousness and fierce inter-denominational conflicts, Nonconformity has 'drawn to itself much of the best life of the community for nearly a hundred years' (90). Here one has almost the total triumph of the 'residual' elements in journalistic culture. Addressed to the readers of *Young Wales* towards the end of the magazine's life, this critique provides a rationale for a search for a new public in Wales which drives the development of these Anglophone periodicals. They simultaneously celebrate the central pillars of nineteenth-century

Welsh society but are also forced to search for a new response to the 'intellectual and ethical difficulties' that arise from social change. Stefan Collini's assertions about the public role of intellectuals in Welsh society are borne out to some extent by the intensity of this debate in a periodical originally aimed at a youthful audience. The theme of negotiation between 'Old' and 'New' repeats itself in another journal linked to Cymru Fydd, this time bilingual and centred about the lives of Welshmen in London.

The London Kelt (1895–1917)

Sub-titled 'Newyddiadur Cymru', with the legend 'Cymru Fydd' marked in the top right-hand corner of the first page, this bilingual weekly magazine (price 1d) announces itself on 12 January 1895 with a full page of advertisements. These include traditional Welsh remedies for coughs and colds, Sunlight soap, shirt makers, tailors, drapers, dairymen and sellers of pianos and harmoniums – traditional occupations for Welshmen in London[44]. 'No effort or expense is spared to make the LONDON KELT worthy of the patronage of our countrymen . . . We have come to stay.'

Unlike other bilingual magazines this one does stay, for more than twenty years until December 1917, including a substantial period after January 1897 as a solely Welsh-language periodical. The tone is gossipy: the front page of this first number offers a *mélange* of news items. It notes the return of Tom Ellis to his Downing Street office and the hospitality afforded Mr Gladstone by the former Welsh leader, Lord Rendel, at his beautiful Riviera residence. There is praise for the Marquis of Bute's 'enterprise and foresight' in building Cardiff up from 10,000 inhabitants to 130,000. The Temperance movement is propitiated in a proposal for a Christmas dinner for young men and women left in London over the festive season: 'a right merry day of feasting and intellectual enjoyment' that will 'keep many of our friends from the tap room and evil doers'. The Annual Soirée at St Benet's Welsh Church offers amateur dramatics, and the Tabernacle at King's Cross will mount its Annual Children's Entertainment.

The second page has a short story by Lilian Bowen-Rowlands: set in Solva, it is about a passionate working woman, Judith, and her resentment of being patronised by the male narrator. There is an item about 'Peggy Lewis', 'the notorious anti-tithe character', who has apparently enjoyed being in prison during the Christmas holiday. Over the holiday Wales lost to England at rugby, but at least London Welsh managed a draw with Tottenham Hotspurs.

The London Kelt is directed to and draws on its intimacy with the compact and influential Welsh social grouping in London. On page 3 it has 'Professional Notices' for tenors and baritones and provides 'News from Wales', worrying about the exposure to corruption of newly elected and inexperienced parish councillors and about the reluctance of the railways to hire labourers who have only a small knowledge of English. 'Personal Notes' record the sickness of Mr Lleufer Thomas, the secretary to the Welsh Land Commission, and the appointment of the Revd Gwynfro Davies of Barmouth as the first Calvinistic Methodist Minister to be made a County Magistrate in Wales. There are several pages of articles in Welsh and a formal report on the Cymru Fydd League's conference in Cardiff, urging the abolition of north/south distinctions within Wales and the desirability of including 'Welshmen in England' in their future deliberations.

In his article about the journal, Tomos Owen points out that the substantial Welsh contingent in London at the end of the nineteenth century may have amounted to as many as seventy thousand: 'consuming this paper, then, becomes part of the project of performing Welshness in London.'[45] As Owen also insists, *The London Kelt* owes much of its appeal to the predominance of Welsh Liberalism, to the level of activity of Cymru Fydd and to the existence of a London-based literary coterie including such figures as Arthur Machen, Ernest Rhys, W. H. Davies and Caradoc Evans.[46] On 1 February 1896 there is yet another note of regret that Lewis Morris, though recently knighted, has not been appointed poet laureate (9). The journal sees its audience as having traditional tastes but being interested in intellectual pursuits.

The predominant material in the magazine is, however, not literary or cultural, but concerned with politics and religion: disestablishment, revivalism, education, temperance, discrimination against the Welsh language, which all appear as repetitive themes. On 12 June 1909, when the National Eisteddfod was held in the Albert Hall, the first-page 'Notes and News' shares its space between two rival topics. There are confident assertions that 'The ancient Britons will reconquer London on Tuesday next' and that 'Welsh will be the only language heard around Hyde Park during the coming week.' At the same time, 'London Milkmen are up in arms over John Burns's Milk Bill,' and are threatening to desert the capital and return to farming in Wales. An account of David Lloyd George's recent ceremonial visit to his home in Llanystumdwy dominates page 2. During the Eisteddfod, the 16 June 1909 issue quotes (from the *Contemporary Review*) W. B. Yeats's desire for 'a way of life in which the common man has some share in imaginative art' (2). For that week only, the magazine becomes a daily production, publishing an illustrated souvenir issue. Immediately afterwards, the *London Kelt* returns to its political preoccupations in the context of the parliamentary battles over Lloyd George's 'People's Budget'.

A mixture of major political issues and intriguing local gossip continues, for instance in 'News and Notes' on 23 March 1912. Here, the government's bill establishing the principle of a minimum wage shares editorial space with the retirement of Mrs Margaret Powell of Builth Wells from her role as the oldest postmistress in Wales (1). The magazine also interests itself in other contemporary Welsh publications. On 3 January 1914 there is a substantial article, criticising *Baner ac Amserau Cymru* which 'has become mediocre and has not progressed with the times'. The article welcomes the arrival of *The Welsh Outlook* 'edited by a group of enthusiasts in the Cardiff area', but recalls that similar journals, such as *The Welsh Review*, Owen M. Edwards's

Wales and *Young Wales*, have all struggled to become paying concerns (2).

In the period immediately before the 1914–18 war, *The London Kelt* begins to increase the proportion of Welsh-language materials, and this emphasis is reflected in a new bilingual title: *Cymro Llundain a'r Celt (The London Welshman and Kelt)*. Hopes that disestablishment will be rapidly achieved in the aftermath of the expected civil war in Ireland are frustrated; instead on 15 August 1914 the magazine fears that 'six months of war will more than wipe out the achievements of nine years of peace' (2). In May 1917, *The London Kelt* becomes a monthly production for the rest of the war. Its last number in December 1917 records growing food problems in London but still loyally praises Lloyd George, who has enraged 'Pacifists and Military Professionals' but 'has succeeded to convince the populace' about the dangers that face the nation. The final issue also discusses a report on 'Industrial Unrest in Wales', criticising the authors' regressive tone – 'Is it really necessary to go back to Offa?' – together with the six-month delay in issuing the document and their failure to consider representations from people 'west of Swansea or north of Cardiff' (3). The article is signed 'Cymru Fydd', thus defiantly echoing in this last issue *The London Kelt's* original affiliation.

The London Kelt hovers between Wales and London, past, present and future, 'Old' and 'New'. Its occasional strap line 'Cymru Fu; Cymru Fydd' (Wales Past, Wales Future) reflects a preoccupation, sometimes a touch of irritation with tradition (as in 'Is it really necessary to go back to Offa?') on the one hand, and contemporary politics and future aspirations on the other.[47] It attempts to drive the 'emergent' into the 'dominant'. The *Kelt* is to have an afterlife as *Y Ddolen* in the 1920s and 1930s, as *Y Ddinas* between 1945 and 1949 and finally as the *London Welshman* from 1959.[48] Overlapping *The London Kelt* is another unusual and short-lived Liberal miscellany, this time published in Cardiff.

The Welsh Review (1906–1907)

In chronological terms, this monthly periodical is self-evidently a twentieth-century production. But in spirit it still belongs to the nineteenth-century tradition of Welsh liberal miscellanies in English. It is, unusually for the period, published from Cardiff. It carries no front cover, is priced 3d, and it is presented in two densely printed columns, sporting a red title on buff-coloured paper. In the first issue of March 1906 (twenty-six pages in length) the advertisements appearing on the back cover are for Everyman's Library, *The Christian World*, and *The South Wales and Monmouthshire Training School of Cookery and Domestic Arts*; they testify to solid middle-class affiliations. The most unusual characteristic, however, is that there is no named editor. [49] However, editorial intentions are clearly announced in the 'Notes of the Month':

> Not a day passes but some new periodical is launched until the stream becomes thick with craft of all shapes and kinds . . . The mission of this periodical may be summed up in a sentence: it is to articulate that new spirit which is animating the life of Wales . . . It is to provide one new bottle for the new wine: one medium for the new spirit: one exponent of that quickened sense of destiny which is so thoroughly possessing the heart of our people. (22–6, 22)

By the end of its short life *The Welsh Review* adopts the ambitious subtitle *The National Organ of Wales*, implicitly challenging comparisons with *The Red Dragon*, *Wales* and *Young Wales*. Nearly half the first issue in March 1906 is devoted to political articles. It opens with an anthropological essay by Professor W. Boyd Dawkins on 'The Origins of the Welsh People' (1–3). This links the Silures to 'the Iberic peoples of Spain' and argues that 'the small dark men of Scotland, Devon, Cornwall, Yorkshire and Derbyshire' are all of the same stock. Together they comprise 'the Celts and Gauls of history' supplying 'the vanguard of the great Aryan army which ultimately conquered the whole of western Europe'.

An unsigned article on 'Welsh Ministers of State' (4–5) is headed with a photograph of Lloyd George at his desk. A strong patriotic message claims George Eliot, Oliver Cromwell and William Morris (among others) as having unacknowledged Welsh descent. England acknowledges Welsh superiority in 'football, singing, and preaching' as well as in 'pulpit oratory'. Lloyd George is now commanding a great Department of State – the first Welshman to do so since Leoline Jenkins under Charles II. However, there will be no more 'Parnells of Wales'. This was 'the foolish dream of callow youths. It was magnificent but it was not politics'. The Revd John Thomas from Liverpool, writing on 'The Mission of Wales' (6–7), reinforces the unionist message: 'Let no one imagine that national patriotism in respect to Wales is incompatible with true British patriotism on the part of Welshmen.' He argues that the 'national soul is concerned with the pursuits and delights of the mind, with religion, poetry, music and literature'. A former Cardiff MP, J. M. McLean, also expatiates on 'The Welsh Party as a National Force' (8–9), remarking on 'the rapid growth of a vehement spirit of nationalism in Wales' and linking it to the election of 'a serried phalanx of radicals' excluding 'a single Conservative dissentient.'

There are further articles on contemporary politics, including one by Keir Hardie (13), looking forward to the revival of communal life in Wales, to land becoming common property and religion being freed from state control. J. Hugh Edwards interviews Ellis J. Griffiths (19–21), an academic and barrister, described as 'a son of the soil' who believes that 'politics have now become the passion of the peasantry.' The range of intellectual preoccupations and political commentary is aimed at a highly selective public sphere.

Cultural matters are more lightly covered. But there are 'Welsh Literary Notes' (10–13) recommending Watts-Dunton's introduction to *Wild Wales* in the Everyman edition and suggesting the possibility of Keats having had Welsh blood. A paragraph about Sir Lewis Morris (accompanied by a photograph) records his role as 'a man of affairs', notes his services to education and says that, now approaching seventy, he has decided to write no more poetry but to concentrate on prose. W. Lewis writes 'Welsh Educational Notes' (17–18) arguing that 'the Central Welsh Board and the University Court are too much jockeyed by academic members'; secondary schoolmasters should be represented and their salaries increased above the present £130, which is less than that paid to a colliery engineer.

The Welsh Review becomes steadily slimmer over the next year, and by its final issue in March 1907 has reduced to nineteen pages. It still carries a healthy number of advertisements, however, and it has gained a new front cover with a contents list. This issue is accompanied by a 'presentation plate' depicting Lloyd George addressing the House of Commons. The balance of the contents has shifted, with only two pages directly about politics, and a good deal of biographical material. Ellis W. Davies MP's 'Welsh Political Notes' (55–6) report the creation of a new Welsh Education Department, likely, in his view, 'to alleviate the discontent that is rife in more than one direction'. W. Lewis (honorary secretary of the Welsh County Schools Association) supports this in his 'Welsh Education Notes' (47–8), claiming that most schools are 'on the brink of bankruptcy' as a result of increases in numbers without any increase in available funds. He welcomes the appointment of Owen M. Edwards as chief inspector.

Edwards also features in the article that follows, from a series on 'Welsh Personalities' (49–50), quoting his 'Introduction' to *Wales* in May 1894 with its emphasis on the need of Welshmen to gain a better understanding of their historical heritage. 'Welsh Literary Notes' by L. J. Roberts (57–8) reprints a letter from York Powell about the founding of the Welsh University, this time from the February 1895 issue of *Wales*. *The Welsh Review* here is leaning directly on the earlier tradition of Anglophone periodical writing established by Edwards and his predecessors. Other biographical material appears in L. J. Roberts's opening account of George Borrow (especially remarking on Borrow's command of more than twenty languages, including Welsh), as well as in

'Vignettes of some Notable Welsh Judges' (59–61) and 'Notable Welshmen of the Month' by Professor J. Young Evans (53–5). This puts together brief accounts of a wide range of middle-class notabilities: lawyers, vicars, historians, scholars, preachers, musicians, a bishop and an archbishop.

The biographical material in this last issue of *The Welsh Review* has obvious political resonance, asserting the significance of Welsh contributions to public life, but perhaps also suggesting that the anonymous editor has, as he contemplates closure, a ready supply of this material waiting for publication. The central appeal of the magazine has been from the beginning to those already converted to the bedazzling cause of Welsh Liberalism in one of its most resurgent phases. Its conscious resource to and quotation from its predecessors suggests that a strong literary and cultural tradition has by now become established. Indeed, according to the first editorial, the stream of new periodicals was becoming by March 1906 'thick with craft of all shapes and sizes' and this may have something to do with this offering's short life. The editorial trope on 'one new bottle for the new wine' reflects the continuing significance of the 'Old New' theme in the story of Welsh liberal miscellanies written in English. The final example of the liberal tradition I want to examine returns us to London and to a familiar editorial figure. Again, though chronologically a twentieth-century production, it belongs in terms of style and content to the earlier tradition.

Wales: The National Magazine for the Welsh People (1911–1914)

Edited by J. Hugh Edwards (seven years earlier the editor of *Young Wales*), *Wales* presents itself in the by now familiar manner: two columns of close print, fifty pages long, well supported by advertisements, mounting a picture of Lloyd George in the centre of the first cover. Letters to the editor are to be addressed to St Stephen's Green, Westminster and half the contributions in the first issue (May 1911) are by Liberal MPs.[50] The issue has eight 'preliminary pages', tucked in among the advertisements, including metropolitan anecdotes, notes on 'curiosities', a letter about fashion by 'Lady Gwladys', accounts of Welsh holidays with photographs of Harlech, Tenby, Barmouth, and a poem: 'Another Version of Olwen'. *Wales* obviously wants to appeal to an expected readership that is likely to be fascinated by contemporary details relating to Wales while still seeing it at something of a distance. It appears to mount a particular appeal to women readers. A regular feature of the magazine's style is the inclusion of numbers of 'snippets', brief 'filler' items typically at the foot of a page. Examples include a recent mining disaster in Wyoming (8), the existence of 'a vestry of crossbells in Radnorshire' (15), the fact that Dr. Richard Price was the founder of Hackney College (24), and the publication of a new history of Gelligaer (27). These echo the 'Notes and Queries' elements of earlier journals.

J. Hugh Edwards opens the main text of the magazine with the first in a series about 'Welsh Leaders', a near hagiographic account of Lloyd George, introducing him as 'the modern incarnation of the last and the greatest of the native princes of Wales'. He is 'the little Welshman' who 'has attained the huge position of Chancellor of the Exchequer in the greatest Empire in the world'. He is an example to those who are 'smitten with diffidence and fear in the presence of an Englishman', especially because 'in every speech he continues to make some reference to the little country among the hills' (1–5). The political effect of this double play on the contrast between the 'little' and the 'great' is intensified by the concern expressed by W. Llewelyn Williams in his article on disestablishment. He argues that Wales cannot have Lloyd George and others in ministerial office and at the same time expect recognition as a separate political party along the lines of the Irish Party (11). This unease about the status of Wales is underlined in several critical articles, one about public health in Wales (seen as 'backward' in comparison with England), and another about the Welsh University – facing allegations of improper conduct in examinations – and about its 'very grave' financial position (16–19). An article by Rhys Nicholas on elementary education in Wales complains about the quality of teachers and makes unfavourable comparisons with Scotland (46–9). This first issue of *Wales* seems more ready than earlier magazines to air such criticisms. They overflow into cultural items, where Beriah G. Evans (358) complains about the prominence of 'merely Brummagem imitation of alleged native ware' among novelists, asking where are the Welsh equivalents to Ireland's Charles Lever or the Highlands' Ian MacLaren. He asserts that 'Allen Raine's history is not romantic and her romance, such as it is, is certainly not history.'

These provocations are balanced by a number of positive articles with a nationalist tone. At the end of the issue, Edwards maintains that the periodical 'sets itself to deepen our sense of nationality' and to promote national unity (50). The reliance on accounts of famous Welshmen, a series on 'The Sons of Wales' listing Welshmen who have achieved 'positions of distinction and responsibility' across the globe, and an article by Gwyn Nicholls, celebrating a seventh Triple Crown (20–2) all contribute to this objective. E. T. John writes about Wales and self-government (23–5) and Ellis Davies about the need for land reform (33–4). The magazine clearly wants to be seen as 'progressive'. An article by S. C. Fox about the newspaper proprietor Sir John Duncan (29–32) uses the epithet on three separate occasions in the context of his ownership of the *South Wales Daily News*, the *South Wales Echo* and the *Cardiff Times*.

In 'Welsh Literary Notes', W. J. Gruffydd claims that 1910–11 could be the Welsh *'annus mirabilis'* of modern times and points out that the work of Ceiriog was read by the Welsh peasants and was not, like the poems of Wordsworth and Burns merely 'the solace of the cultured' (43–5). Poetry in England is 'in a decadent state', compared to Wales. Owen M. Edwards 'has breathed new life into a study that greatly needed it and taught the Welshman to regard his country as a living organism and not as a dead *corpus vile* on which the ignorant may experiment'. This piece is unusual in referring to the world of literature outside Wales and in its rejection of English models. This may also account for the absence of any creative writing in the first issue.

Later issues, however, do include some serial fiction, such as one of Mrs Cecil Popham's romances, 'The Two Desires: An Eisteddfod Story' (April 1912, 214–18), about a schoolteacher who falls to his death when the singer he loves says that she is leaving him. Popham is one of the few women writers to appear in *Wales*. Others include Allen Raine, with a chapter from *A Life's Chase* in November 1911. 'Gwenneth' has a series, 'Woman and Her Interests' running for about a year from August 1912, when she is 'given this little corner to serve as a sanctum'. The series mainly deals with fashion or advice on holiday resorts. In March 1914 a weightier series appears, 'Women of Wales', starting with an account of Lady Mond's thoughts about mothercraft and reporting on activities in the Temperance movement in north Wales (34–5).

Other creative writing includes a few sentimental verses after the neo-Victorian tradition, such as Dudley G. Edwards's 'Nature's Little Optimist' in March 1914:

> The primrose drooped her listening head,
> Poor babe benumbed by fears;
> The dew of night fell softly down
> And mingled with her tears. (11)

By way of contrast, however, the same issue has a sardonic poem by W. H. Davies, 'The Welshman's Heaven':

> That paradise the Arab dreams
> Is far less sand and more fish streams.
> The only heaven the Indian knows
> Is hunting deer and buffaloes . . .
>
> The Scotchman has his heaven to come –
> To argue his creator dumb.
> The Welshman's heaven is singing airs
> No matter who feels sick and swears. (65)

In May 1914, J. W. Nicholas ends his serial *The Groesfford Well* in the style of Walter Pater:

> At his bidding her lyre gave way to rapture all its trembling strings and his old age was cheered by the knowledge that in his abode sojourned for a time the very Goddess of Harmony . . . For he knew her true of heart, blithe of wit and clad in triple steel against the darts of temptation. (140)

Wales betrays in these sparse pieces of creative material its consciousness of recent literary trends. In April 1912 it carries an advertisement for *The English Review*, a cultural and radical journal, to which W. H. Davies had contributed an early article about the experiences of the unemployed.[51] Despite the adherence in these periodicals to traditional forms, some awareness of developing new modes, ideas and attitudes seeps through.

As with some other Welsh periodicals in English, the end comes suddenly and is unheralded. The final issue in July 1914 appears confident enough, still fifty pages long, with eight pages of advertisements (rather more than usual), several contributions by MPs and one serial firmly labelled as 'to be continued'. There is an article by W. Llewelyn Williams about the national status of Monmouthshire (238–41), an account of 'The Glamour and Lore of the Cambrian Line', another contribution by Frederic Evans on the topography of Kenfig, and some parliamentary gossip (269–73) from 'Shôn Dafydd', Member for the University of Wales, about the pending wedding of an unnamed Welsh MP.

J. Hugh Edwards's *Wales* is the last example of the nineteenth-century tradition of the Anglophone liberal miscellany, centred in the world of the London Welsh. It marks the transition to the twentieth century proper. In literary terms it retains a conventional Victorian ambience during a period when elsewhere in London the drumbeats of the formation of early modernism were sounding in a new generation of little magazines such as *Blast* or the *Egoist*. At the same period in Ireland W. B. Yeats was producing the magazines of the Irish National Theatre, *Beltaine* and *Samhain*. The arduous search for a circulation that will maintain a reasonable level of advertising revenue without alienating the particular group it aims to serve, gives *Wales* something in common with these more experimental publications.[52] *Wales*, however, like its predecessors among Welsh periodicals in English, only rarely gives a nod to the existence of an *avant-garde*. It concentrates on relaying traditional Welsh materials relating to well-established topics that it judges will be of interest – especially to a diasporic audience.

A tradition of Welsh liberal miscellanies in English has become firmly established in a period of just over thirty years, between 1882 and 1914. This era spans a single generation, and is wholly contained within the formative career span of the iconic Welsh political figure of the period, David Lloyd George, an eighteen-year old solicitor's clerk in 1882 who had become Chancellor of the Exchequer by 1908. Charles Wilkins, founder-editor of the first Anglophone Welsh periodical in 1882, died in 1913 and Owen Morgan Edwards died in 1920. The coincidence of this fertile generation of politicians, scholars and journalists with that of the foundation and expansion of higher education in Wales helped to create a set of contributors and an educated audience that sustained this series of English-language periodicals. While the overwhelming majority of this fraternity was male, there were early publishing opportunities for pioneering women writers in both creative and critical modes. Many of these magazines had relatively short individual lives, but their collective endeavours ensured that, after the foundation year of 1882, there was no period when there was not at least one of them available to serve the newly created Anglophone public sphere, hitherto isolated from Welsh periodical culture. They represent a modest contribution to what Huw Walters describes as 'the great century' for Welsh periodicals, during the latter half of which he has identified almost six hundred separate titles.[53] Despite their shortcomings (including some provincialism, a narrowness of class appeal, and a regular retreat into old-fashioned values and tastes) they have, nevertheless, succeeded in creating a genre of Welsh liberal miscellanies in the English language. While serving faithfully the 'residual' elements in Welsh culture they have, nonetheless, driven forward the cause of 'emergent' ideas and concepts. They have created a new if subordinate public sphere within which intellectual debate can thrive among Anglophone writers and readers. They have produced an expectation that there will be regular periodical spaces where Welsh writers can express themselves in English, and have provided continuing sources of English-language commentary on political and cultural themes within Wales. The next century will benefit from their example.

2
The Independent Periodicals: 1914–1969

For the first half of the twentieth century and up to the end of the 1960s, Welsh periodicals in English continued to live independently, supported by the enthusiasms of their owners and editors and the personal efforts they could make to acquire some financial backing, obtain advertising revenue, recruit writers and readers and maintain subscription levels. These years encompass critical historical events and shifts of opinion: the 1914–18 war, the post-war euphoria of the 1920s, the decline of the Liberal Party, the foundation of Plaid Cymru in 1925, the prolonged recession of the 1930s, leading to the political ascendancy of the Labour Party in Wales. At another extreme of the periodical world (and outside the scope of this study) the period sees the creation of a number of radical, politicised magazines and newspapers. A colourful early example is *Plebs* or the *Rhondda Socialist* (1909), ominously subtitled *The BOMB of the Rhondda Workers* (later retitled the *South Wales Worker* (1911)), originating from passionate differences of opinion within the Workers Educational Movement. The 1939–45 war was followed by the first Labour government, the nationalisation of major industries, the foundation of the welfare state and the expansion of educational opportunity – radically altering the character of the public sphere in Wales. The comparative affluence of the late 1950s and 1960s was associated with major societal shifts. Changes of views on the family, the role of women, divorce, contraception and sexual relationships were associated in Wales with the decline of Nonconformity. Growing tensions between the English-speaking Welsh and the nationalists were dramatized in the conflicting rhetorics of Aneurin Bevan and Saunders Lewis. Kenneth Morgan points out that there was simultaneously a rapidly increasing crystallisation of the polarising concept of 'Anglo-Welsh' culture.[1]

Major periodicals of this period were: *The Welsh Outlook* (1914–33); then an overlapping quartet: Keidrych Rhys's *Wales* (1937–59); Gwyn Jones's *Welsh Review* (1939–48); *The Welsh Anvil* (1949–58) and *Dock Leaves,* later *The Anglo-Welsh Review* (1949–88). The London-based magazine *Life and Letters To-day* (1935–50) also belongs to this era. These magazines are uneven in quality, independent, often highly original but occasionally falling into the doldrums. Their editors take a lofty view of the position of writers, are often scornful of popular taste and are given to occasional political axe-grinding. Wales was not sealed from the intellectual currents of the day. In John Carey's view, 'the early twentieth century saw a determined effort . . . to exclude the masses from culture,' and many modernist writers deliberately cultivated obscurity and irrationality. Many British magazines of this period serve self-selected coteries and promote personal manifestos on behalf of their patrons or editors.[2] Welsh periodicals in English come late to modernism but often exhibit some similar characteristics. The first twentieth-century periodical to be discussed here links the liberal miscellanies of the late nineteenth century to the more trenchant cultural politics of the twentieth.

The Welsh Outlook (1914–1933)

The opening issue of this substantial and long-lived periodical (January 1914) mixes political and religious articles with antiquarian and artistic contributions. It presents itself in an impressive large format, better illustrated than its predecessors though its content has much in common with them. The founders were the mine owner, philanthropist and Liberal politician, David Davies from Llandinam (who covered the magazine's financial losses and dictated its general policy) and its first editor, Thomas Jones, an academic, senior civil servant and adult educator. Jones, known generally as TJ, was also a founder-member of the 'Cardiff–Barry circle' which influenced the magazine from its inception and included several members of the Editorial Board – described by Gwyn Jenkins as 'socialists but gradualists'.[3] The changing nature of life in industrial south Wales and the growth in immigrants put traditional Liberalism under pressure. The original title planned for the magazine was *Red Dragon* – perhaps seen as a connection to the past. In her authoritative article on the magazine, Alyce von Rothkirch discusses the range of contributors, largely a cohort of male writers born between 1870 and 1890, drawn from a middle-class, secular and academic establishment within Wales. She analyses the magazine's content, circulation and readership. Sales figures hovered around three to four thousand for most of *The Welsh Outlook*'s nineteen-year life but fell to around eight hundred by its end. It is doubtful whether any later Anglophone magazine exceeded this by much. Readers came mainly from the educated middle class living in university towns; there was little or no penetration of the south Wales industrial valleys or the 'more rural parts of Wales'. The content remained consistent, concentrating, according to William Watkin Davies, one of its later editors, on 'matters pertaining to Wales – politics, education, religion, music, literature and art'.[4]

The 'Foreword' to the first volume (unsigned, but surely written by Thomas Jones) makes it clear that the editor plans to challenge English hegemony:

> The English Press penetrates every morning into the remotest corners of the land . . . In the presence of these all-pervasive influences can a small nation of two millions sustain any semblance of its ancient self? Can it absorb into itself the immigrants of the mining valleys and share with them its spiritual heritage?

Read against *The Welsh Outlook*'s strap-line, 'Where there is no vision the people perish', and its subtitle, *A Monthly Journal of National Social Progress*, TJ here sets out to address – or even to create – a nascent public sphere in Wales. He challenges his new audience with the culture of the old while still promising a modernising message. The conventional appearance (sober covers, two columns of close print, most articles unsigned) echoes earlier Welsh magazines. In this first issue there are no advertisements; it is priced 3d. The February 1914 issue of J. Hugh Edwards's *Wales* contains a crude *ad hominem* attack on this new rival. It identifies TJ and his colleagues as members of 'The Society for Self Glorification', and alleges jobbery and pharisaism. Gwyn Jenkins says that TJ on his part 'wanted *The Welsh Outlook* to be a standing protest to John Hugh Edwards's *Wales*'.[5] The London-based journal, as we have seen, was to close a few months later.

It is worth looking at the opening number of *The Welsh Outlook* with this in mind. The editor's 'Notes of the Month' (1–6) will constitute the journal's campaigning signature pages throughout its life. TJ deploys a number of pithy short paragraphs on issues of the day. He notes the publication of the 'Living Wage Manifesto', 'a noteworthy attempt to organise Christian opinion', and the creation of a Register of Teachers giving teaching some of the professional cachet attaching to medicine. He addresses the shortage of qualified staff in schools with their 'utterly inadequate' pay scales. 'Dental deficiency' among children is linked to tuberculosis. An exhibition of Welsh Art at Cardiff's City Hall features Burne-Jones and demonstrates Augustus John's 'daring originality'.

A series of articles on religion and politics follow. 'The Religious Outlook in Wales' (unsigned, 9–13) remarks that the Welsh language has been used as 'a mighty bulwark to keep out the good and the evil that the alien might send us', but that defence is now challenged by education and industrial development. The quest for modernisation extends to religion as well as to political matters: 'If Theology still claims to be the queen of the sciences she knows that she must rule as a constitutional monarch' (10). 'The Medical Outlook for Wales' (also unsigned, 14–17) argues that teaching of medicine in hospitals is too traditional, and that funds should be raised for a new Medical School within Wales. The country needs to be self-reliant: 'Chancellors of the Exchequer resemble Providence because they always help those that help themselves' (17). 'Evolution of a Revolution' (27–8), a classic statement of liberal ethics, is a transcript of a speech to University settlement workers in Cardiff by Principal Burrows, which is said to 'reflect closely the aims and desires of *The Welsh Outlook*'. Burrows deplores developing class tensions and stereotyping, and wants to see the 'friendly personal relations' of traditional village life in Wales translated into industrial situations. The 'old' (again associated with the idea of the *gwerin*) is being called into the service of the 'new'.

The remainder of the issue is devoted to a mix of cultural topics. There is a poem in Welsh by R. Williams Parry (18) and an article on 'Modern Welsh Literature' (19–22) by T. Gwynn Jones (recording the growing preference for short stories rather than novels). An unsigned piece about 'Art and the National Life' (25–7) deplores Welsh apathy about art and architecture. 'Some Recent Welsh Plays' ('E.E.', 29–30) criticises representations of Welsh people on the London stage and asserts that 'the Welsh drama is at present in its infancy.' There are four excellent photographs including one of a sculpture titled 'The Miners' and one of miners' housing in Senghennydd. Six pages of book reviews follow (33–9), ranging from the literary (Gilbert Murray's *Euripides and His Age* and Galsworthy's *The Dark Flower*) to the social (research by Fabian women into the conditions of London labourers). Religious topics reviewed include the inspirational doctrines of the New Testament by J. Puleston Jones and *Constructive Natural Theology* by Norman Smyth. There is a review of *Indian Nationalism* by Edwyn Bevan. Articles on cultural topics are usually signed while most political and social articles are anonymous.

The general ethos of the magazine, advocating Christian values, Liberal politics and conventional cultural tastes, is well represented by this first issue. Compared with J. H. Edwards's *Wales*, the new magazine seems more serious, more intensely Welsh and far less engaged with the London political scene. Meic Stephens summarises *The Welsh Outlook* as 'Liberal, internationalist, moderately de-centralist but often rigidly conservative over ideological questions'.[6] In the two years of Thomas Jones's editorship these characteristics become firmly embedded. By the February 1915 issue the magazine attracts advertisements for banks, insurance societies and boarding schools and includes colour illustrations (for example of initial letters from the Book of Kells). There are a few pieces of English verse in the familiar Victorian style; the magazine's modernising drive is not literary but political and social.

The response to the war is more restrained than that of some Welsh-language periodicals.[7] 'Notes of the Month' for February 1915 observes the army's preference for officers who come from the public schools or universities. This discriminates against Welsh candidates (44). An article on 'The European Spirit' criticises German materialism and notes the decline of philosophy in German schools (47–50). A long piece by 'E.E.T.' follows: 'Politics and Philosophy in England and Germany', which attributes Germany's preoccupation with power to Hegel and Nietzche (51–6). 'Hans' by 'T.Q.' describes a Falstaffian German student at the Welsh College of Art (66–7): 'We cannot find it in our hearts to hate him.' Writing in *Planet,* nearly sixty years later, Tecwyn Lewis confirms *The Welsh Outlook*'s argument that waging war against aggression can reasonably be linked to Christian values.[8] However, at the time, a pacifist reader from St Fagans writes saying, 'I have been somewhat disappointed at the *Outlook*'s attitude towards the war' (79), while others congratulate the magazine on opposing the 'Anglification' of Wales and on 'teaching Welshmen to know one another'. Some short unsigned reviews of Welsh-language periodicals (75–6) include praise for Owen M. Edwards and his 'grave and sane words' on the war in *Cymru*. *Y Beirniad* represents 'the worthy product of the higher education in Wales' and *Y Geninen* is

The Welsh Outlook: ed. Thomas Jones, first issue, January 1914 'likened to a huge fisher's net that draws into its meshes many kinds of fish'. *The Welsh Outlook* consciously aims to reproduce the seriousness of these established periodicals in Welsh.

By September 1915 *The Welsh Outlook* is firmly established in form and content as well as political and social stance. It supports Lloyd George's war policy but is sceptical about conscription and worries about profiteering. It rejects jingoism in several articles: one about the differences between German and English ideas of freedom by a leading academic, C. H. Herford (335–40). There are two anti-war pieces, both by women. Romain Rolland contributes 'Motherhood and War: To the Women of Europe', celebrating 'the eternal Antigone refusing to give herself up to hatred' (345). Gwenda Gruffydd from Rhiwbina writes about a Women's International Congress at The Hague seeking to make peace through interventions by neutral nations (366).

By this stage, Thomas Jones is giving almost half the *Outlook*'s space to literary content. He co-opts John Masefield as a Welsh border-poet, on account of his links with Shropshire (351–3), and includes 'Songs of Serbia' (340–2). He publishes a short story, 'The Dream', about a mystic and preacher, and a poem about the destruction of Dante's tomb by the Austrians. The periodical is now more international in outlook and more interested in the arts. TJ moved to London as Deputy Secretary to the Cabinet at the end of 1916. Future, less authoritative editors were to find their working relationships with the proprietor David Davies more difficult.

After a brief interim period under H. J. W. Heatherington (January to April 1917) Edgar L. Chappell took over. Chappell had crossed swords with Davies earlier in 1917, because of his article about 'Unrest in the Coalfield'. However, Chappell sought to maintain the *Outlook*'s judicious flow of opinion while declaring his preference for 'strong, virile, out-spoken stuff'.[9] Chappell's 'Notes of the Month' (June 1917, 201–4) records his expectation of exercising influence over policies affecting Wales. The *Outlook*'s links with the Liberal ministry through David Davies and Thomas Jones would have encouraged Chappell to seek change over a wide range of topics: industrial relations in wartime: civil liberties; post-war reconstruction; devolution of health policy. In 1919 Gwladys Perrie Williams contributes 'Woman's Opportunity' (295–7) urging the women of Wales – who have borne heavy responsibilities in wartime – 'to act as the "flame-bearers" of Welsh traditions'. There is less coverage of the arts, but there is still substantial literary content including an obituary of Edward Thomas (208–10) and more poems – such as 'A Song of Glyndŵr's Rising', in the manner of Thomas Davis's ballads for Young Ireland.

Around this time, however, the board decided on major policy changes. TJ wrote a memorandum advocating less emphasis on cultural topics and concentration on two major drives: 'education and propagandist'. David Davies urged support for Home Rule, progressive reform, opposition to 'syndicalism' and collaboration between capital and labour. Members of the Cardiff–Barry Group were unhappy, and the ensuing reorganisation instituted a change of base from Cardiff to Newtown (nearer David Davies), and a further change of editor with the appointment of T. Huws Davies, a London-Welshman.[10] The January 1921 issue seems to fulfil some of the desired changes. It is shorter (twenty-four pages), more economically produced, with less extravagant paper, and no illustrations. There is only one page of advertisements. 'Notes of the Month' (301–3) has more international content and a section challenging the emphasis on German reparations. There is far less literary material in the issue (scarcely three pages) and more articles on Welsh life and folklore. Huws Davies's valedictory 'Notes of the Month' in the May 1925 issue (118–19) re-emphasises the *Outlook*'s internationalism:

> If this generation has for its first task the recovery of the old Wales, it has for its second the discovery of the new Europe, and it is only to the extent that we become and remain good Welshmen that we shall all prove ourselves good Europeans. (119)

Thus, 'the old Wales' is called into service in the development of 'the new Europe'.

William Watkin Davies, son of an 'old crony of Lloyd George', took over in June 1925 and experienced considerable difficulty in maintaining good relations with the *Outlook*'s supporters.[11] His first 'Notes of the Month' (June 1925), praises his predecessor and promises continuity, though he will aim to 'broaden its appeal and to popularise it, without lowering its intellectual standard' (143). He goes on to discuss the need for a 'Welsh Party' in the House of Commons but immediately qualifies this: it could be an error to create 'too great a stress on Home Rule – overshadowing other issues – which the *Outlook* considers of more vital and lasting importance' (145). In the correspondence section (166–7) he publishes a letter from D. Henry Rees arguing that Home Rule is merely a movement towards the parochial. Like some of his predecessors, he risks the wrath of David Davies. There is no mention of the General Strike until the June 1926 issue, when its collapse can be described, as 'a victory for sanity' (236). This response, ignoring the continuation of the 'miners' stand', may represent belated deference to the magazine's patron.[12]

Soon, however, controversy erupts over Watkin-Davies's adverse review of *Wales under the Penal Code* by Thomas Richards. The author is described in 'Notes of the Month' in September 1926 as 'the very worst type of dry-as-dust specialist' (251–2). In November 1926 Watkin-Davies alleges that 'one of the supermen who misdirect the studies of some of our unhappy youth' is effectively promoting puffery. This accusation led to Silyn Roberts writing a complaint to Thomas Jones, and to threats of libel action by Professor T. Gwynn Jones (a contributor to both the first and the last issues of the *Outlook*). The Davies sisters wanted the editor to be given immediate notice.[13] In August 1927, Watkin-Davies also fell out with TJ because of suggestions about undue secrecy concerning the finances of Coleg Harlech. His position became untenable and he handed over to Elias Henry Jones, the final editor of the *Outlook* in September 1927. David Davies instituted a further board reorganisation, marking the end of his direct interest in the magazine and giving control of its finances to his granddaughters at Gregynog.

Alyce von Rothkirch speculates usefully about the causes of the *Outlook*'s subsequent decline.[14] Key problems included a failure to grasp the pace and direction of change; ironically for an English-language journal, 'assumptions about a culture centrally based on the Welsh language were becoming tenuous.' The shift of opinion towards Labour seems to have been underestimated. Failures to initiate any 'generational shift' among contributors over the twenty years of its publication, to accept the need for more women contributors and to modify its standard range of subjects are all seen by her as damaging flaws.

A glance at the January 1928 number suggests that advertising revenue had become practically non-existent, and that there was an overemphasis on educational issues, comprising nearly one-third of this issue. By January 1930, 'Notes of the Month' have been inflated to a three-page editorial, quite different from the brief paragraphs of the TJ era. The political content is confined to articles about the League of Nations. There are more antiquarian and topographical articles, such as 'The Old Drover's Road to Tregaron' (23–5). The coverage by Gwilym Davies of international questions, especially the disarmament negotiations, continues to the end.[15] These depression years carry understandable concerns about unemployment, but also, as in the January 1932 number, numerous articles that look back nostalgically to 'Days of Yester-Years' (17) or 'School in the Early Eighties' (18–20). A review article about 'Welsh Periodicals' is far more critical than TJ's earlier article in 1915. It describes them as dominated by denominational differences; the splintering of the public sphere into 'five parallel independent streams . . . seems too absurd in such a small country' (28).

The editor's 'Retrospect' (315–26) in the final issue (December 1933) records the impact of the war and the Depression that have 'determined and over-shadowed' the *Outlook*'s life. However, 'all that we have to do, after all, is to hand on the torch' (316). The general tone is depressed. A section on literature by

T. Gwynn Jones confines itself to authors writing in Welsh and complains that there are few poems 'above the level of the barren rhetoric so common in the last century' (318). Sir Percy Watkins sees the last twenty years in education as 'an unproductive record' (321). T. Morgan Jones, reviewing developments in religion, laments the loss of 'the happy days of more uniform opinions' (322). T. Huws Davies declares that 'the present position of Welsh politics is utterly confused' (341). Welsh drama demonstrates 'deteriorating social values' (330). There are more positive accounts of music – a 'miraculous' increase in facilities' (333) – and health: especially progress on tuberculosis (337).

Thomas Jones's original challenge to the penetration of the Welsh public sphere by the English press has lost traction. The concentration on the tastes of a core circulation (around eight hundred) has been aimed at too narrow a base. The magazine's repetitive orthodoxy of opinion has led to a disastrous drop in circulation and advertising. The subordination of editorial opinion to the views of the proprietors and founders has been damaging. There is no recognition of the growing number of writers in English coming from the Valleys and the Borders. These talented pioneers, then in their twenties, such as Idris Davies, Glyn Jones, Rhys Davies or Margiad Evans, have to look elsewhere for publication. The absence of professionalism among its editors has exacerbated these problems. *The Welsh Outlook* has been the sole English-language periodical in Wales for most of its life, and the lack of any contending rival may have bred complacency. There is no immediate successor. The growing cohort of writers in English has to wait for four years before the publication of new journals. Then, however, quite suddenly, in the period between 1937 and 1950, several substantial periodicals enter the field, overlap, and compete for their talents.

Wales (1937—9; 1943—8; 1958—9)

Wales appears on the scene with a thunderclap first issue in the summer of 1937, price one shilling, printed in Newtown, the cover bearing a quotation from Dylan Thomas, announcing a Welsh entry into the world of twentieth-century modernism: 'As I walked through the wilderness of this world, as I walked through the wilderness, as I walked through the city with the loud electric faces and the crowded petrols . . .'. His short story, 'Prologue to an Adventure', is urban, erotic and youthful (1–6). The cover also lists Glyn Jones, Idris Davies, Nigel Heseltine and Vernon Watkins, introducing a new generation of Welsh writers in English. There is no editorial from Keidrych Rhys: the material speaks for itself. Glyn Jones's 'Scene' sounds a modernist voice:

> This is the scene, let me unload my tongue,
> Discharge perhaps some dirty water from my chest,
> The north swells bunioned with Plynlimon whose
> Sides leak water like some rusty old
> Boiler's brickwork . . . (7)

Nigel Heseltine's poems (10–13) echo Eliot's *Waste Land*, dealing with urban rubbish, broken glass, rubber tyres.

Nineteen pages out of thirty in this first issue are given to poetry. In reviews, Aneirin ap Gwyn asserts that 'London street life, even Rugby at Twickenham, v.d. or homosexuality are preferable to the dull-as-dishwater pieces of Non-conformists, helpful professors and officials' (28). 'G.J.' (presumably Glyn Jones) praises Rhys Davies as 'one of the first to get the valleys across on the English' (30). This feisty, almost familial tone is probably what makes Kenneth Morgan declare *Wales* 'a landmark in the dawning of Anglo-Welsh literature'.[16] The consciousness of making quasi-mythical figures out of each other echoes the manner of the 'Auden generation' in England, although this Welsh pantheon includes more working-class contributors.[17] M. Wynn Thomas describes the work of Welsh writers in English in this generation as 'the product of socio-cultural circumstances significantly different from . . . their predecessors', often based in 'the Merthyr–Rhondda axis' and facing 'an old South Wales that is starting a New'.[18] In his essay on Alun Lewis and Alun Llywelyn Williams, he emphasises the extent to which these writers were caught up in the international tensions of the 1930s, convinced that they were a generation facing 'certain and total annihilation', deriving its style from the 'products of literary modernism'.[19]

Keidrych Rhys delays his first editorial until the second issue in August 1937, when he reports that

> All agreed that the Principality had been long enough without a literary journal and that *Wales* supplies 'a long-felt want'. For the present anyway, this review ought to be a sort of forum where the 'Anglo-Welsh' have their say, as poets, story writers and critics, chiefly . . . We are not a literary clique; once more we stress that we are with the People. (36)

He refers to *New Signatures*, the 1931 collection of verse edited by Michael Roberts and John Lehmann, the iconic product of Faber and the 'Bloomsbury Establishment'.[20] He declares a desire to give 'our younger writers' 'an opportunity denied to them by the English Literary Map of log-rolling, cocktail parties, book-clubs, O.M.s and superannuated effeminacy in Bloomsbury editorial chairs' (37). Rhys takes up a provocative stance, fortified by his professional awareness of the journalistic and literary environment. The first critical article in the magazine by H. L. R. Edwards, 'The Allusionist School of Poetry' (40–5), reflects this insubordination, claiming that the irreverent young speak of 'gaffer Eliot'. Rhys sounds a nationalist note in his own poem 'The Fire Sermon or Bureaucracy Burned' (69), which pays tribute to the events at Penrhos Aerodrome in 1936.

This August issue is longer (forty pages as against thirty) and contains more prose writing, including six pages of reviews (one by Margiad Evans) and a new feature, 'Bibliographies of Modern Welsh Authors', opening with Caradoc Evans. It also has more advertising material, mostly for books and literary magazines. Issue 3 (Autumn 1937) is longer again (forty-six pages), with short stories from Rhys Davies and Glyn Jones, and poems by Idris Davies, Vernon Watkins and Glyn Jones. Dylan Thomas also offers poems, together with an excerpt from his projected prose piece, the *Map of Love* (116–22). The prevalent style of *Wales* has been established in Keidrych Rhys's image. The next few numbers are all slimmer; indeed, Rhys's final 'double issue' in March 1939 (co-edited by Dylan Thomas) has only seventeen pages but includes fragments by Kafka, poems by Dylan Thomas, Glyn Jones, Robert Herring, Lynette Roberts, Emyr Humphreys, Vernon Watkins and Rhys Davies. There is, probably deliberately, no editorial and no mention of the international situation, six months away from the outbreak of the Second World War.

The first of Nigel Heseltine's issues of *Wales* (August 1939) has an allusive modernist poem by Hugh MacDiarmid, 'On Reading Ifor Williams's "Canu Aneurin" in Difficult Days' (232–4) that expresses his reluctance to engage with contemporary history:

> Between two European journeys of Neville Chamberlain's
> And two important speeches of Herr Hitler's
> I return to the Taliesin and Llywarch Hen's poems
> Full of *hiraeth*, of angry revolt
> Against the tyranny of fact . . . (234)

Similarly, George Ewart Evans, (responding to a questionnaire from *Wales* about the relations of writers to society) urges that it is 'important to place himself in the main stream of culture from the past'; 'any attitude to the present war-ridden, bourgeois-rotten reality would of necessity be negative' (225). The tensions between the New and the Old surface again, under the pressure of cataclysmic events.

Heseltine prints his predecessor's 'Notes for a New Editor', twenty-one numbered iconoclastic statements by Keidrych Rhys, for example characterising key elements in Welsh society as 'unlovely, soul-destroying and violent Puritanism' (246) and claiming that 'Aberystwyth University College . . . is at present deep in a thick stupor intellectually' (248). Rhys also comments on the deficiencies of the Welsh public sphere: 'Public opinion here is still what four or five knights decide "what should be done" whenever they meet at the cocktail bar of the Royal Hotel' (249). Heseltine prints more trenchant criticism of Welsh life in Idris Davies's 'Morning Comes Again' in his next issue (October 1939):

> The fat little grocer and his praise for Mr. Chamberlain,
> The vicar and his sharp, short cough for Bernard Shaw
> And the colliery-manager's wife behind her pet geranium
> Snubbing the whole damn lot. (270)

This issue begins with Heseltine's editorial, dated 7 September 1939, finally acknowledging the entry into the war: 'Blood and honour are forced on us so lately at peace', ending 'Our fight will be against any establishment of Fascist principles in this country' (254). Heseltine's final issue (the last in this series of *Wales*) has a different tone, still with the emphasis on poetry, eschewing any farewell editorial but opening instead with Keidrych Rhys's 'The Van Pool', adopting an unaccustomed pastoral mode:

> Llansadwrn slept unattacked
> As all pretty hamlets should . . .
>
> Noiseless, Towy winds gently through the land, no flood below,
> No tuneful nightingale charms the forest with her tale.
> Ah! The Mabinogion tales of Wales. (292–3)

Some of the early energy seems to have seeped away. There is no announcement but, apart from a one-page 'Wartime Broadsheet', *Wales* goes out of circulation for three years, restarting in July 1943 as a new series, this time six-monthly, priced 1s. 6d.

This July 1943 issue is ninety-four pages long and well supplied with advertising from prestigious publishers and London and Scottish magazines. Keidrych Rhys's editorial consciously differentiates *Wales* from its earlier history:

> We are primarily a cultural magazine – cultural in the broadest sense . . . non party, independent and progressive. Not like the old magazine which concentrated on 'experimental' writing . . . The pioneer work of the old happy-go-lucky pre-war *Wales* is done – the sapping, the literary fireworks, the frontal attack – all that is over *pro-tem*. Our aims have been partially achieved. (4–5)

Its objective is to be the 'subtle encouragement of all those creative elements in our midst with some sense of nationhood'. So, the reader is to expect a more considered, more conventional version of the magazine. The 'new' of 1937 has become 'old' rather quickly.

The early articles support this sober prospectus. Jim Griffiths MP in 'Wales after the War' writes about industrial reconstruction and the reform of local government (7–10). There are three critical articles about the perceived weaknesses of 'Anglo-Welsh' writing. Wyn Griffith queries the value of the 'Anglo-Welsh' label, seen as 'an easy way of announcing to the English reader that the writer pre-judges the issue by claiming to be different' (15–16). W. Moelwyn Merchant's 'The Relevance of the Anglo-Welsh' cites Saunders Lewis: Anglo-Welsh writing 'enriches the English imagination rather than the Welsh'. Idris Bell ('The Welsh Poetic Tradition') emphasises the importance of continuity and the bardic tradition in Welsh poetry; he 'fears slavish subjection to English models' (38–45).

The poems, too, especially the 'Little Anthology of More Poems from the Forces' (20–33) – which includes work by Alun Lewis, Ewart Evans and Vernon Watkins, speak more of *hiraeth* and alienation and less of rebellion. Vernon Watkins writes lyrically of home:

> Returning to my grandfather's house, after this exile
> From the coracle river, long left with a coin to be good,
> Returning with husks of those venturing ears for food
> To lovely Carmarthen. (29)

WALES

Prologue to an Adventure

As I walked through the wilderness of this world, as I walked through the wilderness, as I walked through the city with the loud electric faces and the crowded petrols

DYLAN THOMAS
GLYN JONES
JOHN PRICHARD
NIGEL HESELTINE
KEN ETHERIDGE
IDRIS DAVIES
LL. WYN GRIFFITH
VERNON WATKINS
CHARLES FISHER
ANEIRIN AP GWYNN
KEIDRYCH RHYS

No. 1

Summer 1937

One Shilling

Wales: ed. Keidrych Rhys, first issue, Summer 1937

There is, as promised, little that could be described as 'experimental'. A sense of endorsing the Old rather than the New, appears again in W. J. Gruffydd's short story, 'Bethesda'r Fro' (45–50), where a patriarchal nineteenth-century figure foresees the forthcoming industrialisation of his valley and 'sank on his knees weeping bitterly'.

Criticism of the 'Anglo-Welsh' idea is repeated in the highly conflicted editorial in the next issue in October 1943:

> The Anglo-Welsh 'intelligentsia' in itself at the moment is so inorganic as scarcely to be more than a group who happen to be connected with a single region . . . they are a bit scared to show where they stand . . . We have at last produced some talent but we can't hope for any sort of patronage . . . What is to be done? I am not very hopeful about the future . . .
> The attitude of once-promising fashionable young Welshmen round Bloomsbury, who show no interest in trying to reach a public here, or any interest whatsoever in Welsh life and native culture results only in a general forgetting of their Welsh consciousness. (6–7)

George Ewart Evans ('An Emergent National Literature') also excoriates his contemporaries: 'Look how different we are with our quaint accent and our harsh flannel style' (50).

This masochism gains *Wales* unaccustomed praise from the English press. The *Times Literary Supplement* finds the magazine 'more serious-minded and substantial'; the *Liverpool Echo* and the *Manchester Guardian* are all quoted in January 1944 as enthusiastic (116). In the correspondence column, however, there are ominous signs. Gwyn Jones announces the restart of his *Welsh Review* (suspended since 1939) and Thomas Jones (TJ) refuses finance from the Pilgrim Trust. In the next number (January 1944) R. S. Thomas questions the wisdom of reviving Gwyn Jones's rival magazine, given the losses *Wales* is known to have sustained on its recent numbers (106).

I have argued elsewhere that the change in the content of *Wales* at this stage is effectively a generic shift, moving away from being a 'little magazine' and reverting to the traditional form of the nineteenth-century 'liberal miscellany.' This process is largely complete by the Autumn 1944 issue of *Wales* where, in his editorial, Rhys accepts the limiting formulation, common in those nineteenth-century predecessors, that

> Many issues of great consequence in the Principality today – issues of values, economics, nationality and assimilation, politics, religion, culture, psychology, inherent in the Welsh temperament – could be of profound interest to the outside world. (5)

This list of abstractions moves away from his earlier emphasis on creative writing and proposes a wider agenda. He engages with E. H. Carr's views on nationalism: 'I assert that complete cultural autarchy is not compatible with the existence of a common European culture' (6). *Wales*, however, still finds space for poems and pictures by Glyn Jones (8–11) and Lynette Roberts (33–4), together with typical short stories. There is a lengthy contribution from Robert Graves (36–50). Perceptions of Welsh institutions are negative. In 'Welsh BBC Programmes', Neville Penry Thomas asserts that 'during the hey-day of mediocrity the Welsh programmes are the most mediocre' (56). Ivor Lewis deplores Bangor's 'stiff adherence to the set syllabus' that produces 'efficient, shrewd-eyed mediocrities'. There are no less than fifteen pages of political reminiscence shared between Lord Clwyd's memories of his parliamentary colleagues (71–8) and John Legonna's 'Political Trends' (79–85).

In June 1946 *Wales* acquires the traditional subtitle shared with many of its predecessors, establishing itself as *The National Magazine*. A year later, in the summer issue of 1947, it celebrates the tenth year since its original founding, with sixty messages of good will from many of its frequent contributors as well as from the editors of the *Observer, Reynold's News*, the *Daily Mail* and the *Western Mail*. However the December 1947 issue announces that it is to become bi-monthly in future. Issues become sporadic and the series comes to an end in October 1949. The tone becomes increasingly elegiac: the editorial for December 1947 places the magazine in the context of the history of the Welsh press since

1770 (330–2). There is a poem by Roland Mathias 'On the Grave of Henry Vaughan at Llansaintffraed' (334). A reprint of a broadcast by Saunders Lewis on 'The Essence of Welsh Literature' celebrates the bardic tradition (337–41). In February 1948, Dilys Rowe offers her 'Thoughts on the Tenth Anniversary of *Wales*' (442–50), expatiating on the 'cultural starvation in Wales', caught up in the 'straight-laced and unnatural mould of nonconformism'. There is a list of contributors since 1937 (487–8). Keidrych Rhys contributes fourteen pages of 'Editorial Flashbacks'. In May 1948, a fourteen-page-long 'List of Subscribers' (554–68) sheds some light on the public sphere within which *Wales* operates. *Wales* takes more than half its 800 regular supporters from outside Wales, almost a hundred of them from overseas. It is bought by many institutions, especially Miners' Institutes and university departments. The reasons for the series coming to a premature close are not very clear; advertising support continues to the end. It may well have been due to changes in the editor's private life: Rhys moved from Llanybri to London in 1950, after the breakdown of his marriage.[21]

When the magazine is revived for its third and final series, nine years later, it is based in the editor's north London home and given another imposing subtitle: *The National Monthly Magazine of Literature, the Arts and Welsh Affairs*. The September 1958 issue has a glossy cover with a photograph by Anthony Armstrong-Jones of HRH Prince Charles at age six, listing all his many titles. Keidrych Rhys's editorial (4–6) emphasises that *Wales* is not subsidised but intends to give 'astringent expression to the lively original and authoritative viewpoints of those who really care about the country's future'. It will be 'a popular magazine, aiming to cover literature, criticism of the arts and affairs'. He will aim to sell *Wales* to 'one-hundredth of our three and a half million compatriots in the world'. (Meeting that ambition would have required sales of 35,000 copies, well beyond the best achievement of any Welsh magazine.) The editorial also contains an invitation to Lord Raglan to 'defend his controversial standpoint' on the Welsh language.

This first issue is not noticeably more 'popular' in tone, having at least twenty pages of serious political commentary. There is a lengthy essay on 'Welshness in Wales' by James Morris (13–23) suggesting that 'the basic character of Wales (often shifty and secretive, often charged with maudlin sentiment) survives the varied onslaughts of modernity'. Personal memoirs feature substantially: Huw Menai's experiences in a draper's shop (31–4) and Murray Tulloch's reminiscences of bird-watching (39–45). There is only one piece of short fiction, Rhys Davies's gothic account of 'The Wedding at the Lion' (51–62).

In the following issue (October 1958) Rhys (3–8) records a number of readers' criticisms, distrustful of market influences, especially of the 'plushy glossy' appearance of the new *Wales*, and its alleged approximation to the ethos of the *Western Mail*. For his part, the editor expresses scepticism about the quality of typical short stories on Welsh themes, agreeing with Cyril Connolly's account of them as 'stagy exports'. There is another piece by Huw Menai, this time on 'The Bilingual Mind' (8–14), followed by Lord Raglan's 'I Take My Stand', a contribution that is to haunt *Wales* for the rest of its life. Raglan argues provocatively (15–18) that Welsh is essentially a minority foreign language within Wales, that academics who publish in Welsh 'cut themselves off from the international fellowship of scholars', while others cultivate the language mainly to secure preferential treatment in applying for certain posts. They aim 'to create enmity where none existed'. No Welsh books were taken out of the library in Barmouth for a whole year; and 'most of the speakers of Welsh are . . . illiterate or semi-literate'. He concludes (18) that 'it will be a happy day for Wales when that language finally takes its proper place – on the bookshelves of the scholars.'

In the November 1958 number Rhys records the support of *Baner ac Amserau Cymru* for his challenge to Raglan (14). He also gives space to the 'icy courtesy' of Emlyn Williams's rebuttal of Raglan (16–21), ending, silkily, with the comment that Raglan has shown that, contrary to his own assertion, the language of the Philistines is not yet dead (21). In a 'Stop-Press' (69 and 75) Rhys announces that Raglan is to sponsor a debate in the House of Lords on the desirability of letting Welsh die out, arguing that it is illegal to insist on it being taught against parental wishes and that teaching it actually handicaps children by making them 'inefficient'. The next editorial (December 1958) observes that the article has 'served to inflame the hotheads of a few' (4), praises Raglan for having the courage to make his case and takes a Voltairian stance: Rhys does not agree with him but supports his right to express his views. Raglan has 'stirred many minds on the subject.' Subsequent issues, however, play the Raglan intervention down, ignoring it in editorials, which are now preoccupied by social and industrial questions. Tudor David in 'The London Squelch' (January 1959, 70–3) refers to Raglan's 'egregious farrago' and attacks the suburban London Welsh fraternity, which, he says, 'inhabits a cream cake world' and harbours opinions even more extreme than Raglan's. The article continues to rankle. In June 1959 Owain Glyn Williams writes of 'the English tittering and Raglanising about the Welsh language' (73). Raglan is defended in September by 'Janus' who describes the 'choleric responses' to the original article as the product of a 'gang of bigots and nepotists that ruled the official cultural roost for so long in Wales' (20).

During the rest of 1959, *Wales* mingles serious political commentary with relatively trivial (or 'popular') material. Editorials become prolix, largely devoted to social and political issues such as NCB closures (February 1959, 6–10) or unemployment levels (April 1959, 6–12). The magazine becomes less stable. There is a three-month hiatus after the June 1959 issue, and the September number covers three months. The October 1959 issue opens with a listing of the MPs just elected: '"Thirty-six Tickets to Westminster" – all first class with £1000 a year basic and tax-free allowances at the rate of £750 per annum'. In his piece, 'The Never-Never Land', Alun Richards maintains that the work of 'the literate post-war generation' in Wales is 'as unreadable as the later surrealist stories of Dylan Thomas'. Anglo-Welsh writers 'stand gabbling like the spurious traditions of a barely credible past' (29). There are few poems and the short fiction is undistinguished: a short story by Val Baker, 'Oranges' (30–6), about strip poker after a party and Charles Jones's 'Chief Petty Officer Kosco Ross' (53–62) about a night out in Bute Street.

The final number appears in January 1960. There are no farewells, but a passing reference in a contributor's note to a 'printing dispute' which 'must have been a great trial to you' (85) may explain the recent suspension of publication. Keidrych Rhys reverts to the Raglan incident yet again in his final 'Editorial Comment': 'No sooner had the hubble-bubble and racket over Lord Raglan died down than one becomes aware of new eruptions . . .' (11). Glyn Jones, present at the end as in the beginning, provides a study (15–17) of the 'Literary Scene' in Wales, while Alun Richards's downbeat comment (16–18) again invokes the Raglan article:

> The Anglo-Welsh School as far as I am concerned is over. There are the Welsh, the Welshie-Welsh who in Lord Raglan's inimitable phrase, 'by their knowledge of Welsh obtain preference for posts for which they are otherwise ill qualified' and thirdly those few serious contemporary writers in the Welsh language. (18)

This critique of the 'Anglo-Welsh School' and the tilt at the freemasonry among Welsh-speakers reflects the critical tone of *Wales* in its final year.

The magazine has shifted ground on several occasions, particularly in its attitudes to the London Welsh. In its early stages, *Wales* had enjoyed, together with Gwyn Jones's *Welsh Review*, 'stylistic membership of an artistic metropolitan *avant garde*' and had been closely allied to periodicals outside Wales, such as the *Dublin Magazine* and *Life and Letters To-day*.[22] However, its earlier devotion to modernism faded with time as Keidrych Rhys sought a more popular audience. *Wales*, like many of its predecessors, betrays some of that over-concern which Tony Brown has noted with the '*interpretation* of Wales to England' and the insistence on the continuity of Welsh tradition.[23] These are themselves tropes that have repeated themselves regularly in the earlier miscellanies. The history of *Wales* further illustrates the tensions in these periodicals between 'Old' and 'New', 'residual' and 'emergent' and the feverish instability of the Anglo-Welsh public sphere.

Life and Letters To-day (1935–1950)

Edited by Robert Herring, *Life and Letters To-day* demonstrated a continuing interest in Anglo-Welsh writing and produced five numbers devoted to Welsh writers between March 1940 and September 1948.[24] Alvin Sullivan points out that the magazine had an earlier history, from 1928, when it was founded by Oliver Butt, with Desmond MacCarthy as editor. It was closely involved with modernism and published Lawrence, Forster, and Virginia Woolf. After Robert Herring took over in 1935, the magazine proclaimed a special interest in younger writers.[25] Its contribution to Anglo-Welsh writing is acknowledged by many. Glyn Jones says of it that

> One felt a great sense of relief, almost of self-indulgence, at having two literary magazines to which one could submit one's work, when for years and years one had, perforce to send it to often indifferent, hostile or uncomprehending editors in London or America.[26]

Robert Herring had no personal Welsh connections, nor did his backers, but he was a close friend of Keidrych Rhys, whose *Wales* is presumably the other literary magazine that Glyn Jones had in mind. *Life and Letters To-day*, at this stage of its life, was financed by the poet, Winifrid Annie Ellerman, known as 'Bryher', a wealthy American bohemian.[27] The first Welsh issue, in March 1940, appears in *Life and Letters To-day*'s smart yellow and black formal cover with a Contents page largely written in Welsh. The editorial (*Golygyddol*) says:

> A Welshman allows life to words . . . and therefore they move, and do not always mean the same thing, what is true now not being true a few minutes hence or thence. Don't ask an Englishman to know this because he can't follow; his Pegasus is a hack, not a steeplechaser. (218)

This exoticism might lead one to expect an emphasis on the wilder side of the Anglo-Welsh tradition. What follows is, in fact, quite different. In addition to creative writing, mostly in a realist vein, by such established Welsh writers as Alun Lewis, Dylan Thomas, Glyn Jones, Keidrych Rhys and Vernon Watkins, there are also scholarly articles about Welsh culture. Examples, from this issue, include articles by J. Hughes Jones on the Gregynog Press (226–35), by H. D. Lewis on the use of Welsh as a medium for scientific and practical, as well as literary discourse (236–43) and by Nigel Heseltine about the history of Taliesin and other Welsh bards (244–5).

In the March 1943 issue (sub-titled 'Cambria') the emphasis is on the contemporary. A section on 'Welsh Poets' has work by Henry Treece, Vernon Watkins, and Alun Lewis. Robert Herring himself is co-opted for the occasion. R. S. Thomas publishes 'A Peasant', introducing the figure of Iago Prytherch:

> Iago Prytherch his name, though, it be allowed,
> Just an ordinary man of the bald Welsh hills,
> Who pens a few sheep in a gap of cloud.
> Docking mangels, chipping the green skin
> From the yellow bones with a half-witted grin
> Of satisfaction . . . (154)

This iconic poem marked a distinctive shift in Thomas's poetic technique and a 'quantum leap' from his earlier work.[28] It is preceded by Walter Dowding's essay on the 'The Evolution of a Nationalist' (135–48) describing his conversion to nationalist thinking during wartime and developing an 'argument for a sane, creative nationalism' (148). Gwyn Jones completes his 'Notes on the Welsh Short Story Writers' (156–63) with an account of Glyn Jones ('as precise as twice-twos and odd as moonlight') and his criticism of the 'slabs of proletarian realism' that is produced 'in the hands of the incautious' (161). Some of the short fiction in this issue (by Rhian Roberts, Reginald Moore and Con Morgan) only narrowly avoids falling prey to this tendency.

In the September 1948 issue, where 'the accent lies more on the past than the present' (165), Selwyn Jones writes about Thomas Gwynn Jones, born in 1871, comparing him to the 'wild Irish' poets who survived the English policy of breeding illiteracy in their country' (178). 'The Women of Llyn-y-Fan' by Gwyn Williams (185–99) deploys the myths of Lake women, developing Freudian and Frazerian interpretations; Gwyn Jones's article on 'Culhwch and Olwen' (200–12) suggests that the Welsh Arthur is the 'fabulous barbaric chieftain of a barbarous fantastic court' (211) rather than a figure of courtly romance. There is also some contemporary material, for example short stories by Con Morgan ('Stranger Within' 213–19) and Cledwyn Hughes, 'Sheikyn the Gypsy' (227–43). Both of these are dark tales of murder and betrayal in rural Wales, with echoes of Caradoc Evans. There is no contemporary poetry, but the review section includes a piece by Denis Botterill, writing about Margiad Evans, R. S. Thomas and Wyn Griffith (252–60).

Life and Letters To-day provided Welsh writers with access to wider markets. Meic Stephens emphasises the extent to which writers like Glyn Jones and Dylan Thomas had 'London-oriented' aspirations and the attractions that the international ambitions of *Life and Letters To-day* would have had for them and for their contemporaries. The back cover of the summer 1937 issue lists seventy-five overseas locations where the periodical was read. Its Paris correspondent was Sylvia Beach. He also points out that there is hardly an issue that does not carry something by a Welsh writer.[29] The magazine's Welsh role owes everything to the personal enthusiasms of its patron and its editor. It offered an extension of the Anglo-Welsh public sphere within which there was less room for the distracting internal polemics that featured in the later series of Keidrych Rhys's *Wales*.

The Welsh Review (1939; 1944–1948

Edited by Gwyn Jones, an academic, anthologist, novelist and critic (described by Dai Smith as 'the Anglo-Welsh Colossus himself'), the *Welsh Review* presents itself as a classic serious miscellany, more concentrated on literary material and criticism than its contemporary, Keidrych Rhys's *Wales*.[30] In his retrospect, *The First Forty Years*, Gwyn Jones traces the origins of twentieth-century Anglo-Welsh writing to the existence of a 'strong, patient, passionate, rebellious, idealistic, and *kind* generation [which] coincided in its parenthood with the great flowering of Welsh secondary education between the wars' (11). He seeks to defuse tensions with Welsh-speaking Welshmen. He hoped in the *Welsh Review* 'to give to Welsh writers in English the sense that they belonged with and to each other – I wanted all my writers and readers to feel that, despite the barrier of language, they belonged with and to Wales.'[31]

The first issue in February 1939 has an imposing appearance, somewhat reminiscent of the earlier *The Welsh Outlook*, using a large print face, fifty-six pages long, a substantial monthly magazine with a subscription of 12s. a year, based at the editor's home in Rhiwbina Garden Village, Cardiff. There are several advertisements, for *Wales*, for *Life and Letters To-day* and for books and paper manufacturers; there are woodcuts and other illustrations. Gwyn Jones's lengthy opening editorial (3–7) describes the magazine as 'a journal for the English-speaking Welshman' but not designed as a successor to *The Welsh Outlook*: 'it is a new journal for a new day' (3). He chooses not to mention the existence of Keidrych Rhys's *Wales*. He is confident that his group of young contributors, already 'interpreting Wales to the outside world', will 'soon be recognised as the most valuable leaven to English literature since the Irishmen opened insular eyes at the beginning of this century'. He responds to three questions often put to him. The *Review* is in English because a bilingual model would fail financially; there are, however, a million potential readers in English needing such a magazine

(4). The *Review*'s 'height of brow' is determined by its intellectual stance: 'briefly we speak to and for people of mind'; it is not 'the mouthpiece of a coterie' (5). Its political standpoint is 'humanitarian': it is to stand for 'tolerance, progress, knowledge, freedom of thought and expression and a firm belief in the dignity of mankind and the unqualified wickedness of all that outrages it' (6). This highly traditional liberal-humanist manifesto is sensitive to the international issues of the day, as Europe struggles with the aggressive development of Fascism.

This first issue concentrates on literary materials. Fiction, poetry, criticism, Welsh drama, excerpts from Welsh broadcasts, and book reviews, make up most of the content, but there are some articles on social and political topics. The short stories tend towards the south Wales working-class grotesque, as in Glyn Jones's 'An Afternoon at Uncle Shad's' (8–15), where two boys see their Uncle, 'gone bloody dull since he lost his job', ineffectually trying to kill himself: 'the fool couldn't even cut his throat tidy.' The poetry in this first issue is conventional and light in tone, lyrics by W. H. Davies and Huw Menai. A contribution by 'Gwerinwr' (42–3) registers concern for the future of the Welsh language and another by 'Gwrandawr' (44–5) claims that the BBC is 'still only scratching at the surface of Welsh ingenuity and talent.' The reversion to Welsh pseudonyms in these cases reflects Gwyn Jones's more traditional editorial approach. Gwilym Davies, the established commentator on foreign affairs from *The Welsh Outlook*, reappears with a wide-ranging article, 'Beyond Our Frontiers' (38–41). He reports the views of an Italian Fascist on the weakness of French and British policy (advocating compulsory emigration of the unemployed to Canada and Australia). There are four pages of book reviews.

The editorial of July 1939 observes: 'These are not good days for literary journals. The publishers of books say that these last nine months are the worst they have ever known' (303). Gwyn Jones notes the closure of *Criterion* and the *London Mercury* and he appeals for more subscribers. The tone is less optimistic than the magazine's opening salvoes, and Gwyn Jones accuses British capitalists of irresponsibility:

> We are suffering grievously from the betrayal of British interests by the new-style imperialist, who grants to aggressor states the exact rights of smash-and-grab we found so profitable during our own empire-building days, and the old-style businessman who will not bate twopence-halfpenny of his trade with indecent nations, though he sharpens their bayonets at the same time. (305)

The emphasis on 'our own empire-building days' links Wales to British political history more directly than would have been comfortable for most of Gwyn Jones's predecessors and contemporaries. Peter MacDonald Smith insists that 'Gwyn Jones's instinct was to shrink from forming opinion . . . The first series was not notable for its forthright views.'[32] However, this issue does address social issues in Peter and Richenda Scott's article on 'The Brynmawr Experience', welcoming 'the idea of setting a derelict town to work to rebuild its own life' (336), and it gives Gwilym Davies space to speculate on the effects of Fascist victory on the eventual formation of the 'United States of Europe' (344). But the emphasis is mainly on literary matters, taking up more than three-quarters of the magazine.

By August 1939 Gwyn Jones has shed his early optimism about the million potential readers. He says in his 'Editorial' (3–5) that 'it will be clear from its contents so far that the *Welsh Review* or any journal like it depends for support upon no huge audience but upon one thoughtful and faithful' (3). The extensive reach of *Life and Letters To-day* seems to be beyond his grasp. In October 1939, the editorial underlines Gwyn Jones's hatred of war – 'indeed this is not a subject I can trust myself to write on' (125) – and asserts that defeat would mean 'the annihilation of liberal thought' in Britain and France. In a postscript he proclaims that 'the *Welsh Review* stands for just those values of creativeness, tolerance, goodwill and understanding that we are fighting this war to maintain.' Once again the emphasis of the issue is literary. There are short stories, including a Lawrentian contribution by Alun Lewis (128–39) which is marred by stereotypes: 'a shrivelled little Jew'; a charming milkmaid; a sexy Breton onion-seller. A poem by Idris Davies strikes a simplistic note:

> Once in a mining valley
> I heard the nightwinds say:
> 'Beyond our sunless sorrows
> There dawns a kinder day'. (140)

The general quality of creative writing does not live up to the editor's original prospectus. He seems to sense this himself when writing an article 'The Future of the Industrial Novel' under the pseudonym, 'Mulciber' (154–8).[33] He still wants the work of Welsh novelists to be based in the 'things they know with their very bone and sinew' (155). However, he argues a case for them to get away from the family as their 'circle of interest', and to reflect the epic sweep of the history of the south Wales coalfield. The next contribution, 'Pikelets and a Penny' by Charles Davies (159–64), illustrates this lack of ambition: it is another child-centred tale about a poor boy refused 'a pennyworth of Mrs. Hollingsworth's black peppermint sweets'.

The November 1939 issue is the last of the first series, though it does not proclaim itself as such: indeed, it contains an announcement of the contents of the planned December number (217). The editorial is preoccupied with problems caused by the influx of evacuees:

> Liverpool and Birmingham have emptied their slums . . . The Englishman is a coloniser of unescapable [sic] efficiency . . . Surely he is an unthinking man at a desk who threw into Welsh homes a horde of monoglot children. The arrangement cannot work out well for host or guest. (183–4)

This implied xenophobia is uncharacteristic of the *Welsh Review*'s usually liberal responses. The issue betrays a sense of being under some pressure, overtaken by the unwanted events of the day. Apart from the presence of a long poem by Hugh MacDiarmid (93-6) the creative writing appears nostalgic. There are short stories about Welsh rural life; letters from Brenda Chamberlain recording walks in the Western Highlands (197-205); an account of Chartist history (218-24) and an article by Gwilym Davies (225-7) regretting the abandonment of the Twentieth Assembly of the League of Nations. The book reviews (128-40) include a tribute to Seumas O'Sullivan's *The Dublin Magazine*. Gwyn Jones himself contributes two reviews, one of *The Loneliest Mountain and Other Poems* by W. H. Davies and another of *The March of Literature* by Ford Madox Ford. Alice Rees Jones says of *How Green Was My Valley* that 'the Welsh reader will be irritated by its constant errors' but that they will enjoy it if they 'forget that it is supposed to be Welsh' (237). *The Welsh Review* then goes into hibernation for nearly five years.

The second series opens in March 1944 as a quarterly magazine, now priced 2s. 6d, with an editorial (3-6) promising more attention to new writers: 'a journal which prints only the arrived men fails in one particular duty: it is no encouragement to young writers' (1). Gwyn Jones compliments Robert Herring and *Life and Letters To-day* for its hospitality to Anglo-Welsh writers, especially its contribution to the reputation of Kate Roberts. The magazine is longer (seventy-six pages). Its content is still dominated by literary material, with new poems by Brenda Chamberlain, short stories by Kate Roberts (translated by Wyn Griffith) and Glyn Jones. There are nearly ten pages of book reviews, including one of Margiad Evans's *Autobiography* (66-8) and a cool critique by Gwyn Jones himself (69-74) of Idris Davies's *The Angry Summer*: 'its level is not uniformly high' despite its accurate portrayal of Valleys life. The issue's sharp increase in attention to women writers represents a distinct shift in gender priorities.

By December 1944, most contributions still come from established writers: Glyn Jones, Idris Davies, together with distinguished guests: T. S. Eliot's essay 'What is Minor Poetry?' (256-7) and Sir George Stapledon's piece on 'The Changing

Countryside' (283–9). However, there are also some new names. John Ormond Thomas's early 'Birthday Poem' (252–5) is lengthy, self-conscious but carefully controlled. 'Oranges', a tale by Robert Gwyn (247–9), about life among the peasantry in the Spanish Civil War and a short story by E. Eynon Evans 'On Driving a Bus' (295–300) make good Gwyn Jones's earlier undertaking to publish new writing.

The end of the war in Europe is a difficult moment for Gwyn Jones: his June 1945 editorial says:

> I thought it would be easy to write a set-piece on the end of the war in Europe and the final shredding of that black and horrid cloud which has overhung the lives of men for twenty years. I must be held excused: I find I cannot do it. (79)

However, he goes on to demand 'stern justice' for 'every brute . . . from the commandants down to the menials', picturing them as 'spruce, handsome metallic creatures of both sexes every moment of whose training had been designed to make them indifferent to suffering and contemptuous of pity' (80). The editorial switches abruptly to praise the achievements of Lloyd George (recently deceased) and to thank Mrs Alun Lewis and Mrs Caradoc Evans for releasing their husbands' letters to the journal. Excerpts appear from Lewis's letters from India (83–93) and from Caradoc Evans's journal (103–11).

In 1946, *The Welsh Review* begins a series of 'Welsh Profiles', which are unsigned and may be written by Gwyn Jones himself. These include political figures (Aneurin Bevan, James Griffiths), together with literary personalities (Arthur Machen, Jack Jones) and sportsmen (Jimmy Wilde). E. Glyn Lewis's lengthy article (176–86) in the autumn 1946 issue worries about the lack of encouragement to

> regard the contribution [of Anglo-Welsh writers] as a coherent autonomous body, characterised by identifiable common features, which declare a distinctive racial origin, and which serve to distinguish it from other, perhaps more important, but essentially different, influences. (176)

Lewis regards writers like Rhys Davies and Gwyn Jones as drawing Wales back into 'the mainstream of literary culture of which at one time she was a most important tributary' (177). He concedes that 'it is obvious that the production of such a fine flower of sophistication as Henry James would have been impossible in Wales' (178). He argues that in modern Anglo-Welsh writing 'the emphasis is upon the creative impulse in language . . . illustrated in the surrealism of the twentieth century as in the metaphysics of the seventeenth century' (179). Writers like Dylan Thomas and Caradoc Evans demonstrate 'a keenness of introspective analysis, and an extreme subjectivity of attitude which is at times full of dangerous implications' (182). However, they have a sense of 'a sacramental universe' that parallels that of Vaughan and Traherne. In the same issue H. E. Bates reviews Kate Roberts's *A Summer Day* and announces the presence of 'a Welsh renaissance, nourished by a soil at last almost free of the sourness of industrial depression' (217).

Later issues, however, sometimes seem to reach backwards. In the winter 1947 issue, Gwyn Jones reprints the scripts of five radio programmes about 'The Welsh Literary Tradition' (231–53) that recognise the primacy of literature in Welsh. To include these he holds over until later pieces by 'new writers making their mark' (231). He includes instead another 'Welsh Profile' on Arthur Machen, a retrospective on the history of the University College of Wales by Thomas Jones and an account of 'Welsh Voices in the Short Story' by Michael Williams. There is a sense of reduced energy, although the 'new writers' (including Gwyn Thomas, S. Beryl Jones and Lawrence Hockey) do appear in time.

The editorial for winter 1948 announces the suspension of publication because of paper shortages, cost increases and a decline in subscriptions (230–1). Gwyn Jones is content to 'let our thirty numbers speak for themselves'. In this last number, he seems to indulge his own tastes. It opens with H. Idris Bell's translation from the Welsh of Saunders Lewis: *Amis and Amile* (233–55) – a long verse drama that dominates the issue. There is an unsigned biographical piece on Augustus John (256–9) and another on Jimmy Wilde, the last of the 'Welsh Profiles' (260–5). A thoughtful essay on Dylan Thomas by E. Glyn Lewis (270–81) sees him as a 'religious poet', essentially 'a mythopaeic poet', strongly influenced by Protestant theology. Two short stories continue the preoccupation with south Wales working-class experience, David Vernon's 'The Chair' (282–4) is about a fratricidal murder, and Hugh Edwards's 'Rum and True Religion' (294–7) celebrates a sailor uncle's favourite toast. Margiad Evans's short story, 'A Party for the Nightingale' (285–93) varies the tone. The poetry is sparse. Henry Treece's 'Cornish Village' (265) and a sequence by Peter Hellings, 'Enemies of Forgetting' (266b9), are attractive but conventional. The issue (and the *Welsh Review* itself) closes with eight pages of book reviews (298–306), all concerned with books about medieval literature. Idris Bell reviews a new translation of *The Mabinogion* by Gwyn Jones and Thomas Jones (a de luxe version published by Golden Cockerel at 30 guineas).[34]

Like his predecessors and contemporaries, Gwyn Jones has wrestled with the problem of finding a sufficient audience. His theoretical market of a million or so Welshmen who are primarily English-speakers has actually produced fewer than a thousand who are ready to purchase his literary magazine. For some of the time, too, he has had to share that public sphere with Keidrych Rhys and Robert Herring. The weight of the magazine's content often reflects his academic interests in literary matters, and Gwyn Jones shuns any attempt to emulate Keidrych Rhys's late attempt to recruit a popular readership. Between them, however, *Wales* and *The Welsh Review* have created a presumption that there is a need within Wales for at least one periodical that will give publishing opportunities for Welsh writers in English while facilitating debate on literary and social topics. Though relatively small there seems to be an active and resilient 'counter public sphere' that demands attention. The appeal of *The Welsh Review* is addressed to the group of intellectuals that Collini suggests is strongly represented in Wales.

A similar constituency is addressed by the next magazine to appear in Wales, on this occasion specifically aimed at the relatively new graduate population.

The Welsh Anvil: Yr Einion (1949–1958)

Edited by Alwyn D. Rees for the Guild of Graduates of the University of Wales, *The Welsh Anvil* aims, according to his first editorial, 'to foster discussion among old students of the Welsh University' (vii). It was planned as a biannual journal but in practice appeared once a year. There is little creative writing; articles are about education, literature, Welsh affairs or the progress of academic studies. Rees does not attempt to cater for 'the minutiae of research' but is interested in 'what the physicist may have to say to the artist or philosopher' (ix). Optimistically, the editor sees himself addressing 'some 14,000 Welsh graduates' – regarded as a palpable extension to the public sphere in Wales. It also represents another attempt at a bilingual periodical.

The Welsh Anvil has sober buff or green covers and no advertisements. Almost one-third of the first issue is in Welsh though this proportion is not maintained. W. J. Gruffydd (Liberal MP for the University of Wales) asserts (23) that the Westminster government regards insistence on Welsh problems as 'an intolerable nuisance' and has a consistent policy 'to keep the Welshmen quiet'. Ieuan E. John writes on 'Soviet Russia and Eastern Europe' (33–45) and Glyn Jones urges the claims of five first books by Anglo-Welsh writers, including Roland Mathias, R. S. Thomas and Gwyn Jones; Gwyn Thomas (60) is described as 'a newcomer who can write'. None of these writers 'follows tamely in the track of the earlier Anglo-Welsh'. Arthur Pinsent (81–96) advocates more research in the social sciences, observing that there are few university graduates engaged in public life in Wales (94).

Ioan Bowen Rees, writing in July 1952, challenges Glyn Jones's 1949 article, arguing that Keidrych Rhys's journal *Wales* and

Gwyn Jones's *Welsh Review* may have been 'coaxed upon them from without' (20) and that 'the Anglo-Welsh . . . are perilously near complete absorption into English life' (24). Both these editors have 'set up a school without pupils', failed to find a distinctive public and 'have died of a poor circulation' (27). The debate is taken up again in December 1954 when Raymond Garlick in turn challenges Bowen Rees by listing seventy Anglo-Welsh poets beginning with Davies of Hereford (76–84). Given the *Welsh Anvil*'s annual periodicity, it is remarkable how Alwyn Rees manages to maintain a flow of literary discussion over such a long period. *The Welsh Anvil* was revived in December 1958 (after a three-year gap) giving most of its space (11–40) to an unsigned article discussing the implications of a proposed new University College using Welsh as the medium for instruction. There is no signal that this is to be the last issue, but no further numbers appear. However, the existential challenge to the Anglo-Welsh literary community, inherent in the *Welsh Anvil*'s protracted debate, is met head-on by the next periodical to be considered, which was to be the foundation stone of a renewed Anglo-Welsh periodical tradition.

Dock Leaves (1949–1958)

Raymond Garlick's first editorial, in the Christmas 1949 issue, announces *Dock Leaves* as: 'the work of a group of writers living in the Southern part of Pembrokeshire and meeting at regular intervals to discuss their craft and art' (1). Published from Pembroke Dock, the magazine is to appear three times a year. The group in question was brought together by Roland Mathias, the head teacher at Pembroke Dock High School, who had recently appointed Garlick to teach English.[35] The members met monthly to discuss each other's papers on a wide range of cultural topics.[36] The origins of *Dock Leaves* are therefore intensely local, encapsulated in the punning title (Mathias's idea) and the symbolism of its misty green cover with a tower, sun, sea, trefoil leaves and astronomical instrument. The initial issue was recorded in the January 1950 issue of *The Penvro*, the school magazine, which noted the familiarity to pupils of most of the contributors to the first issue (only thirty pages long).[37] These local writers included Olwen Rees, the writer of four poems (three in Welsh) and a sonnet, 'On Hearing Beethoven's Fifth Symphony', in romantic style:

> Here are great rocks and peaks, and valleys deep
> And mighty winds roaring with brassy voice,
> High surging seas drum-beat the shore and leap,
> Glad in their strength and tumult to rejoice. (4)

The Penvro also mentioned the Revd L. Alun Page, whose piece on 'The World of T. S. Eliot' (4–9) reacts against modern values: 'the desert is in the heart of suburbia, the land of the decent godless people.' Mrs Nora Davies contributes a poem, 'About Seeing a Coloured Woman in a London Church' (20–2). Mathias and Garlick each contribute four poems and a short story. Mathias's poems include 'A Letter' (9–10), a conversational piece about a lodger's quarrel with his landlady: 'I am no more a scullion than I was/ Brained out a bit as a haulier over at Roose [*sic*]', while Garlick's includes 'Orchestra':

> All wood and wire, ruled by a wand.
> He drags up sound from its rock roots and wrings
> Music from mere matter. (25)

Mathias's story, 'Block System', (12–20) is about a London-Welsh milkman's exploitation by a committee: 'In the droop of his shoulders was the cost of living.' Garlick's 'The Golden Mountain' (27–30) centres on a dying Welsh farmer who refuses to betray the presence of gold on his land 'to the stranger from the south and east'. Both writers underline a key theme running through this first issue: the opposition of rural and metropolitan, provincial insider and exploitative outsider.

The second number is twice the size, and carries illustrations by Eric Peyman and Kenneth Cooper. The editorial defines its objectives:

> Although the first purpose of this Review must be to provide, in the face of the appalling publishing situation for present-day creative writers, a vehicle for poetry, short stories, essays and criticism of quality – no matter from what direction they may come, it must also be interpreted as Pembrokeshire speaking to Wales. (1)

Welsh national feeling is described as largely sentimental; it has 'no hard core of will'. Indeed, 'if Wales has been betrayed, she has betrayed herself' (3). As well as local contributions it includes translations from Mallarmé and a review from the Glynn Vivian Portrait Gallery by Arthur Giardelli (25–30) describing woodcuts by David Jones. The cover bears an encouraging message from the Irish poet, Austin Clarke, expressing fellow-feeling: 'here we have young Welsh writers looking for an example of what we might call literary Home Rule.'

Dock Leaves embarks on a familiar trajectory among little magazines in Wales and becomes successively more like a review, weighty in content and solemn in tone. The editorial in January 1951 still refers to it, however, as wending its way 'from a remote and western corner of Wales' (1), a 'small, quiet land' where 'the tranquil life of the poet and the painter, the musician and the scholar and the teacher is pursued still.' The editors publish an 'Annual Subscription List' (46–8) with about a hundred entries, mostly from within Wales but also including about half a dozen overseas subscribers. The issue has photographs of a recent production of *Murder in the Cathedral* at the Grammar School and an article by Walter Dowding (31–6) arguing against a bilingual policy for Wales.

In May 1951 *Dock Leaves* acquires the traditional style of subtitle, *A National Review in English of Welsh Arts and Letters.* A. G. Prys-Jones writes on 'Anglo-Welsh Poetry' (5–9), arguing that it is important as a 'growing contribution to . . . English Literature' and that it gains extra strength from the 'Welsh literary renaissance' currently being experienced in the native language. Roland Mathias publishes his short story, 'The Eleven Men of Eppynt' (13-26) about the struggles of villagers in the snow, 'ordinary men, devoid of heroism but dogged and going home'. The spring 1953 issue has an ambitious editorial about floods in the Netherlands, Mau Mau murders in Kenya and the death of Stalin. There are now fewer local contributions, more criticism, more reviews. Roland Mathias has another story, 'Ffynon Fawr' (30-9) about ghosts emerging form a ruined farm by a lonely reservoir. Bobi Jones again sounds the note of opposition to metropolitan standards:

> Anglo-Welsh literature . . . must be regarded as a justified retreat from the cosmopolitan disintegration and proletarian mass-production of London and its fashions, towards a regeneration within a society which has not yet completely lost its character. (25)

This issue publishes a new 'List of Subscribers' (55-60), which by now includes over 250 names, including university libraries in Wales and overseas. The magazine has moved well beyond its original role as a vehicle for local writers, although Sam Adams notes that Roland Mathias himself published fifty-one contributions in the course of *Dock Leaves'* twenty-two issues.[38]

In the 'Dylan Thomas number' in spring 1954, Raymond Garlick sets the work of the recently deceased poet in a tradition of Anglo-Welsh writing claimed to reach back to the seventeenth century. He seizes the opportunity to set out the magazine's manifesto on behalf of this heritage, describing Dylan Thomas as speaking to his fellow Welshmen

> in the only language most of them possess, not primarily of the Wales of the ancient tongue but of that other Wales which, speaking an idiom of English, lives a life whose values and characteristics are not those of England: the Wales of the majority of Welsh people, the Wales of Dylan Thomas. (2)

The number has encomiums from such literary figures as Louis MacNeice, Saunders Lewis and Aneirin Talfan Davies.

There is some internal evidence of the practical and financial difficulties of maintaining the magazine. The summer 1954 issue draws attention to the 'annual Dock Leaves Day' to be held on 22 October, 'an autumn *Kermesse*, an amalgam of fete, sale of work, tea party, writers' convention and funfair' (1) designed to raise sufficient funds for at least one of the three issues in the year. In 1954, too, Raymond Garlick moved to a new teaching job in Ffestiniog.[39] Problems with postal rates lead to skipping the summer issue in 1956 and to reducing the frequency to twice annually thereafter. The winter issue of that year (where this change is announced) nonetheless runs again to over sixty pages, has some advertisements and an insert with photographs of statues by Jonah Jones, accompanied by an article on him (33–4). There are over ten pages of reviews and the contents place great emphasis on poetry and short fiction. In the following year, 1958, Roland Mathias left Pembroke Dock for a new job in Belper in Derbyshire.[40] The links between *Dock Leaves* and Pembroke Dock were thus severed.

Raymond Garlick's editorial in the final issue of *Dock Leaves* for 1957 apologises for its late arrival, which is due to 'the removal of the editorial chair from one machine-for-living-in to another' as he settles in to Blaenau Ffestiniog. There is no reference to the forthcoming change into *The Anglo-Welsh Review*. This last issue relies to some extent on transcriptions of radio broadcasts, one a talk by Sir Ben Bowen Thomas on bilingualism in education (6–12) and another an extended 'radio poem for five voices', 'The Golden Bird' by George Ewart Evans (13–27). There is a piece by Brenda Chamberlain (34–5), accompanying four black- and-white reproductions of her paintings, followed by Rhys George's commentary (36–43), describing the development of her style from figurative to abstraction, remarking that 'one does not expect that Wales will be appreciative of her new work.' There are more poems including 'The Ballad of Felix James', a series of literary 'in-jokes' about Amis, Wain, Osborne and 'The Movement'. Reviews include Roland Mathias on Ted Hughes's first collection, *The Hawk in the Rain*, generally approving but suggesting that Hughes may have too many 'attitudes' and that 'he falls under suspicion of posturing' (59).

Dock Leaves has established itself over the best part of a decade as a space within which Anglo-Welsh writers can find themselves, has exceeded its origins in Pembrokeshire and is speaking to a growing audience in Wales, England and overseas. The founders are moving on in terms of their individual careers but still retain ambitions linked to their original objectives. This is the genesis of their new production, retaining the core characteristics of *Dock Leaves* but with a more formal presence, designed to address a wider public.

The Anglo-Welsh Review (First Period: 1958–1969)

The transition to the new title is seamless, Raymond Garlick remaining as editor, continuing the numeric series, and retaining the reference to the Dock Leaves imprint and the printer H. G. Walters of Narberth in Pembrokeshire. In his first editorial, Garlick justifies the change of title by a need to appeal to the 'uninitiated' and to give extra respectability to the concept of the Anglo-Welsh (3). This new title is to last for thirty years. Together with the ten years of *Dock Leaves* it will dominate its founders' working lives. It is to see a transformation from Anglo-Welsh magazines as small-scale private enterprises, struggling financially through limited lives, dependent on private subscriptions, donations and occasional subventions from the Arts Council, to a new, quasi-institutionalised form of literary journalism, reliant on regular public patronage. It is eventually to be joined in this respect by two other major Welsh periodicals in English, *Poetry Wales* (from 1965) and *Planet* (from 1970), together creating the template for literary journalism in English-speaking Wales for more than a generation. It is effectively to be succeeded by *New Welsh Review* in 1988. However, it will be almost ten years before the Arts Council establishes its Literature Committee in 1967 and thus makes this crucial intervention. In 1958, however, Raymond Garlick still faces all the problems of producing and distributing the magazine twice yearly, now operating in isolation at a considerable distance from his publishing base.

The magazine has a new cover, red, black and white, featuring a red dragon and some symbolic gold leaves. At one hundred pages it is almost twice the size of *Dock Leaves*. The first lengthy editorial (3–8) argues the need to remove any pejorative sense from the term 'Anglo-Welsh'. It is especially important that this is recognised by the University; the editor is much encouraged by the W. D. Thomas memorial lecture on this theme by Gwyn Jones, published in 1957 as *The First Forty Years*. Garlick also pays tribute to the role of Keidrych Rhys and *Wales*, describing the rival magazine as 'vigorous, catholic, controversial and colourful' and welcoming its imminent return to print (7).

It is perhaps fitting in this context that the first set of poems in *The Anglo-Welsh Review* (by Vernon Jones) contains one on Caradoc Evans:

> He is gone one long decade
> His rancour whistling in the wind.
> He is gone beyond my shout of praise.
> I was too young and threats of war
> Obscured his passing in that gaunt
> Parish on that grudging day . . . (10)

The accent on poetry continues with an article by Islywn Jenkins on 'Idris Davies: Poet of Rhymney' (13–21), headed by a quotation from a letter from T. S. Eliot: '. . . my own impression of his poems remains the same: that they are the best poetic document I know about a particular epoch in a particular place.' There are more poems, several short stories, articles about music and painting (with illustrations) and about twenty pages of book reviews (78–100), three by Roland Mathias.

In his second issue (Winter 1958) Garlick introduces the convention (familiar in other reviews such as the *Dublin Magazine*) of dividing the contents page by sections: Literature; Painting and Music; Biography. In an article ten years later in *Planet*,

Garlick records his pleasure in these first issues of *The Anglo-Welsh Review* which 'represent the realisation of what I wanted in the magazine – in terms of typography and format as well as internal structure'.[41] He experiments with another division of the subject matter in his third issue: 'At Home', 'Abroad' and 'Reviews'. His lengthy editorial (3-9) sees the new magazine in a tradition extending from *The Welsh Outlook* through Gwyn Jones's *Welsh Review* and Keidrych Rhys's *Wales* – which 'has helped to make Anglo-Welsh writing cohere' (3). The issue extends to 120 pages, with numbers of formal essays (for example on Ibsen and on Arthur Giardelli) with a good deal of travel writing about visits to Israel, Montparnasse and Holland. The editorial in his final issue (Spring 1960), before he left Wales for a teaching post in the Netherlands, expresses Garlick's concern that academicism is affecting the nature of Anglo-Welsh writing: 'The young man who, twenty years ago, might have tried his hand at poetry or a novel, will probably be found trying his hand at a thesis today' (5).

However, the longest article in this issue is itself an academic study by Roland Mathias (23-37), discussing the evaluation of Edward Thomas by F. R. Leavis and Geoffrey Grigson. Garlick worries, too, in his last editorial, about London publishing houses resisting writing where Welshness is dominant. He concludes, presciently, that 'for Anglo-Welsh writers however only the Arts Council represents a source of support.' Raymond Garlick's issues of *The Anglo-Welsh Review* established a weighty presence and a sober presentation that was to be little altered over three more decades despite a succession of different editors.

The subsequent editors include Roland Mathias (1960-76), Gillian Clarke (1976-84) and Greg Hill (1984-8). Gillian Clarke also co-edited some of the later Roland Mathias numbers, and John Davies, Tony Bianchi, Greg Hill and Huw Jones acted as co-editors for some of the later issues. The presence of this quorum of committed individuals played a major part in assuring the continuity of the periodical. Roland Mathias's period as editor accounts for more than half the life of the magazine and, considering also the influence he exerted over Raymond Garlick, who started out as his protégé, he stands out as the key editorial figure and a major contributor.

His first editorial (11/27: 5–14) looks back to *Dock Leaves*:

> Raymond Garlick has faced bravely the difficult task of pressing the right of Welshmen whose first language is English not merely to be Welshmen but to have a literary and cultural contribution to make to Wales which is something more than merely alien and English. (7)

However, Mathias immediately begins to impress his personal touch on *The Anglo-Welsh Review*. Sam Adams pays tribute to his editorial mastery, seeing the *Review* as both 'a personal platform, but also a work of service and self-abnegation'.[42] The magazine becomes more intensely literary, with fewer articles on social or political themes. Over time it grows even longer, so that, when the period of regular Arts Council subsidy begins in 1967, it often extends to over two hundred pages, including some fifty pages of book reviews.[43]

One innovation was the introduction of biographical studies of Welsh writers, artists and musicians, past and present. There are some issues (such as no. 34 in 1964) where as much as a quarter of the magazine is devoted to life-writing of this kind, occasionally in the form of obituaries. It is rare, during Mathias's editorship, to find an issue without such material, but the incidence of this kind of writing declines sharply after his departure. This biographical record of literary, artistic and cultural achievement is similar to material in some Scottish and Irish journals of the period: it made a substantial contribution to Mathias's objective of regularly enhancing the image of the Anglo-Welsh.

By issue 29 (1962) the difficulties of financing *The Anglo-Welsh Review* had become acute. The editorial (3–9) explains that subscriptions are only meeting about half the minimum costs. There is a need for readers who will pay more than the present subscription of 6s. 6d per year. In *The Lonely Editor*, Mathias points out that the sales of *The Anglo-Welsh Review* never exceeded eight hundred copies, half of them outside Wales.[44] He worries that Arts Council support had recently been reduced and might cease altogether. In fact, despite his fears, the new Welsh Arts Council and its predecessor had, according to Sam Adams, been providing grant aid since 1959 and increased its support steadily over time.[45] In the event, the Welsh Arts Council's appointment of Meic Stephens as Literature Director in 1967 and his creation of the Literature Committee in the same year was a critical development which facilitated a higher proportion of funding for literary magazines in Wales, compared with other parts of Britain. It established a pattern of subsidy for magazines in both languages that was to last effectively for a generation.[46] Sealing this compact, Roland Mathias became a member of the Literature Panel in 1969 and was later chairman for three years. At this mid-point in its history, therefore, *The Anglo-Welsh Review* is poised to enter a new phase of its existence marking a precedent for other Welsh periodicals in English.

For more than fifty years from the beginning of the twentieth century, Welsh periodicals in English have relied on the efforts of a group of individual editors, often well known to each other, sometimes helped by financial support from wealthy individuals such as David Davies or from institutions such as the Guild of Graduates, together with a sprinkling of enthusiastic individual supporters and fund-raisers. There have also been individual, maverick productions, outside the main focus of this study, such as Harri Webb's *The Welsh Republican – Y Gweriniaethwr* (1950–7). This is a four-page broadsheet, produced every two months, price 2d or 3d. Founded by a breakaway group from Plaid Cymru, it lasted for just thirty-seven issues and was 'socialist, secular, anti-royalist, and disrespectful'.[47] Its editorial for October/November 1950 announced that a condition of membership of the movement was a refusal to serve in the 'English Imperial Armed Services' (4). The August/September 1955 number attacked the Labour Party which, it claimed, believed that 'all the mildewed pomp of Court and Crown is sacred' (2).

Within the mainstream of Anglo-Welsh periodicals, however, editors steadily moved away from the earlier reliance on a liberal political consensus in Wales and invested more heavily in literary and cultural materials. They have successfully, despite opposition, established a concept and practice of Anglo-Welsh writing. This has become increasingly reliant on a limited public sphere within Wales itself and, with some exceptions (including Keidrych Rhys and Robert Herring), a generation of editors based within Wales have reduced their magazines' reliance on a London Welsh audience or on support from the diaspora. There are still, however, regular appeals to established values and invocations to traditional figures; the tensions between 'Old' and 'New' have not departed. There are more women writers, and Gillian Clarke has set a precedent for future women editors. The intellectual tone has become increasingly modernist and the appeal of the magazines has been concentrated on a newly established minority audience of intellectuals; Owen M. Edwards's attempts to create an appeal to a broader community have not been replicated. It has become clear that reliance on the Anglophone public sphere is leading to increasing difficulty in sustaining independent periodicals financially. The need for the intervention of public bodies has been recognised and this signals a new era in the history of Welsh periodicals in English.

3
The Late Twentieth Century: 1969–2012

In the second half of the long twentieth century in Wales the country's traditional economic base was devastated by closures in the mining and steel industries. The periodicals lived through the behavioural shifts associated with the 1960s. During these years Plaid Cymru achieved its first successes in parliamentary elections, and the Kilbrandon Report of 1973 'made devolution into a serious issue.'[1] The magazines witnessed two referenda on devolution, the 'failed' vote in 1979, and the positive decision in 1997 leading to the establishment of the National Assembly for Wales. Meanwhile, the use of the Welsh language has strengthened, especially in the areas of education, legal status and broadcasting. John Davies sees the 1960s as a decade during which 'the Welsh cast aside the leadership of the London Welsh' and a more confident culture emerged. He suggests that the foundation of the English section of Yr Academi Gymreig in 1968 and the initiation of the *Writers of Wales* series in 1970 marked a substantial improvement in relations between Anglo-Welsh writers and writers in Welsh.[2]

The period since 1969 has also seen a decisive and unprecedented long-term intervention by public bodies in the operation of the public sphere in Wales. The Welsh Arts Council (and more recently the Welsh Books Council) has exercised responsibility for funding major periodicals in Wales in both languages. The transfer between the two bodies in 2003 was organised so as to be seamless, with all long-term funding arrangements guaranteed. *The Anglo-Welsh Review, Poetry Wales* and *Planet* all received regular aid from the Arts Council on an annual basis until, in 1988, following a commissioned report by Rhodri Williams, *New Welsh Review* replaced *The Anglo-Welsh Review* and a revised system of three-year renewable franchises came into operation. The Literature Committee also made some limited finance available on a more *ad hoc* basis to selected periodicals (usually described as 'little magazines') such as Peter Finch's *Second Aeon*.[3] The publishers and editors of these more experimental productions were, therefore, mainly dependent on their own personal efforts to boost circulation and ensure their continuity. However, there were always some independent periodical ventures that fell entirely outside the Arts Council's funding criteria. Quite well established examples in the twentieth century included the north Wales magazine *Mabon* that was funded by the North Wales Arts Association, the controversial current affairs periodical *Rebecca* and the short-story magazine, *Cambrensis*. Although most of these had relatively short lives they were still able to produce creative ripples in the Anglophone public sphere. Independent magazines still exist in Wales, including at the present time such further examples as the current affairs review *Agenda* or the general interest magazine *Cambria*. At the same time internet access has broadened to an extent where most periodicals have established websites and digital publishing has developed, offering a challenge to the primacy of print culture. The continuing claims of such magazines for audiences and for public funding alongside the three major franchised journals recur throughout this period.

There has been an ongoing debate about the effects of state-sponsored aid for periodicals. Wolfgang Gortschacher in his magisterial review of little magazines argues that subsidies inevitably lead to more conventional attitudes and less creative eccentricity.[4] In similar vein, Peter Hodgkiss, writing in *Poetry Wales* in autumn 1978, observed that 'the majority of British poetry in "approved publications" presents a bland and toothless face' (49). Meic Stephens, however, in an interview in the same issue, entirely discounts the suggestion that Arts Council subsidy stifles experiment, arguing that on the contrary, 'if you leave literature ... to the operation of the market, what you are in danger of getting is conformity' (26). Each of these generalisations is open to challenge: as we shall see, the Arts Council involvement in the long-term magazines was largely 'hands-off' and allowed the various editors to introduce significant changes reflecting cultural shifts over time and their own personal priorities. This is accompanied, however, by an inbuilt respect for the already established characters of the publications, and this does lead to some degree of conservatism and institutionalisation. These tendencies can be seen all too clearly developing through the history of the second phase in the life of *The Anglo-Welsh Review,* one of the first beneficiaries of Arts Council funding from 1969 onwards.

The Anglo-Welsh Review (Second Period: 1969–1988)

The summer 1969 issue illustrates Roland Mathias's mature style and owes something to the confidence stemming from the new funding source. The issue is bulky, at 243 pages, including fifty pages of book reviews. There are no advertisements and there is an acknowledgement of the new level of financial help from the Welsh Arts Council (and also from a dozen Welsh Church funds). The editorial (3–9) marks the twentieth anniversary since the founding of *Dock Leaves* in 1949 by giving a detailed account of the original founding group in 'a time of many beginnings'. Mathias traces the history leading to 'the era of comparative affluence' that has followed the recognition by the Arts Councils that 'creative writing is for the most part just as uncommercial a venture as art, music or drama.' The ability of the magazine to pay its contributors 'is the first and most golden miracle'. Analysis of the contents of the issue shows the continuing primacy of literature, with over 180 pages (nearly three-quarters) devoted to creative writing, criticism and reviews. There is the traditional biographical article, on this occasion about the eighteenth-century philosopher Richard Price, and there are shorter, well-illustrated contributions on art and music. Mathias includes over fifty pages of poetry, including work by R. S. Thomas, Alison Bielski and Ruth Bidgood. The tone throughout is authoritative, clearly in command of the intimate public sphere that it is addressing. But there is already some sense of an over-prescribed approach: successive issues take the same shape, themes are regularly repeated and there are fewer new contributors.

By spring 1974 Roland Mathias is sharing the editorial burden with Gillian Clarke. The style has changed little in five years: again some 230 pages with now as many as seventy pages of reviews. Mathias placed great importance on the reviewing process, although he also recorded that Gillian Clarke joked at one stage that 'she took over just in time to prevent me from having reviewed a book about snails because it was written by a Welshman.'[5] The brief editorial (3–4) concentrates on the recent death of Cyril Hodges, praising him for his poetry but also for his generous private patronage. In the summer issue of the same year the editors criticise a BBC lecture by Iestyn Evans, arguing (4) that 'he reveals himself as standing outside the Welsh heartland and its values,' especially the three-quarters of the population that 'already live in urban Anglicisation'. The editors also draw attention (6) to the death of B. L. Coombes and the appointment of David Jones as a Companion of Honour. *The Anglo-Welsh Review* now sounds like the semi-official voice of a coterie, becoming a journal of record, orchestrating an orthodoxy of Anglo-Welsh opinion and taste that is not to be lightly challenged.

The editorial in Gillian Clarke's first solo issue in autumn 1976 (3–7) pays tribute to Roland Mathias, who has trained her to care about the details of punctuation and typography, 'never angry, never arrogant . . . without a hint of the headmaster, the tone always that of a friend and colleague'. She goes on to announce a change of ownership of the *Review*, passing to the safe-keeping of Gareth Walters of the Five Arches Press in Tenby – now the magazine's publisher. She also notes the new involvement of John Davies, from Prestatyn Comprehensive School, as reviews editor. However, Clarke is preparing some innovations. She is concerned about the dropping circulation, drawing attention to some 'finger wagging' from the Welsh Arts Council, and declares her intention to do away with the 'editorial block' with its symbolism of harp, dock leaves and a Sunderland aircraft (a relic of the war) which has traditionally appeared at the head of every issue, recalling *Dock Leaves* days. This decision on the part of the new editor is seen as iconoclastic and arouses instant opposition from traditionalists, including Mathias himself. However, the overall presentation and contents of the *Review* are substantially unchanged. Clarke's issue 58 in 1977, for example, is still over two hundred pages of solid literary material, with more than eighty pages of reviews. The editorial (4–7) is mainly concerned with language issues, in the context of parallels suggested by a recent Serbo-Croat visit and a contemporary dispute about compulsory Welsh in schools in Aberystwyth. Her issue 65 in 1979 is a special number for women writers. Its editorial (1–2) claims that 'there has always seemed a high proportion of women poets in the Anglo-Welsh magazines in comparison with other British journals, and here three out of twelve poets and three out of six prose writers are women.' The issue features articles on Lynette Roberts and Katharine Philips ('Orinda'). Clarke's editorial also notes some negatives in relation to women writers in Wales: 'excluded subjects', a lack of appreciation for 'domestic topics' and a low level of public recognition for women writers. It urges the case for 'a lively correspondence on this subject' but, typically, none ensues. The history of Welsh periodicals in English is littered with similar frustrated editorial pleas for readers' comments or for contributions on particular themes. It hints at a relatively passive readership.

Greg Hill's issues (1984–8) follow a similar pattern to that set by his predecessors, though by now the *Review* has reduced in length to around 150 pages, about half of which are given to book reviews. Hill took seriously the admonition to review any relevant publication and began to list all reviews formally at the front of the magazine. His editorial for issue 79 in 1985 expresses his concern about the recent withdrawal of Arts Council bursaries for writers and the alleged diversion of these funds to the relaunch of *Planet* (4). The problem of finding cash for paying contributors within the magazine's financial constraints leads to 'the enforced amateurism of much literary practice in Wales'. This issue has over forty pages of poems massed together at the front of the magazine (5–48), then three short stories placed together over about twenty pages (48–69). An article about R. S. Thomas by James A. Davies follows, involving very detailed exposition and close readings (70–83). Then reviews take up the rest of the issue (84–125). This layout is over-formulaic and, while providing the regular subscriber with a consistent, expected experience, might not appeal to any new audience.

Throughout the 1980s, indeed, the Arts Council's Literature Committee had become increasingly concerned about the regularly subsidised magazines, especially about weaknesses in their financial management, about some aspects of their quality and about their ability to command reasonable levels of circulation. Separate internal reports by Tony Bianchi and Ned Thomas had proposed more stringent controls and more regular interventions.[6] Eventually the Literature Committee commissioned a formal external report by Rhodri Williams. A well-established television journalist, Williams had begun his career with the investigative journal *Rebecca* and was to go on to become the Director of Ofcom Wales. In his immensely detailed report to the Arts Council, he produced some serious criticisms of the financial management and the marketing of the magazines. He found that editors often regarded these managerial matters as beneath their attention. He reserved some of his sharpest comments on the actual content of any magazine for *The Anglo-Welsh Review* which, he says,

> belongs, as it were to a past age and has not succeeded in developing in a way which will attract new readers. The magazine's old-fashioned

and uninteresting appearance reflects the nature of its contents, on the whole. (26)

The Arts Council decided to withdraw funding from *The Anglo-Welsh Review* (and also from the Welsh-language journal, *Y Faner*), changed its system of support to a series of renewable three-year franchises and called for applications for a new literary magazine, eventually to become *The New Welsh Review*. [7]

Greg Hill's issue of *The Anglo-Welsh Review*, 86 (1987), records the decision of the Arts Council to cease its support at the end of the year. Hill accepts some of the criticisms in Williams's report, especially those about the *Review*'s erratic appearances (blamed on the printer), but he remarks that the complaints were 'rooted more in objections to our image than to what we actually publish' (7). Indeed, Rhodri Williams's comments (though generally just) do seem to miss the point that *The Anglo-Welsh Review* belongs to 'a past age' not only in the sense that it has not been modernised; it directly emerges from, and in many ways consciously seeks to preserve, the tradition of earlier Welsh periodicals in English. It is now, however, itself the 'residual', no longer the 'emergent'.

The editorial in the final issue, edited by Greg Hill and Huw Jones, records the magazine's historic role:

> With this, our final issue, nearly forty years of consolidation comes to an end. The idea of 'Anglo-Welsh' literature was still a dubious one at the beginning of the period . . . By now the history of that literature has been written and a tradition established. (7)

The *Review*'s continued preoccupation with the status of 'Anglo-Welsh' literature is now less relevant than it was when it succeeded *Dock Leaves* in 1958. That this is so is a measure of the success attributable to the promotional energies of Raymond Garlick, Roland Mathias and their successors. *The Anglo-Welsh Review* has survived into an era where it has no longer for some time been the sole vehicle for Welsh writers in English. Other publications (some also subsidised, like *Poetry Wales* and *Planet*, and others more maverick, such as *Second Aeon*) have entered the field during the twenty-five years of the *Review*'s existence. As early as 1988 *The Anglo-Welsh Review* is to have a lineal successor in *The New Welsh Review*, already, however, deliberately planned and financed in a different style. But before turning to this new production I need to consider the two other franchised periodicals that began as contemporaries of *The Anglo-Welsh Review*.

Poetry Wales (1965–)

The life of *Poetry Wales* spans nearly half a century, under eight different editors (as well as four guest editors). Like many poetry magazines, *Poetry Wales* (Spring 1965) started life as a slim production, just eighteen pages, priced 3s., published twice yearly by the Triskel Press (an imprint owned by the first editor, Meic Stephens, who ran the magazine more or less single-handed). Meic Stephens had a ready audience among members of Plaid Cymru, among whom he had some agents selling the magazine. The first issue opens with a characteristic well-made lyric, 'Nocturne' by Alison Bielski:

> The city cry is loud tonight,
> Out of streets and lighted windows
> A slow moan moves on the wind . . . (3)

Bielski's opening contribution and Ida M. Mills's 'Requiem' (7) can be seen as favourable omens for the future of women poets in *Poetry Wales*. Indeed Bielski establishes a regular presence in the magazine through the 1960s, alongside Sybil Hollindrake, Ruth Bidgood and Brenda Chamberlain.

Other poems in the opening issue have stern national resonances, like Peter Gruffydd's 'The Small Nation':

> Yet there are few things small in you,
> Except that vital tree, courage.
> Your poets scourge you and, with each

Welsh Periodicals in English

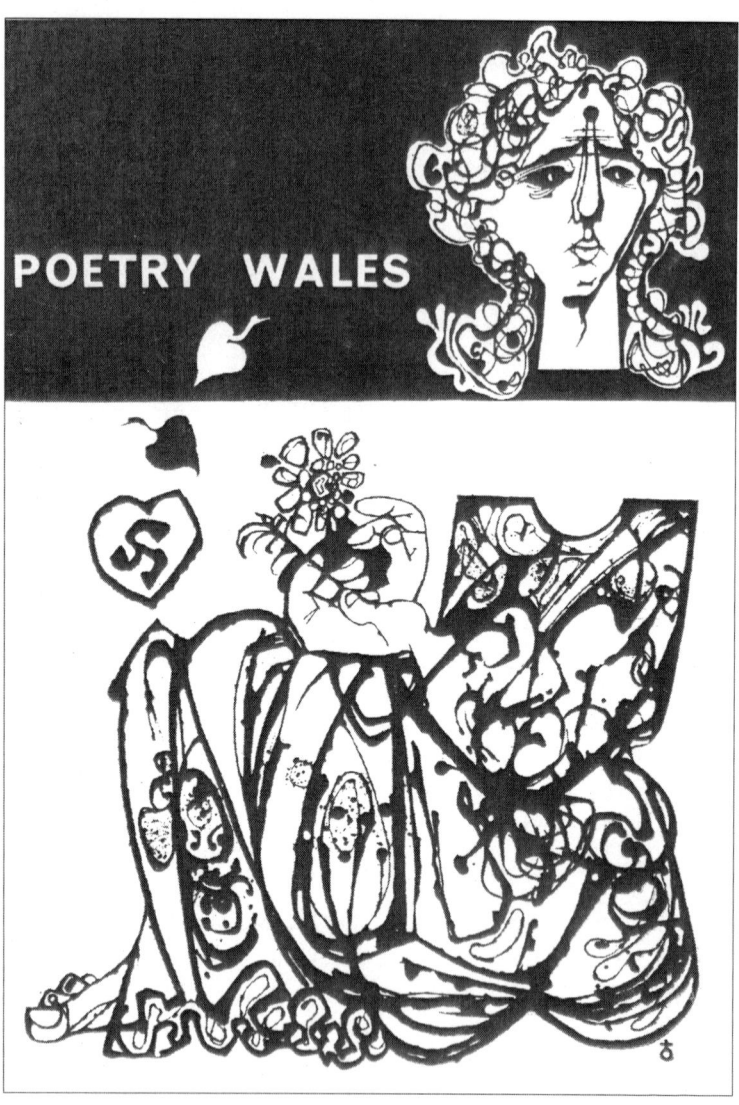

Poetry Wales: ed. Meic Stephens, first issue, Spring 1965

> Crack of rage, you bow further
> Into the dirt. All the scaly ways
> Of selling are scored in your present face . . . (5)

This angry tone is heard again in Herbert Lloyd Williams's "Depopulation', where 'the bleak hearts' of those that leave Wales 'speak/the bitter language of the dispossessed' (15). Meic Stephens avoids any editorial at this stage.

The second issue, in the autumn, has grown to thirty pages and includes some book reviews (25–9). The close of Meic Stephens's own 'Ponies, Twynyrodyn' evokes a passionate sense of community:

> These beasts are our companions,
> dark presences from the peasant past,
> these grim valleys our common hendre,
> exiles all, until the coming thaw. (22)

Bryn Griffiths's 'A Note for R. S. Thomas' repeats the intransigent theme:

> We have always been in retreat, but never beaten.
> Two thousand years of assault and conquest
> Have failed to kill this race rooted in rock;
> Failed to end the dying cadence of our song;
> Failed to extinguish the slow flame of speech. (23)

The third issue (now forty pages) has the first editorial (2–3), where Meic Stephens announces that the first two numbers have sold out, acknowledges some Arts Council support, and situates the magazine in the tradition of earlier twentieth-century productions:

> We are not crowing. It is still too soon to say whether there is a permanent place for such a magazine in contemporary Wales. But, lifting our daicaps to the memorable example set by *Wales* and the *Welsh Review*, we match our hope with firm intention to do our blue best. Our shutters are open and the door is on the latch . . . with Arianrhod, the bitch-muse, on the cover, our first commitment, as our title has it, is to the craft. Our second is to the country. (3)

He declares that future issues will do more to celebrate Welsh-language writing: 'the senior literature'. *Poetry Wales* becomes a bilingual production for a relatively short period. The work of Gwilym Rees Hughes as Welsh editor (1967–74) allowed the 1971 'twenty-first birthday issue' to record that as much as a third of the contributors up to then had written in Welsh. This is roughly contemporaneous with the most active period of the Welsh Language Society; subsequent editors, however, reduced the Welsh content sharply.[8] They became more concerned with improving the always fragile status of Welsh writing in English within the national culture. This became a persistent theme in *Poetry Wales*. Ned Thomas, writing twenty-five years later, still saw such writing as 'making a culture in English out of the not immediately promising material', and Kirsti Bohata remarked as late as 2004 that 'Welsh writing in English remains in a precarious and persistently marginal position in Wales and beyond.'[9]

Following his appointment as literature director of the Welsh Arts Council, Meic Stephens passed the editorship to Gerald Morgan for the winter 1967 number. While maintaining a policy of 'arm's-length' control, guaranteeing editorial freedom, Meic Stephens later acknowledged that he kept a 'fatherly eye' on *Poetry Wales* throughout his tenure.[10] Stephens published an important valedictory article on 'The Second Flowering' (2–9). He had been initially concerned with 'perhaps a dozen young poets who . . . might have been dubbed Anglo-Welsh'. Now, however, he wants to respond to a challenge from Gwyn Jones in the *London Welshman* to bring about the creation of 'an exciting and authoritative journal' to provide space for 'young creative writers.' He discounts Raymond Garlick's 'over compensatory' claims about a tradition going back to the seventeenth century and is 'not looking for a school or a movement' with 'a single manifesto'. He wants to serve a group of poets who 'are willing to associate as Welshmen and have their work discussed with reference to the culture of Wales'. He links this to a recent growth in national consciousness. While not a formal

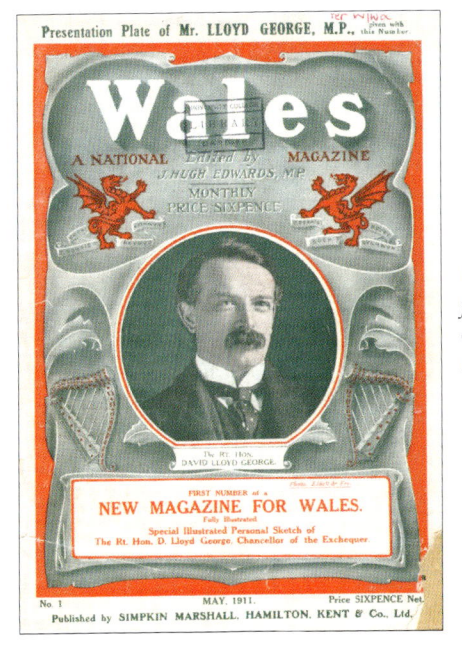

Wales: The National Magazine
for the Welsh People,
ed. J. Hugh Edwards,
first issue, May 1911

Wales: ed. Keidrych Rhys,
first issue, October 1959

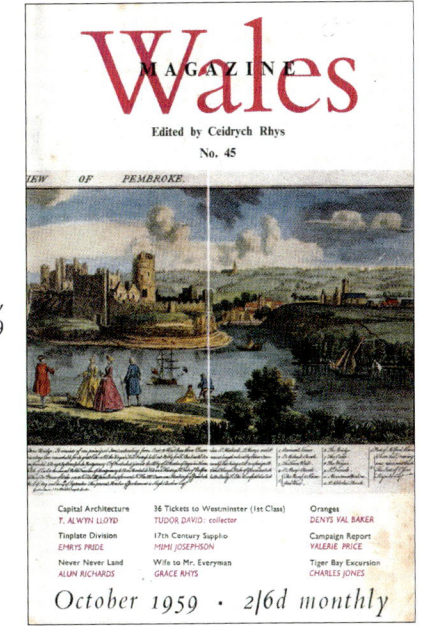

Second Aeon: ed. Peter Finch, issue 14, 1972

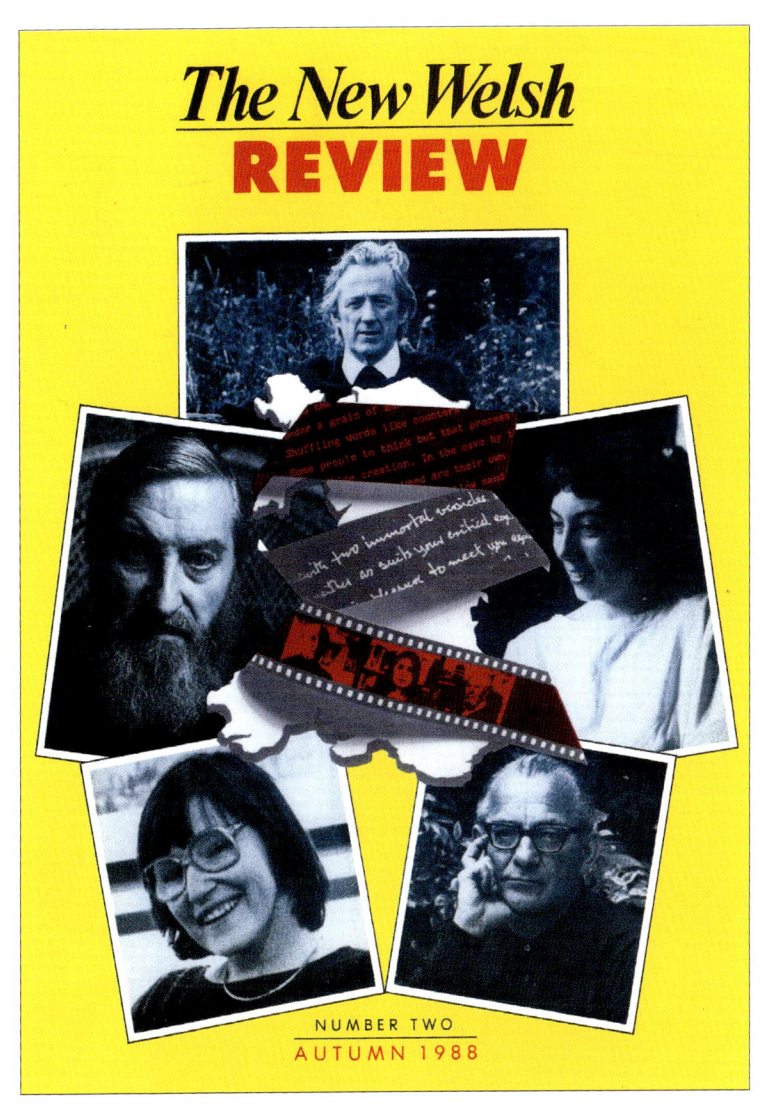

The New Welsh Review: ed. Belinda Humfrey,
second issue, Autumn 1988

Dock Leaves: ed. Raymond Garlick, first issue, Xmas 1949

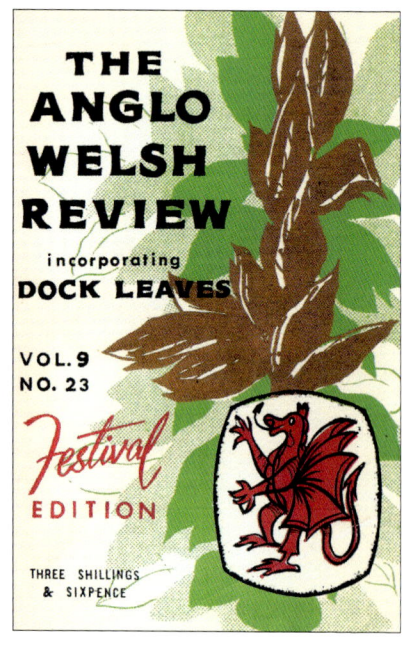

The Anglo-Welsh Review (incorporating *Dock Leaves*): first issue, Spring 1958

'manifesto', this article nevertheless effectively defines the role of *Poetry Wales* for a generation.

Under Gerald Morgan, the magazine expands to around sixty pages, increases its price to 5s. and publishes some experimental work, such as 'Calligrammes' by Meic Stephens and Alison Bielski. When Morgan has to give up the role Meic Stephens returns as editor in spring 1969 (with the permission of the Arts Council). The summer 1969 issue is again preoccupied with the place of *Poetry Wales* in the history of Welsh periodicals in English. The editorial (3) pays tribute to forerunners like Keidrych Rhys's *Wales*, *The Welsh Review*, *Dock Leaves* and *The Anglo-Welsh Review*. Gerald Morgan reviews the recent reprint of *Wales*, claiming it as 'the first Welsh literary periodical in English' (perhaps discounting its predecessors as not 'literary'). Anthony Conran's second article on 'Anglo-Welsh Poetry Today' (9–12) argues that the influence of R. S. Thomas is such that without it 'I doubt very much that we'd have much left of *Poetry Wales*'.

Poetry Wales became a quarterly in 1970. The '21st Birthday' issue in winter 1971 affords an opportunity for stocktaking. Meic Stephens refers to his recent interview with John Tripp in *Planet* where he had defended the policy of the Arts Council in funding only the literary elements in magazines, warning that 'The Arts Council can't be expected to go on increasing its subsidies if its support isn't matched by sales to the public.'[11] However, despite still disappointing sales, *Poetry Wales* has published over 130 poets, 550 poems, and reviewed over 150 books. Stephens publishes supportive pieces by writers including Glyn Jones, Pennar Davies, Leslie Norris, Roland Mathias, Raymond Garlick, B. S. Johnson and Duncan Glen. Warning notes are struck, however, by other contributors. Anthony Conran warns that 'English gold [presumably channelled via the Arts Council] is a dangerous ally for those who fight England' (26), while Jeremy Hooker worries that the burden of heritage may be 'heavy as a sarcophagus and with a whiff of decomposition about it' (32). He points out that 'Anglo-Welsh writers form a fairly small group, and perhaps they are too kind to each other.' This is to become a continuing area of anxiety in Welsh periodicals in English, through to the present day. The editor invites an extension of this debate, asking for readers' letters for publication. However, these, as might have been forecast, never appear.

Meic Stephens introduced a number of 'special' issues, including the celebratory R. S. Thomas number (Spring 1972) with eight new poems and a number of critical views from Tony Conran, Roland Mathias, Jeremy Hooker and Dafydd Elis Thomas, among others. He promises that the next issue will be 'an ordinary number' and that the autumn issue will contain the work of 'poets who have never appeared previously in the magazine' together with critical comment on their work. The next year would have a special 'Love poetry number'. The autumn number keeps his promise, listing thirty-four new poets. They include Tony Curtis, Nigel Jenkins, Moelwyn Merchant and Robert Minhinnick. There are two more 'special numbers', one on David Jones (Winter 1972) and another on Dafydd ap Gwilym (Spring 1973). The 'Love Poetry' issue does not get produced, however.

Sam Adams (previously the reviews editor) takes over in summer 1973 and immediately warns readers not to expect sweeping changes: 'Do not look for a brand new *Poetry Wales* . . . we could honestly say that we liked the magazine as it was' (3). Adams continues with the pattern of 'ordinary numbers' mixed with special issues, such as his Dylan Thomas number in autumn 1973 or the issue about T. H. Parry-Williams in summer 1974. J. P. Ward, when he becomes editor in summer 1975, also takes pleasure in the 'clear identity' of the magazine, reflecting the 'clean, lean poetry' of *Ten Anglo-Welsh Poets,* a recent anthology edited by Sam Adams. The argument about 'Anglo-Welshness' has been thrashed out over a decade, so that less editorial material on that topic is now needed and 'an emerging plurality of interests' is becoming apparent. The magazine has avoided becoming 'merely provincial'.[12] Ward's interest in expanding the magazine's links to the diaspora is illustrated by his 'U.S.

Miscellany' in the winter 1978–9 issue. He contrasts the vivacity of the 'Irish-American or Scottish- Canadian traditions' with the 'stay home' attitudes of the Welsh. His inclusion in this issue of three sonnets by Seamus Heaney is seen by Peter MacDonald Smith as 'a declaration of his intention to "internationalise" the magazine'.[13] Ward devotes two issues (Autumn 1979 and Winter 1979/80) to 'Critical Issues'. He reassures his readers at the outset of this experiment that 'This magazine is not becoming a magazine of prose,' but he wants to provide opportunities to explore structuralism and other developing aspects of critical theory. The 1979–80 issue has a section on 'Poetry and Politics' which includes an essay by Terry Eagleton, 'Marxism, Nationalism and Poetry' (30–8). It ends by quoting Walter Benjamin, arguing that 'tradition must be blasted out of the conformity which threatens to overwhelm it,' and seeing this as 'the most urgent task of a contemporary political poetry'. It is perhaps ironic in the light of this that *Poetry Wales*, at this stage of its existence, is still publishing mostly traditional material and that it is sufficiently insulated from current political events to have refrained from mentioning the failure of the 1979 referendum on devolution.

Cary Archard takes over in the autumn of 1980, again without instituting any personal change of direction. His editorial in June 1983 argues for a stronger publishing base in Wales and insists that 'irregular, small magazines' (by implication different from *Poetry Wales*) are better equipped to be risk takers. He takes particular satisfaction, in his editorial for January 1985 – the first issue of the twenty-first year – in the achievement of *'continuity'*. At least four of the poets in this issue also appeared in the first volume in 1965. His anthology *Poetry Wales: 25 Years* contains a high proportion of poems with social content, reflecting the social turmoil in Wales during the period.[14] Cary Archard sought to increase diversity, for instance by including dialect poems. He encouraged a further increase in the proportion of women poets, including, among others, Jean Earle, Sheenagh Pugh, Joyce Herbert and Christine Evans. Prose pieces increased significantly and made up nearly half of the anthology. He established a lively correspondence column including, for example, some passionate letters (January 1984, 43–7) about John Pikoulis's objections to the exclusion of Lynette Roberts from the Academi and his adverse review of Elizabeth Bishop.

Cary Archard's editorial for his last issue in winter 1986 refers to the practical difficulties of combining the editorship with his teaching job. By this point, *Poetry Wales* has grown to 130 pages. He lists seventeen contributors, only one of whom is said to be new to *Poetry Wales* (130). Sheenagh Pugh has an article in this issue about the poetry festival in Darmstadt (71–5), where she remarks that there were seven hundred entries and that 'fewer were academics than might have been the case in Wales . . . where every second poet seems to have been a teacher or lecturer'. Indeed, the unusual long-term continuity of style in *Poetry Wales* may owe something to the professional background of the editors. Tony Conran has harsh things to say about 'the stuffy teacher-dominated Cardiff scene in the late sixties and seventies' and is highly critical of the Arts Council's 'worthy but irrelevant' attitudes which he attributes to the dominance of teachers like Mathias, Adams and Archard. While he wants to avoid devaluing the work of Meic Stephens 'as editor or cultural commissar' he believes that 'one can look a long way either in *Poetry Wales* or in the poetry books subsidised by the Arts Council for any intellectual excitement or significant experiments in form.'[15] Meic Stephens directly contradicts this analysis in *Planet* in October/November 2003, regarding Conran's assertions as 'misleading and factually wide of the mark' (101). Tony Conran does seem to ignore the fact that almost all editors of *Poetry Wales* were practising poets as well as teachers. The Rhodri Williams report in 1987 mentions Cary Archard's belief that 'editing a quarterly magazine of 130 pages was an '"impossible task" for one man' and recorded his criticisms of the publishers, Christopher Davies.[16] The magazine is said to have about five hundred regular subscribers, about two hundred of these overseas. It had attracted several generous letters of support. Despite the magazine's initial failure to respond to his initial requests for information, Rhodri Williams recommended a number of practical improvements and thought an increase in financial support was justified.

Mike Jenkins takes over as acting editor in 1986. There is now less investment in maintaining continuity, and his editorship reflects his personal position as a committed socialist and republican. Some of Mike Jenkins's issues welcome the experimental, for example in Spring 1987 where Peter Finch writes on 'Performance Poetry in South Wales' (40–7). The same issue has Christopher Mills's 'Never Forget Your Kaairdiff':

> Aark aark d' lark
> Frum Kaairdiff Aarms Paark
> I'll aave a Claarksie pie
> An an aaaf an aaf a Daark . . . (16)

The next issue (Summer 1987) discusses the need for more political verse in Wales. Robert Morgan's poem on 'The Dismantling of Penrhiwceiber Man' (19–20) denounces mass redundancies. Jeremy Hooker contributes an article on 'Resistant Voices: Five Young Anglo-Welsh Poets' (Robert Minhinnick; Nigel Jenkins; Mike Jenkins; Steve Griffiths; John Davies) and concludes:

> Poets of the new movement are more tenacious of present social reality, more inclined to defend or to wrestle with what they actually have . . . and to resist the judgement of 'traditional' Welshness as well as the condescension or indifference of English centralism. (93)

Brian Aspden, in 'Doctor's Papers' (95–103) accepts that

> It is a fault of Anglo-Welsh writing that when we turn to politics we leave poetry behind and wave banners of emotion and sincerity instead as though damp gunpowder and rusty bullets don't matter if the cause is right. (100)

He cites Osip Mandelstam, Rimbaud, Lorca and Neruda, 'writing for a people against suppression' but concludes that 'these voices are a long way from Wales' (102).

The January 1987 number introduces a new, larger format. The editorial discusses the role of women poets and pays tribute to the feminist movement in Wales. Eight out of eleven of the poets in this issue are women, including Ruth Bidgood, Catherine Fisher and Fleur Adcock and there is a lively symposium on the topic (30–57) which includes Sheenagh Pugh arguing that it is questionable whether such a thing as women's poetry exists. This increase is short-lived, however. The next issue has only two women poets out of twenty-six. One of Jenkins's special issues (September 1991) is devoted to 'The Poetry of Scotland', suggesting that 'Scotland and Wales, both on the brink, both searching for a new identity . . . have produced poetry in which global and local cannot be separated' (2). His final editorial in April 1992 expresses gratitude for having been allowed to 'sound off' as a 'socialist republican'. Mike Jenkins has presided successfully over the effects of the Arts Council's change from annual subsidies to a three-year franchise.

Richard Poole's view of the world is less politicised. His first editorial, 'A View from the North' (July 1992) debates the proposition, attributed to R. S. Thomas, that English-language writing is to be seen as English literature, and therefore not fully Welsh. Writing from his base in Coleg Harlech, Poole suggests that the collapse of basic industries in the south has meant that 'its literate auto-didactic proletariat has dwindled' (2). Meanwhile (3) 'the Welsh-speaking heartland of the North' is in full reaction against English influences. Poole rejects a 'damagingly inward-looking' literature and insists that 'a healthy culture interacts with others, it does not stick its head in a bucket of sand.' He revisits these arguments in January 1993 through a translation of Bobi Jones's article 'Demise of the Anglo-Welsh' (14–18), originally published in Welsh in *Barddas* in April 1992. Jones asserts that 'the last quarter-century has been quite disastrous in its erosion of the special identity of the English-speaking Welsh,' attributing this mainly to the marginalisation of work that 'fails to conform to metropolitan expectations'. The 'second flowering' produced a set of writers who were 'altogether less cartoonist, more realistic, more politically engaged and less romantic' than their predecessors. But many of the present generation who have little emotional commitment to Wales risk being over-influenced by a 'powerful neighbour' and 'making the same noise as the incomers' (15). Bobi Jones lists a number of exceptions to this trend and believes that the resultant split of opinion questions the possibility of a 'national aesthetic'.

Later issues continue to discuss these themes. Examples include the 'Special R. S. Thomas Number' in July 1993, a sometimes hostile treatment of the poet, where Robert Minhinnick argues (13) that 'R. S. Thomas the cultural icon has displaced R. S. Thomas the poet,' Barbara Hardy sees him as 'fuelled by hostility more often than love' (21) and John Pikoulis argues (31) that he 'seems to regard failure as a necessary pre-condition of spiritual renewal'. This pessimistic tone is echoed in the 'Thirtieth Birthday Issue' in July 1994, where Richard Poole's editorial (2–4) complains about the omission of *Poetry Wales* from Ian Hamilton's *Oxford Companion to Twentieth Century Poetry in English* and identifies a number of 'howlers' in Hamilton's treatment of Welsh writers.

Poole's editorial in October 1995, entitled 'Cornflakes and Universities' (2–4) accuses fellow academics of 'a new intellectual authoritarianism' and launches an attack on the relativist ideas of postmodernists. Poole and *Poetry Wales* opt out of the preoccupations of 1990s academia and prefer to stay within a more traditional intellectual framework. Thus, the debate about 'identity' is taken up again in this issue in Anne Stevenson's review article, 'Identity, Language and Welsh Poetry', about David Lloyd's anthology, *The Urgency of Identity* (38–43). She criticises Lloyd for his plunge 'thigh deep in label-land' and denies the relevance of postcolonial terms to 'the Wales–England relationship'. This leads to indignant responses in Richard Poole's final issue (April 1996). By this time there is a lively correspondence column in *Poetry Wales* and Mike Jenkins accuses Stevenson of adopting an 'imperialist viewpoint, which illustrates clearly why Welsh writing in English is generally excluded and scorned over the border' (3).Another letter from Eddie Wainwright attacks the women's movement (made up of 'Piranha feminists'). Poole's editorial stance here illustrates to some extent the validity of Stefan Collini's assertions about the more active role of intellectuals in Wales but also suggests that this position was under constant pressure.[17]

For its next five numbers, until October 1997, *Poetry Wales* relies on a sequence of guest editors. This intervention creates a pivotal effect, taking stock of the earlier history of the magazine, but also introducing some new themes, stemming from their individual preoccupations, and preparing the way for significant shifts of emphasis under the next full-time editor, Robert Minhinnick. This process begins with the return of Cary Archard for the July 1996 issue, complimenting Richard Poole on 'his thematic approach which introduced a striking coherence and richness to the magazine' (2). Archard again successfully advocates a conscious effort to increase the representation of women poets. The last three of Richard Poole's issues had four or five women poets (about 20 per cent of the total) but the guest editors almost double this proportion, and Robert Minhinnick's issues maintain this new level.

Deryn Rees-Jones (October 1996) believes that 'Welsh language poetry in translation is still scandalously ignored' (2). Duncan Bush (January 1997) deplores 'familiar bigotries' and praises recent editors for their new 'confidence and cosmopolitanism' (3), contrasting them with 'all those embattled hag-ridden . . . patriots' from 'the grim old days'. Bryan Aspden (April 1997) strikes a pro-European note, citing the revival of literature in bilingual Flanders, dedicating his issue to Saint-John Perse and suggesting that 'Wales has seemed to be on the verge of being a nation at a time when we are no longer sure that nations are what we want' (3). Paul Henry (July 1997) takes worries about changing family relationships as his theme, concerned that 'the greed ethic sanitised by successive Tory governments has gnawed away at society to such an extent that family is barely synonymous with community in Wales' (2). In this issue, too,

Robert Minhinnick, who is to become the next editor of *Poetry Wales*, begins his review of Meic Stephens's edition of *The Collected Poems of Glyn Jones*, by remarking that Stephens 'exercises an extraordinary control over the legacies of Wales's greatest writers, whilst maintaining a Byzantine influence throughout Welsh literature' (33).[18] His own editorial policy will challenge the implied status quo.

The beginning of Minhinnick's tenure as editor coincides with the successful referendum result of 1997. He immediately begins to question established beliefs and practices, and to assert the new. His first editorial in October 1997, subtitled 'A Country That Said Yes', sets the leitmotif of his approach: 'There is no profit and no future in the dour regional introspection that underlies much art in this country' (2). Minhinnick urges writers to visit New York, Ireland, Edinburgh: 'Then come back and for all our sakes share what has been discovered.' Nigel Jenkins obeys this instruction in his account of a recent tour of the United States in the company of Menna Elfyn and Iwan Llwyd (44–8), observing that 'we weren't on anybody's syllabus.' Minhinnick also institutes presentational innovations: the traditional list of contributors is replaced by brief biographies in the margin of the text and there is a new feature, 'The Back Page', which features highly personal views. The January 1998 editorial, 'The Road Ahead', reinforces these initiatives:

> *Poetry Wales* . . . is an international magazine with an international reputation . . . Poets do not belong to the magazine as they once did . . . The first editorial promise is to dispense with surmises and summations of what makes a Welsh person, a Welsh writer, or a Welsh landscape, Welsh . . . The Referendum vote . . . has ended an era of introspection and ludicrous Welsher than thou. (2)

The contents of the issue go some way to fulfil these undertakings although familiar voices still appear. Mike Jenkins has six poems of working-class life in Merthyr (5–6) and John Goodby thirteen small poems in 'A Bestiary'. M. Wynn Thomas's piece about Roland Mathias (21–6) appears as a tribute to the past.

Indeed, the reader has to wait until page 32 to find the first new poet, Owen Sheers, but there are then twenty pages of new writers.

Minhinnick's emphasis on internationalism continues throughout 1998 and 1999. The April 1998 issue is dedicated to four persecuted poets from Hong Kong. Minhinnick publishes poets with connections to Utah, Uganda, Hungary, Turkey, Russia, Jamaica and Cyprus, and makes passing references to Slovakia and Pakistan. But he balances this with an extended feature on T. H. Jones (24–33). In his 'Back Page' Minhinnick promises that, in the light of the Gulf War, the April 1999 issue will be devoted to 'Poetry and War'. In his April editorial, he observes (2) that, while war has been the subject of poetry since Homer, it is nevertheless 'difficult ground' for him, personally. He dedicates the issue to those killed in the Iraq conflict including the civilian victims of allied bombing. Poems, such as Vernon Scannell's 'A Binyon Opinion' (4), debunk the patriotic myths of earlier wars. John Lucas's 'Deathfeast' (5–8) is a long poem by *Poetry Wales*'s standards, about the slaughter in Greece in the Second World War. An essay by Duncan Bush on Siegfried Sassoon's war poetry (11–16) emphasises 'the gulf of experience between those who are doing the fighting and dying and those who are encouraging them in this pursuit' (13). There are pieces about Auschwitz and poems about My Lai, Korea and Vietnam.

In October 1999 Minhinnick's editorial 'Militant Millennium Musing' (2) celebrates the prospect of new collections by Owen Sheers and Frances Williams during the millennium year. He suggests that they, together with Samantha Wynne Rhydderch 'and a handful of others' can be seen to 'constitute a new group of poets from Wales' though they are currently 'unknown outside this magazine'. At around this time, Minhinnick instituted a series of overseas 'launches' for individual issues, in European and American locations.[19] The October 2001 issue (launched in Manhattan) has an editorial (2–5) describing a writers' conference in Lahti, 'one hundred kilometres north of Helsinki', with references to Albania, Russia, Belarus and Lithuania, discussing the *stupidities* of literary globalisation (developing brands like McDonalds or Pepsi) and the role of poetry in relation to it. Hardly any of the poems in this issue are located in Wales: Samantha Wynn Rhydderch's 'The Hunt' (6–7) with its references to Cwm Tudu, *Dafydd y Garreg Wen* and Cei Bach is an exception. Minhinnick still has some older contributors (J. P. Ward, Sheenagh Pugh) but combines them with Owen Sheers and a couple of poets said to be entirely new to *Poetry Wales.* Pascale Petit writes three poems 'after Frida Kahlo'. There are writers from New Mexico, New York and Paris. The appeal of exotic locations and international resonance is fully exploited.

As he approaches the fortieth anniversary of the magazine, in 2005, Minhinnick includes a series of pieces involving previous editors, thus balancing his innovations by maintaining some of the continuities that have been such an important element throughout the history of *Poetry Wales.* In spring 2003, there is a letter from Sam Adams, criticising an earlier unsympathetic review of Roland Mathias's *Collected Poems.* The tensions between 'Old' and 'New' surface again; older concerns about the dilution of Welsh content or the shunning of nationalist themes meet contemporary assertions of the importance of international reach. The 'residual' framework within which Mathias operated appears at odds with the 'emergent' demands of a society working in the context of globalisation. The summer 2004 issue (which has contributions from Meic Stephens and Sam Adams) also has an extended essay on Lithuanian poetry and the autumn 2004 number (with pieces by Cary Archard and Richard Poole) is dedicated to contemporary Brazilian poetry. John Powell Ward's piece in spring 2005 admits to personal reservations about the glossiness of the new presentation of the magazine but still pays tribute to Minhinnick's success in making *Poetry Wales* into 'a truly international magazine which commands massive respect everywhere'.

One of Robert Minhinnick's last editorials, that for summer 2006, marks the eightieth birthday of Raymond Garlick, defining him as 'the *Poetry Wales* writer par excellence' (2). In his last issue (Spring 2008) Minhinnick once again engages with Meic Stephens in a discussion on Stephens's new anthology for the Library of Wales series (6–9). Minhinnick suggests that the selection is overblown, 'a massive over-statement', 'an attempt at the "democratisation" of literature'. Meic Stephens defends his project robustly: 'We are too used to small statements in Wales and I refuse to be coy about the size of the book.' There is some suggestion that *Poetry Wales*'s new-found internationalism may be superficial. Behind the verbal sparring lies a difference in perception about the urgency of native poetry's demonstration of indigenous worth and an alternative view that sees it better when viewed in a worldwide scene. This perception anticipates Matthew Jarvis's recognition of Minhinnick's regular insistence on seeing Wales, 'in an international context – but not in any neutral way'.[20]

In the summer of 2008, Zoë Skoulding becomes editor. In her first editorial she recognises the presence of the historical frictions that have been generated by the long history of the magazine:

> *Poetry Wales,* as a name, brims with paradox: it evokes a nation, but one that is in conversation with rather than identical to *Cymru*. It is in English but not English, while the foreigner who haunts the etymology of *Wales, Pays de Galles, Gales* has come via mainland Europe. Whenever Wales was, wherever it comes from, it's as much a future destination as a description of the political or geographical boundaries within which poetry might happen, although it is that too. (2)

Skoulding observes that the magazine 'has in the past offered a located perspective on ever-expanding horizons' (3). She has valued Robert Minhinnick's emphasis on seeing Wales in an international context.

In her regular two-page editorials Zoë Skoulding emphasises the importance of continuity, remarking on the magazine's traditional links with secondary education in Wales (Autumn 2010, 2–3) and on an 'enabling tradition' reflected in frequent contributions from past editors (Spring 2011, 2-3). Skoulding continues to explore international linkages when she gives ample space to Richard Gwyn's thoughts about Latin American poetry (Winter 2010–11, 30-5) and to comparisons between Bangor ('The Athens of the North') and the city of Athens itself, now enduring severe economic stress (Summer 2011, 2-3). The critical material in the magazine is given higher priority, for example the broad perspective afforded by a substantial series of articles by Matthew Jarvis on the development of Welsh poetry in English, spread over four issues in 2008–9, and a piece on Hélène Dorion by Patrick McGuinness (Spring 2011, 9-14).

The poems themselves have less obvious Welsh resonances; a casual reader, skimming the magazine at random, might not realise immediately that it acts as a national platform. However, most contributors are Welsh or have Welsh affiliations. Most of the poets are well-established figures, many with collections or poetry prizes. But Skoulding emphasises that one characteristic of *Poetry Wales* is that many readers also seem to be writers and, as practitioners, are personally involved in the subject matter of the magazine.[21] One effect of this is the creation of 'a daunting submissions pile'. Steven Hitchins, for example, in an unsolicited offering, had struck a new note in writing about place using collage techniques in his poem, 'Petrol Voices' about Pontypridd (Winter 2010–11, 56). The first stanza reads:

> Through the rain-slashed glass the river's level with the tracks.
> Pontee, this is you is it?
> Ditches of empty lucozade bottles.
> Pearly petrol puddles.
> Delivery van glides overhead, a white box in the sunlight.
> Come on sweetheart, you are lovely.
> You are my darling, why are you crying?
> Ambles overhead, a white box in the sunlighter.
> You are my darling, is it?

This explores new ways of approaching a topic that has become something of a cliché in 'Anglo-Welsh' writing.

The 'old' has lost some ground to a more contemporary emphasis. *Poetry Wales*'s prevalent style is now cool and removed from the magazine's earlier preoccupation with 'political polemic'. There are fewer poems about personal relations. There are exceptions, for example the bawdry in Dannie Abse's version of 'The Summer Frustrations of Dafydd ap Gwilym' (Spring 2011, 4–7) or John Goodby's erotic travesty, 'The Sweet Sour Grove', derived from an ancient Welsh text by Gwerful Mechain (Spring 2012, 8). Zoë Skoulding enjoys seeing contemporary situations 'bounced off' such ancient Welsh texts, seeing such offerings as highlighting the hybrid relations between English and Welsh. Her special interest in publishing translations from Welsh alongside other languages, arises from 'a desire not to be trapped in a binary division between languages'. She insists that 'Wales is always a conversation' within which cultural identity is developed 'in dialogue with the other'. Poetry has a central position in Wales, derived from the Welsh-language tradition and having something in common in these respects with Central European countries which also owned linguistic divisions.

She had commissioned some challenging experimental work such as the piece by Harry Gilonis in summer 2008 (32–7), which once again derives itself (without being a direct translation) from ancient Welsh poems: the eighth- to ninth-century *englynion*, known as the *Canu Heledd*. In cases like this, where a commission has been given in order to expand the horizons of what is possible in Wales, she has invited accompanying introductory material. This recognises that the general readership of *Poetry Wales* may not be familiar with the techniques of contemporary innovative poetry.

Reviews in *Poetry Wales,* as is often the case with Welsh periodicals in English, are usually supportive in tone. The few exceptions, like Lyndon Davies's reservations about the introduction to Carrie Etter's anthology, *Infinite Difference* (Autumn 2010, 67–8), stand out sharply. Davies praises the poetry in the anthology but questions the theoretical stance taken by the compiler. This is not wholly untypical. In the summer 2011 and

2012 issues about a dozen books are reviewed in each, by six different reviewers. All the reviews are favourable, with only one exception, again involving comments about an anthology: Andy Brown's review of Harriet Tarlo's *The Ground Aslant: An Anthology of Radical Landscape Poetry* (Summer 2011, 66–8) again questions the 'radical' nature of the work claimed in its introduction. The message conveyed collectively in these reviews is that most published poetry has merit but that the theoretical grounds for this belief are sometimes unstable.

Poetry Wales is the oldest of the three franchised periodicals, and has over the best part of half a century become established as the leading vehicle for poets in Wales. It has demonstrated the changes in fashions of writing over many decades, been a vehicle for the preoccupations of eight different editors, and has acquired iconic status and institutional *gravitas* in the process. Before considering the development of *Planet* (the next magazine to receive substantial public support) I would like to look briefly at two independent rivals, the maverick *Second Aeon*, edited by Peter Finch in the sixties and early seventies, and the bilingual *Mabon*, another competitor, produced in north Wales at about the same time. Both these magazines challenged the dominant ethos of the Arts Council's Literature Committee.

Second Aeon (1966–74)

Second Aeon, edited and published by Peter Finch, ran alongside *Poetry Wales* for most of its first decade. It is an example of an independent production outside the mainstream of the Arts Council's attention, mostly dependent on private charity, including a major contribution from Cyril Hodges.[22] Despite many fierce objections by Finch it was always judged by the Arts Council as falling into its marginal 'little magazine' category. It started life as an example of 'typewriter art' confined to six foolscap pages and one hundred copies, insisting on a lower-case format throughout. By 1974, however, it was running to over a hundred pages, claiming an extraordinary level of readership of 2,500, and including critical essays and book reviews as well as poetry. It was given to experimentation with alternative literary forms, especially concrete poetry and sound poetry. Iconic figures appearing in translation in just one issue (18, 1974) include Mallarmé, Celan and Pavese. Finch was in full revolt against the traditional values of *The Anglo-Welsh Review* and, by implication, of the Arts Council itself. The same issue's review of 'The Small Press Scene' (107–48) deplores:

> [*The Anglo-Welsh Review*'s] ever unchanging format, almost 30 packed pages, mid-stream to dullness, boredom and screaming welsh sheep. so much could be done with the resources available, it's a great pity.

Kris Hamensley remarked of it that '*SA* is the summit of all the efforts and visions of that large number of unschooled poets in the land. In *SA* can be seen the unliterary un-academic (in the nicest possible way).'[23]

There is significant overlap between the poets writing for *Second Aeon* and for *Poetry Wales:* for instance, Peter Gruffydd, John Ormond, Dannie Abse and Alison Bielski all wrote for both magazines. John Powell Ward says that there was 'perhaps a tacit agreement between us that the two modes and styles . . . ensured that the two traditions would continue'.[24] *Second Aeon* attracted some extravagant praise from critics, even being described by Martin Booth as 'the most important magazine of the period' in Britain.[25] This may have been an overstatement, but it is still a significant accolade from an established representative of a metropolitan coterie. The magazine was always dependent on Peter Finch's energetic activity and it folded when he accepted the role of manager of the Oriel Bookshop, which was financed by the Arts Council, thus making the clash of interests unacceptable. Another close contemporary of *Second Aeon* was the more conventional bilingual magazine, *Mabon*.

Mabon (1969–1976)

Mabon was published by the North Wales Arts Association and aimed to provide a platform for young writers in the region. The first issue is bilingual but later numbers appear either in English or (more often) in Welsh editions. Tensions between north and south soon appear. English poetry is represented in the first issue by poems by R. S. Thomas, including the otherwise unpublished 'Some Place':

> In Wales we ride round
> And round; the perimeter
> Is alien, the centre
> Too close. Somewhere
> There must be an area
> Of calm, pure, clean
> Air for the spirit
> To inhale. (37)

Most contributors are well-established writers, including Harri Pritchard Jones, Emyr Humphreys, Owen Dudley Edwards and Harri Webb. The spring 1971 issue has an editorial (2–4) commenting on the 'lack of healthy controversy in the English-language literary periodicals' and denying (maybe tongue-in-cheek) that this is in any way due to the inbred character of the Arts Council: 'In Wales it would be difficult to make up a Literature Committee if all those writers who had received subsidies in one way or another were to be excluded' (3). In reviewing Raymond Garlick's *Introduction to Anglo-Welsh Literature*, Tony Conran is much more critical, suggesting that

> Dylan Thomas and R. S. Thomas have compromised their heritage, and made it possible for the present bubble of Cardiff points of view to dominate the Anglo-Welsh scene. In the nature of things the class poetry of the Anglo-Welsh bourgeoisie can never be a progressive force in the world (58–62, 62).

Conran anticipates here his controversial assertions about the middle-class, schoolmasterly character of the Anglo-Welsh

Welsh Periodicals in English

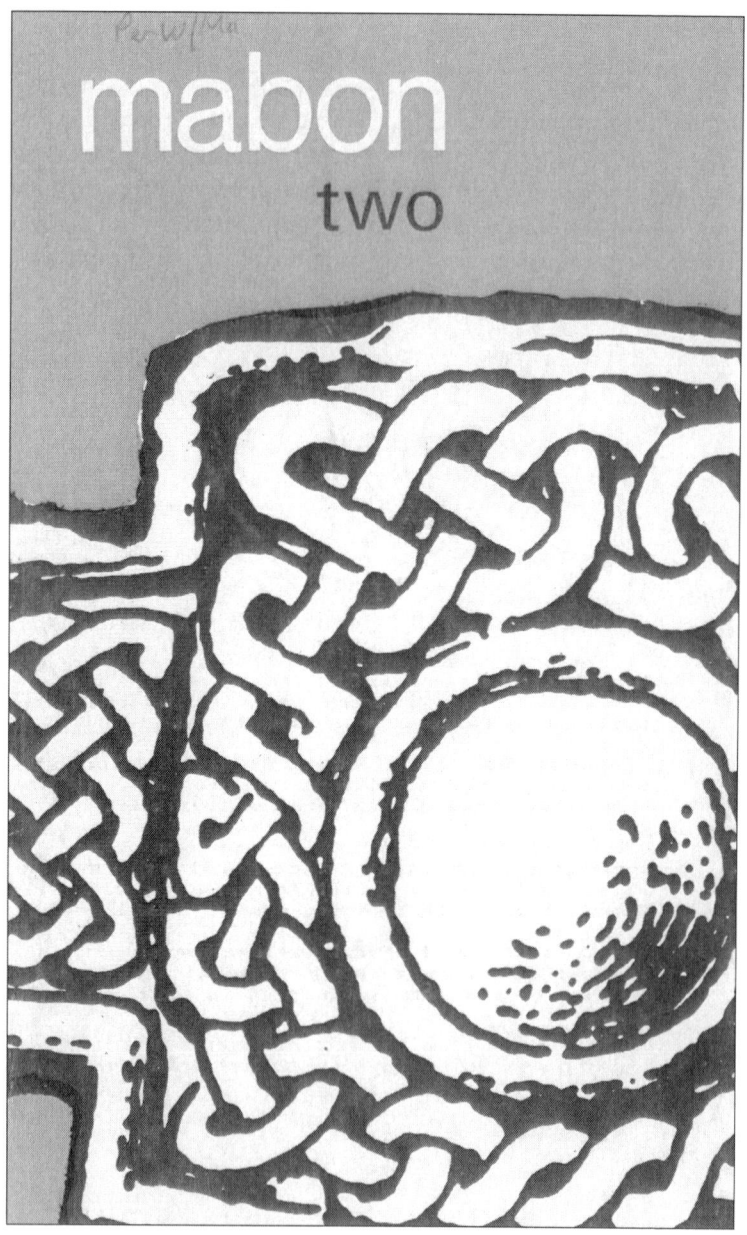

Mabon: ed. Gwyn Thomas and Alun R. Jones, issue 2

magazines sponsored by the Arts Council that were to surface again, thirty years later in 2003, in a public argument with Meic Stephens.[26]

The Spring 1972 issue (edited by Alun R. Jones and Gwyn Thomas) has Conran's 'Elegy for Brenda Chamberlain' (2–3) alongside an obituary on her by Kyffin Williams (4–5), together with an excerpt from her journal. Saunders Lewis introduces the centrepiece of the issue, 'Two Letters from David Jones' (15–25). Conran became guest editor for the spring/summer 1973 issue of *Mabon*, forgoing any editorial comment, but trenchantly reviewing Islwyn Jenkins's editing of the *Collected Poems* of Idris Davies: 'grossly misleading to the general reader and virtually useless to the scholar' (47). Some of Conran's provocative spark is to feature again in the next major periodical to be considered.

Planet (1970–80; 1985–)

'*Planet*', said Roland Mathias, 'was the opposite of introvert'.[27] With Ned Thomas as its first editor it was grounded in a passionate proclamation of a new politics in Wales.[28] The first issue in August 1970 demonstrates the strength of feeling that is to be the provocative hallmark of the magazine and it also presages how much of a true miscellany *Planet* is to be. The cover has a satirical cartoon of George Thomas, recently Secretary of State for Wales. The price is 5s. Ned Thomas's opening article in August 1970 (4–8) condemns 'The George Thomas Era', especially its tokenism in parliamentary gestures falling short of devolution. The two articles that follow are about Scottish nationalism (9–13) and peacekeeping in the Middle East (14–17). Then there are poems by R. S. Thomas and Raymond Garlick (18–20), a piece by Dafydd Iwan on conservation (21–6), and an interview with the editor of *Communes*, a publication that wants 'to create a federal society of communities' (27–32). The miscellany continues with a biographical article by Gwyn Jones on Jack Jones (32–7), the interpolation of further poems in

Welsh Periodicals in English

Planet 1: ed. Ned Thomas, first issue, August 1970

between an essay about 'the restless wilderness' that is John Tripp's dystopian vision of Port Talbot (38–41), thoughtful reviews of Welsh National Opera's recent productions (46–51) and Alun Richards's salty short story about a mismatch between Mavis and her rugby-playing fiancé (52–64). There is a confident advertisement for *Planet* 2, followed by reviews of books (65–84), including a study of education in Communist China, a biography of Caradoc Evans, two publications about Irish politics and Raymond Garlick's *An Introduction to Anglo-Welsh Literature*. The presentation is glossy, with good-quality paper, cartoons and photographs, but there are few advertisements. The magazine is to appear six times a year. Ned Thomas is quick to nail to his mast a characteristic mix of political campaigning, cultural criticism and creative writing that is to be characteristic of *Planet*.

Planet is the first Welsh periodical in English to have begun life with an assured income. Ned Thomas had been in correspondence with Meic Stephens at the Arts Council at least since April 1969, outlining specimen contents, negotiating the terms of financial support, promising a 'fully designed' production and agreeing the format for pre-publication leaflets to be circulated at the National Eisteddfod, paid for by the Arts Council.[29] Some important issues that feature in this correspondence include the proportion of 'literary' content, the ways in which a distinction can be made between this and 'cultural' material and the insistence of its producers that *Planet* is not to be categorised as a 'little magazine'. Ned Thomas takes the long-established *London Magazine* as the standard of presentation he is aiming at. This correspondence continues after the initial launch, with Meic Stephens generally approving but warning that the material about George Thomas is regarded as 'offensive' by some and regretting the absence of any clear 'manifesto'. Ned Thomas argues that the George Thomas material has 'sold a lot of copies' and maintains that 'the editorial philosophy' excludes a manifesto: 'I believe the age of thundering is over.' The first issue gains national publicity, the *Guardian*'s critic describing it as 'a left-leaning *Encounter*'.[30] *Planet* has made a better-prepared, more widely publicised and more ambitious entry on the scene than has been the case for any of its predecessors.[31]

Ned Thomas's collection of essays, *The Welsh Extremist*, appeared a year later and in some ways supplies the 'manifesto' lacking from the first *Planet*. It has a revolutionary tone, declaring unconditional support for the demonstrations by Cymdeithias yr Iaith Gymraeg (the Welsh Language Society). The section on 'Wales and the Anglo-Welsh' reflects John Tripp's critique of the cultural life of Port Talbot that appeared in the first *Planet*, seeing it as an example of 'the new relatively affluent working class of Western Europe, living what seems to be a life of passive alienation'. Thomas here expresses doubt about 'whether Anglo-Welsh writers exert much influence in Wales'. Their relatively poor sales, he says, 'reflect the lack of psychological and institutional cohesion in the English-speaking community in Wales'.[32] Thomas is plainly dissatisfied with the penetration of the public sphere achieved by his predecessors.

The first sixty-nine pages of the June/July 1972 issue are devoted to the politics of the language issue and are written in crisis mode. Ned Thomas, uncharacteristically, exercises his editorial privilege to open with his own one-page satirical squib, 'Mission' (3), which imagines Saunders Lewis rebuffing aliens from a spaceship who offer to 'wipe out London'. He tells them not even to wipe out Cardiff: 'We'll sort it out ourselves.' Thomas follows this immediately with a piece, 'Laws and Order' (4–8) in which he discusses the recent application of English laws to Welsh-language campaigners. Issues of civil liberty dominate this debate, given the 'weak identification with the community' of the judges, politicians and police involved. He advocates 'sociological background training' for the police: 'Policemen, too, have the right to understand. We are advertising this *Planet* in the *Police Review*.' This urbane tone in support of a nationalist theme is new to English-language literary journalism in Wales. The articles that follow include statements from protesters relating their treatment by police and prison officers (9–16); arguments for a Welsh Council of Civil Liberties to follow the Scottish pattern (17–19); a case for Welsh language courts (20–6); and a criticism of the conduct of judges (27–32).There is a piece by Raymond Garlick, 'The Good Tourist's Guide to the Courts' (33–8), which provides five pages of satirical definitions such as: 'BABOON: English legal jargon for a non-violent Welsh speaker who, with considerable moral courage, rises in a law court to utter a dignified protest against the perpetuation of judicial injustice' (33). This is followed by a series of edited extracts (46–58) from a lengthy correspondence between Margaret Davies (a Swansea magistrate sympathetic to Welsh- language protesters) and the then Lord Chancellor, Lord Hailsham (the original user of the term 'Baboon'). Taken together, these pieces make up one of the most sustained political polemics to appear in any Welsh periodical in English. The rest of the issue becomes more 'literary'. Jeremy Hooker's 'Welsh Ambassador' (64–9) marks the centenary of the birth of John Cowper Powys; a short story by Rodney Hyde Thompson (70–6) is about the problems of second-home ownership in Wales; there are book reviews (77–88), all of which deal with political, sociological or nationalist themes. *Planet* is keeping faith with its undertaking to include a proportion of literary content, but maybe more in the letter than the spirit.[33]

Ned Thomas took the view that his first twelve issues of *Planet* (up to the June/July 1972 number, above) were successful in taking a consistently militant stance, but that thereafter there was some falling off in quality until the new enlarged format in 1976 helped to recruit a readership with broader and more sophisticated tastes.[34] This expansion justified extra pages and a price increase. An increased emphasis on internationalism appears in the February/March 1977 issue which, in Ned Thomas's leading article, looks at Anglo-Welsh literature as 'a production and reflection of a colonial predicament' (1). Examples from Ireland, Brittany and Jamaica illustrate the concept. The creative writing includes prose pieces by John Ormond and John Tripp, poems by Richard Poole and Leslie Norris and a short story by Ron Berry. They fill thirteen pages out of fifty-two, a quarter of the magazine, just fulfilling the agreement with the Arts Council. However, there are no book reviews in this issue. The May/June 1977 issue intensifies the discussion; this emphasis on international comparisons yields a massive fifty-page report (53–102) on the 'November Conference'. This report 'ranged over a wide field from internal colonialism to the rights of the Welsh and Gaelic languages, from the question of Cornwall to the multi-national states like the Soviet Union.' Some flavour of the debate is given in Brian Davies's contribution, 'Socialism and the National Question: Towards a New Synthesis' (55–9):

> So, on the one side we have a revolutionary working-class internationalism with no real sense of Welsh identity, and on the other a national consciousness which shuts out the historical experience of its own working class . . . some synthesis would be useful. (59)

This is a wholly different universe of discourse in Welsh periodicals in English. It leads to a deliberate shift; the next issue bears the ambitious subtitle: *The Welsh Internationalist*, which proclaims a characteristic element in *Planet*'s future appeal.

Planet approached the devolution referendum in 1979 in measured terms. Ned Thomas's editorial in February 1979 (2–3) is headed 'Two Cheers for Devolution?', the implied reservations being about the weakness of the measure of self-government on offer from 'an assimilationist state'. There are two lengthy 'conversations', one between Leo Abse and Gwyn Erfyl, and another between Tom Ellis MP and Dylan Iorwerth. JohnTripp collects diverse voices from around the pubs in south and west Wales. In the next issue (May 1979) coming after the loss of the devolution vote, the unusually lengthy introductory piece, 'Mr Morris and the Elephant: The Referendum, the Election and the Future of Welsh Politics' (2–8) is by John Osmond. He sees the event as marking 'the end of the metaphor of Wales as a Nonconformist, radical, one-class single-party state, complete with a Welsh-veneered collaborating elite working at long range in London' (5). The result 'should be welcomed as extinguishing such cosy projections' (8). Osmond here is attempting to close down much of the traditional territory of Welsh periodicals in English.

The January 1980 double issue announces the closure of the magazine. Ned Thomas denies that this is due to financial crisis or intervention by the Arts Council. Nor is closure a response to the unsuccessful referendum. He suggests that *Planet*'s readership is made up from 'Welsh speaking intelligentsia, their Anglo-Welsh equivalent (an undefined though not negligible group) and liberal or left-leaning English people within Wales'. He now believes, however, that a more 'popular level of Welsh life' needs to be accessed and is distressed that the Arts Council has decided against subsidising the current affairs journal, *Rebecca*. Ned Thomas here quotes Raymond Williams on the need for a broader understanding of the role of the arts within 'the deepening cultural crisis' in Wales.[35] Differences of views about the definition of 'culture' and the place of political discussion in relation to it have lurked behind the continuing discussions about what is 'literary' between *Planet* and the Arts Council.

Planet is revived after five years in June/July 1985, reverting to its smaller format, but now priced £1.50, and rather longer – 130 pages. Ned Thomas appears as managing editor with John Barnie as his assistant. In the course of a later interview with Daniel Williams, Barnie points out that Ned Thomas's professional experience as an editor in London was a rare phenomenon in Wales and that working alongside him was a formative experience.[36] In his editorial titled 'As I was saying . . .' (3–5). Ned Thomas takes up the discussion immediately where he left off in 1979: 'Is Wales the same place? Are we the people that we were?' He asserts that the nationalist agenda of the 1970s has been 'relegated' and in his interview with Kim Howells (6–11) claims that Wales, in the aftermath of the miners' strike, has 'discovered and begun to tap a sense of community much larger than that of the traditional tight-knit pit village'. The distribution of political, social and literary material in *Planet* has changed. Articles about the Chartists share space with poems;

a review of Dai Smith's television histories is immediately followed by R. S. Thomas's 'Ystrad Fflur'. Political pieces about the Russian peace movements (57–65) and on 'A Nuclear-Free Pacific' (68–71) are alternated with an interview with Kate Roberts on 'The Craft of the Short Story' (39–48) and with 'Rejoice', a satirical short story about a Falklands veteran addressing school children (72–95). There is less emphasis on the language question; the cartoon character, 'Dai Dialectic' sends himself up as planning to write the 'True Confessions of a Bourgeois Cultural Nationalist'. A closing news commentary, 'Matters Arising' (119–30) allows further editorial comment on current affairs in Wales. The magazine feels more relaxed, more literary and less of a campaigning vehicle.

Over the next five years, during which Ned Thomas continues as editor, *Planet* remains concentrated on current issues within Wales, although each number carries at last one searching article about an international question; European perspectives are frequently adopted. The Rhodri Williams report in May 1987 is complimentary about *Planet*'s professionalism and quotes Ned Thomas as providing 'discussion and creative material at quite a profound intellectual level' which will challenge 'an appalling intellectual deficiency in contemporary Welsh culture' (58). This element of missionary intensity links to an associated determination to work beyond the usual boundaries of contemporary periodicals. Ned Thomas's final issue as managing editor in August/September 1988 leads with a lengthy editorial (3–10). He discusses Wales 'in its modern European context – the perspective which *Planet* has always taken' (4). R. S. Thomas's translated lecture, 'Unity', considers the question 'from three points of view: the unity of being, the unity of humankind and the unity of a nation' (29). John Barnie's article, 'The King of Ashes' (later to serve as the title piece in his 1989 book of essays), is a study of 'Aniara' by the Swedish poet, Harry Martinson (52–65), a fictional enactment of nuclear holocaust. The creative content is now relatively low: two short stories, 'Murder' by Graham Allen (43–7) and 'The Sideboard' (66–8) by

G. O. Jones. There is no original poetry. All the books reviewed (90–104) are Welsh in their origin, and the end piece, 'Matters Arising' (106–20), also deals exclusively with Welsh affairs. *Planet* is still conducting expert balancing acts, between the political and the cultural, the creative and the factual.

The dozen issues between the end of 1988 up to August/September 1990 are jointly edited by John Barnie, Gwen Davies and Ned Thomas. The most obvious change is a sharp increase in the number of poems published. In December/January 1988 there are five consecutive pages of verse, including work by Peter Finch and Joseph P. Clancy. Ned Thomas still helps to set the tone, for example in his article 'If East is East, Perhaps West is East' (February/March 1990) dealing with the collapse of Communism. But in the October/November 1990 issue Ned Thomas disappears from the credits. There is no announcement or note of appreciation for the founding editor's work. However, he becomes a 'Patron' of *Planet* and continues to make frequent contributions.

After a two-year interval, John Barnie becomes the sole editor from the April/May issue of 1992. There is a brief note on the last page (120) paying tribute to Gwen Davies's work since 1985, and especially to her care of *Planet*'s current affairs coverage since Ned Thomas's departure. John Barnie is a Welshman, brought up in Abergavenny, who, according to Clare Morgan, characterises himself 'as an outsider – and a Post-Modernist outsider at that'. Morgan notes his interest in ecology and his sense of himself as balancing Romantic essentialism with 'a social/economic determinist stance'.[37] His early numbers betray these emphases. Creative writing and 'literary' content are still kept close to the 25 per cent level. But the heart of the magazine remains in the social and political arenas. Despite its regular publication of creative work by Welsh writers, it seems unlikely that many people decide to subscribe to *Planet* primarily for the sake of the poetry or the fiction.

Ned Thomas immediately contributes two keynote articles. One, 'R. S. Thomas: The Question of Technology' (April/May

1992, 44–60) is concerned with the poet's extension of the range of 'rational discourse'. Another on 'Political Trends in Europe' (June/July 1992, 3–6) defines the problems in asserting the idea of Wales as 'a democratically autonomous greenish and leftish European region' – comparable with Brittany, Lombardy and Catalonia. Val Feld's 'What Chance for Women?' (June/July: 38–43) suggests that traditionally in Wales, the predominance of heavy industries meant that 'the public sphere was the male domain.' Internationalist ambitions are sustained by articles on Canada, Mexico and East Germany.

John Barnie introduces more material into *Planet* about the visual arts, working closely with Peter Lord. The April/May issue in 1992 has the first of Lord's series, 'Two Pictures in a Tradition' (35–8) and Dai Smith's profile of Ernie Zobole (45–51). Barnie has a special issue in 1992 with translations from recent writers in Brittany, Galicia and Denmark. In his interview with Daniel Williams he describes these innovations as giving him particular personal satisfaction. His editorial style has been consistently more philosophical than his predecessor's and less involved in direct political skirmishing.

In the context of the forthcoming 1997 referendum Barnie demonstrates his suspicions of mainstream politics: he distrusts the newly elected Blair government, seeing it as 'sky blue instead of true blue; but . . . blue all the same' (June/July 1997, 6). In the same number John Osmond campaigns for a national newspaper for Wales (23–4) contrasting *The Western Mail*'s view of Wales as a 'region' of Britain with the less parochial approach in *The Irish Times* or *The Scotsman*. In the teeth of opposition to devolution on the part of the London tabloids, Cardiff needs to reinforce 'the sense of a confident identity', which currently 'remains elusive'. In the next issue (August/September 1997), Barnie, in 'For "Wales" See *Wales*' (3–4) presses hard for a 'Yes' vote.

Although the devolution discussion dominates these issues, *Planet* still pays close attention to a broad range of Welsh cultural life. June/July includes tourism and has a further piece about gender politics – Kathryn Jones and Delyth Morris: 'Public Welsh' (82–7). October/November includes 'Making it New', a profile of Ed Thomas (10–16) and 'Spiritual Realism', where Richard Poole discusses the work of bilingual poets. John Barnie continues to address himself to an imagined readership whose vision exceeds the party political. *Planet*'s emphasis on the international is to some extent held in abeyance. In February/ March 1999 Barnie's piece, 'On the Waterfront', is bitterly critical of the decision to reject Zaha Hadid's design for the new Opera House, seeing this as capitulation to the populist stance of *The Western Mail*:

> Because what Wales is best at is farce – the dreaming up of grand projects which then collapse in a scrum of bickering, self-doubt and inverted snobbery, all of which amount to a kind of concealed self-loathing . . . As a start we might try taking our culture more seriously, especially in the English-language world of the majority. It would be good, for instance, to rid ourselves of the anti-intellectualism which is endemic in Wales, worn by many as a badge of pride. (3–4)

Planet challenges Collini's suggestion that intellectuals are generally respected in Wales and continues to make its appeal to a self-conscious minority.

Barnie himself takes broader views than he credits to the majority of his countrymen. His long editorial piece for the millennium issue, 'A Card from the Horizon', (December 1999/January 2000, 3–11) is an example. He invokes a perspective reaching back to classical Greece and Rome, describing a cultural model which 'provided a durable basis for European high culture for eight hundred years' (3). After an intense scanning of that history, touching on Christianity's 'time–dependence', Darwinism, the development of science and technology, and modernism, 'our switch from a past-centred to a future-centred culture' (8), he concludes that 'relearning how to feel will be one of the great tasks of the coming century' (11). This is a world view that escapes from the narrower preoccupations that have haunted

Welsh periodicals in English. It can, however, still be seen as an intensified version of the 'Old/New' debate, taking it several stages beyond the familiar tensions between the traditional and the modern, and seeking to widen the frontiers of discussion within and beyond Wales itself. By his last issue, in October/November 2006, Barnie confidently deals in his opening piece 'Maps' (3–6) with the intransigent problems of the Israeli/Arab conflicts, as witnessed on a recent visit intended 'to help counter the alleged anti-Israeli bias of the Welsh media'. He resists the organisers' pressures to accept the public face of the Israeli case: 'But Israel, the state is not innocent' (6). He urges the Israelis 'to act on the discomfiting self-knowledge which awareness of the truth brings'.

John Barnie has seen *Planet* through to the end of the twentieth century and beyond. His long editorship (sixteen out of *Planet's* thirty years of publication) has changed the periodical, widening its world perspective while maintaining *Planet*'s commitment to reflecting the political and cultural life of Wales. His editorship is bracketed by two collections of essays, *The King of Ashes*, which reflects his views in the 1980s, and *Fire Drill*, which deals with issues he feels important in the first decade of the twenty-first century.[38] In the earlier book Barnie describes his younger self as living 'in a permanent state of irritability' prior to his period in Denmark, which gave him new insights into the psychology of different languages (18). He struggles with large issues such as the nature of nuclear devastation, as dealt with in the title essay, which was one of his earliest contributions to *Planet*. The later *Fire Drill* tries to resolve some of 'the disjunction between the visceral contingent aspects of our lives and the greater patterns of human and natural history of which we are only intermittently aware' (11). The thinking in these studies underpins his editorial contributions. His personal processes of growth have translated themselves into the magazine's content. However, he still retains editorial scepticism about the 'low circulation of the literary magazines' (100) in what he terms a 'Junk Society' that is inclined to mock intelligence. He wryly cites *The Western Mail*'s levelling comment that *Planet* is 'the magazine for clever people' (106).

In December/January 2006-7 John Barnie's wife, Helle Michelsen, takes over as editor. She has undertaken work for the magazine since 1985 and has been an associate editor since 1988. Her opening editorial 'Back to the Sixties' (3-5), takes education as its theme, claiming that an 'empty bureaucracy . . . has produced a strange intellectual desert where teachers and students wander forlornly'. This is supported by articles about Coleg Harlech and a reprint of a paper by Raymond Williams. The past is once more used to highlight the deficiencies of the present. Under Michelsen, in spring 2009, *Planet* changed from a bi-monthly periodical (six issues a year) to a quarterly, expanding by thirty pages to 160. Michelsen introduces a new email exchange feature, in this issue a discussion on the state of the arts between Richard Poole and Anne Stevenson (58-67) centring about the idea that the present may be a 'time of cultural decadence' in the western world. Content remains consistent in Michelsen's editorship, with about 40 per cent devoted to social, political and international materials, around 30 to cultural and literary matters and another 20 per cent given to creative writing and reviews. John Barnie's emphasis on environment issues is maintained. In her last editorial (Autumn 2010, 4-5) Helle Michelsen suggests that politics have come full circle since Ned Thomas launched the magazine in 1970, when people were angry and worried about jobs. She reverts to the importance of tradition: 'What we need in Wales is to have an understanding of our past and how it has shaped our present, and to make a concerted effort to take the best of that past with us into the future.'

In her first two issues (February and May 2011) Jasmine Donahaye aims for a more consistent and simpler design incorporating a restrained masthead and a quieter layout. *Planet* now displays a shift towards more cultural materials with less emphasis on political matters. Donahaye discontinues the 'Scene' section, devoted to contemporary listings, abandons the traditional subtitle *The Welsh Internationalist* (after more than thirty years) and reserves her editorial input to a brief 'Afterword'. The cartoon figure 'Dai Dialectic' disappears and there are more substantial academic contributions (incorporating endnotes in some cases). Longer review articles are now carried in the body of the magazine. Some characteristics remain unchanged: most of the contributors are Welsh and about half the topics appeal directly to Welsh interests. *Planet*'s reviewers remain firmly on the side of the writers, satisfying themselves with occasional notes of reservation whilst being generally favourable in tone. *Planet* continues to produce an imaginative website, containing a podcast, details of books available from the publishing arm and offers of free online articles. There are also recorded interviews with past editors.

After a year and a half, however, Jasmine Donahaye decides to resign her editorship following the February 2012 issue, citing the difficulty of realising her editorial vision within the existing structure and ethos. In the 'Afterword' to this, her last issue (150-3) she remarks that

> . . . our critical culture is not well developed. In the fields of arts, of literature and of Welsh scholarship in English, there are not enough people who understand the particularity of the cultural context, and often the same reviewers' and commentators' names keep recurring. Sometimes as a result it looks like a closed shop – or as if the few are talking about themselves only to one another. (152)

This ambivalence about a closed circle in the English-speaking public sphere in Wales is not new. Ever since Owen Morgan Edwards's *Wales* the power of a close-knit community has been the subject of both favourable comment and critical reservations. The encouragement of relatively generous critical standards has been seen by some as encouraging new entrants to the field while others (in tune with Jasmine Donahaye's remarks) have discerned exactly the opposite effect: a stultifying intimacy that tends to exclude new writers. It is unusual, however, for such trenchant criticism to be welcome in the comment pages of the magazines themselves.

This editorial frankness reflects some of Donahaye's frustration with what appeared to her as 'an oppressive weight of tradition'. The decision-making process, arising from what she sees as the 'pseudo-collective structure' of *Planet* – in which the staff, the outgoing editor and one other long-standing member make up the board – together with the board's desire for continuity rather than change (all taken together) led to 'a culture of stasis' in which there was a tendency towards compromise and minor modification as against radical rethinking. This was reinforced by the long-standing funding arrangements operated at the Books Council. There was a strong imperative against organisational change and against any change that might risk alienating existing readers. There was also nervousness about shifting from the 'bitty' miscellany form, despite the required change to a quarterly periodicity and the possibility that this offered of a more serious review carrying considered, rigorous and substantial articles.[39]

Emily Trahair takes over as acting editor for the May 2012 issue, before being appointed as editor in time for the next issue. Commenting on *Planet*'s management organisation, Trahair argues that the presence of staff members on the Management Board constitutes a co-operative element and that, given the low wages and long hours staff are exposed to, this ethos 'enables high levels of motivation, that are essential for the longevity of the magazine and feeds into its creative dynamism'. All staff are involved in editorial discussions and 'contribute to *Planet*'s eclecticism'. However, the Management Board has no editorial input and the editor always has ultimate control of the magazine's contents. As editor she feels able to develop her unique imprint on the magazine. She feels that *Planet*'s structural ethos is particularly forward-looking and essential for maintaining its creative independence. [40]

In Emily Trahair's first issue (May 2012) the subtitle *The Welsh Internationalist* is reinstated. Trahair sees this both as confirming *Planet*'s Welsh focus and also as giving 'a sense of the myriad forms of engagement with the world that emanate from the vantage point of a stateless nation'. In the 'Afterword' in the next issue of the magazine (Summer 2012, 154–7). Trahair argues that this subtitle has a renewed relevance for post-devolution Wales. *Planet*, she believes, should explore the interfaces between politics, culture and the arts, between academia and mainstream culture. It should present the reader with 'startling juxtapositions between "modern" and "traditional"'. She envisages *Planet* as 'a magazine and not a journal'. This implies a popular as well as an academic appeal and a desire to restore the 'spark and vitality' of the original bi-monthly production. The reintroduction of the 'Welsh Keywords' series has Richard Glyn Roberts and Simon Brookes examining the origins and the meanings of the word 'Cymry' (11–18). The series is inspired by Raymond Williams's *Keywords* and offers contemporary perspectives on contested meanings of words in Welsh.

Trahair's first issue also introduces, as a significant innovation, a new 'Focus' section – some dozen pages (52–75) – distinguished by a larger typeface and featuring a series of short pieces about contemporary concerns: the nervous reactions in Spain to the prospect of Scottish independence; an experiment in Aberystwyth in the use of digital technology in relation to the Welsh language; brief items about popular music, TV and visual arts, together with a report from 'Cuts Watch Cymru' about the challenges to Welsh society posed by reductions in welfare spending in Wales. Alan Bilton contributes three brief satirical stories (101–11) – anecdotes about occasions of personal discomfiture in the current economic crisis – and there are just three pages of poetry. There is a photo-essay (76–95) illustrating the thesis that 'storytelling is a visual art.' Heiko Feldner contributes a critique of 'Capitalism as a Religion of Self-Destruction' (112–17), citing Walter Benjamin; Trahair's 'Afterword' (156–8) comments on this, remarking that, despite the availability of so much information on the internet, 'there is a widespread sense of being fundamentally *unheard.*' Ten reviews (140–55) include Rachel Trezise writing about *All Things Betray Thee* (a new Library of

Wales edition) and Harri Roberts's excoriating condemnation of Linden Peach's *The Fiction of Emyr Humphreys*. The miscellany genre within which *Planet* was originally conceived is once again invoked in these pages. The overall impression is lively, active and concerned. However, although Emily Trahair hopes to take advantage of the longer, quarterly periodicity of *Planet* to commission longer and more in-depth articles, there is little space in this crowded issue for developing ideas at any length.

Planet's history is in some ways emblematic of the experience of the three franchised periodicals in modern English-speaking Welsh culture. It has jealously sought to preserve an independent view of Welsh society, in its later life steering away from direct political associations, living on an edge between its social concerns and its related cultural interests. It has solicited an educated audience concerned with intellectual developments while still seeking to publish some creative writing and working to retain a liveliness that will give it a popular appeal. Before I turn to the overlapping history of *The New Welsh Review* (the last of the franchised periodicals) I would like to look quickly at three other more independent periodical publications that also emerged in Wales during the late twentieth century.

Rebecca (1973–1993, with breaks); *Arcade* (1980–1982); *Cambrensis* (1988–2006)

Rebecca was edited by Paddy French and had a subtitle *A Radical Magazine for Wales*, clearly enjoying its reputation as 'the scourge of the Welsh Establishment'. It gained a reputation for investigative journalism, with a number of revelations about prominent business men and politicians, some of which led to prosecutions of those involved. In the spring 1978 issue the editorial complains that various companies and institutions have made attempts to silence the magazine (2). In spring 1980 *Rebecca* mounted its Corruption Supplement which included allegations about the property dealings of prominent public figures, including

Leo Abse. In September 1981 it produced an exposé of 'the secret world of Welsh freemasonry', identifying influential individuals in the police, the judiciary and in local government. The July 1982 issue attacked the policy leading to the Falklands War, listing all the names of Welsh servicemen killed during the hostilities. *Rebecca* concentrated on current affairs reporting; it had little coverage of the arts and no creative writing content.

The Literature Committee of the Arts Council approved some funding in 1979, subject to *Rebecca* improving its coverage of the arts, but later that year the Arts Council itself reversed that decision and decided that the publication should not be funded.[41] An editorial (by Gillian Clarke) in *The Anglo-Welsh Review* (66, 1980, 2–4) describes a Radio Wales television programme, 'Late Billing', in which Meic Stephens and Paddy French debated the Arts Council's decision. Clarke expresses concern about the 'sudden narrowing of the definition of literature' implied in this change of stance. Is the Arts Council excluding journalism, however valuable, from consideration? The definition of 'cultural' material in *Planet* was, as recorded above, a topic for regular debate between its various editors and the Literature Department. Tony Bianchi regards the decision about *Rebecca* and the later withdrawal of support from *Arcade* as critical developments in the history of subsidised magazines in Wales. The implied restriction of Arts Council support to material conventionally recognised as literary and artistic effectively ruled out broader interpretations of culture for the next thirty years.[42]

Arcade (1980–2), a fortnightly, did initially secure Welsh Arts Council support. John Osmond's first editorial (31 October 1980) is headed 'An Act of Faith' (10) and sets out the magazine's financial construction in unusual detail (including the personal contributions of its editor). There was a group of supporters that included Ned Thomas and Robin Reeves, forming an expert editorial board that could sack the editor. Osmond assesses the magazine's future needs in detail. *Arcade* will require sales of at least six thousand per issue to survive. The editor regards 'the notion of "Anglo-Welsh" as outmoded and crippling', and he will seek to project the culture of 'a predominantly urban, industrial community'. Osmond later claimed that 'for much of the twentieth century Wales has been a nation in retreat' within which 'the majority English-speaking Welsh have the double dilemma of an "externally manufactured" image on the one side and an internal but inaccessible sensibility on the other.'[43] *Arcade* tried to counter these cultural dilemmas.

This first issue is typical. A newspaper format, with a colourful cover, subtitled *Wales Fortnightly* and promising a look at 'Our Rugby Obsession', it presents a mixture of news items and comment, adopting a consistent left-wing perspective, but less preoccupied with investigations of corruption than *Rebecca*. It has reviews of theatre, music and films, and a page of listings of current events in south and mid-Wales. The editors devote half the magazine to literature and the arts. It is priced at £14 for an annual subscription. This lively presence is maintained throughout its thirty-four issues. The final issue in March 1982 announces the 'surprise decision' of the Arts Council – apparently again reversing an earlier, more favourable indication – and attributes it to sales falling to around the three thousand mark. Osmond seeks an investigation by the Welsh Select Committee into the Arts Council's decision-making process. Ironically, this last issue also contains a biographical piece by Nigel Jenkins about Meic Stephens (4–6). This avoids the temptation to deliver 'a hatchet-job from sour grapes *ARCADE*' and provides a balanced picture of the way that his forceful personal character is reflected in his poetry, his editorship of *Poetry Wales* and his role as head of the Literature Department. The supporters of *Arcade* thus make a generous separation between different aspects of the roles Meic Stephens has taken in his various manifestations as creative writer, anthologist and editor on the one hand and arts administrator on the other. This owes much to their recognition that, despite his being the instrument of rejection of their case for continued funding, he still maintains a key leadership role within the Anglo-Welsh community that provides the rationale and readership for these magazines. Some of the more positive aspects of the closeness of personal relations within the 'subaltern counter public sphere' in Anglophone Wales are represented here.

The short story magazine *Cambrensis* is an example of successful persistence and popularisation in the independent little-magazine genre. Edited by Arthur Smith from Bridgend, it lasted for sixty-seven quarterly issues over eighteen years (1988–2006), specialising in short stories, all less than 2,5000 words. It had small-scale aid, initially from the Arts Council and later from the Welsh Books Council. An early number, Summer 1989, has sixty-three pages, fifteen stories, including one, 'Plumbers and Sauce', by Peter Finch (38–46). By the end, in July 2006, it has expanded in size, has eighty larger pages and, in addition to a dozen stories, carries a number of feature articles and book reviews. Although well-known writers appear in *Cambrensis* (including Mike Jenkins, Herbert Williams and Alison Bielski), most of the contributors are new to Welsh writing in English. Its eccentric and devoted editor, who undertook all the editorial tasks without assistance, succeeded in providing opportunities for new writers on a scale that few better-funded twentieth-century periodicals could match.

New Welsh Review (1988–)

New Welsh Review has a complex history spread over more than twenty years, directed by seven different editors between 1988 and 2011, each working within successive franchises. Following the Rhodri Williams report, *New Welsh Review* set out with the intention of differentiating itself sharply from its inheritance. Belinda Humfrey's submission to the Arts Council for its first three-year franchise proposed a magazine that would be 'specifically literary', employing 'outstanding literary talent in its management as well as its content'. It would be supported by an Editorial Board, upon which the Welsh Academy and the

University of Wales Association for Welsh Literature in English would be represented. It would employ an assistant editor – probably a postgraduate – who would do much of the practical work, and it would have a well-developed marketing strategy. It would have a print run of a thousand copies initially, increasing to fifteen hundred by the end of its third year.[44] These ambitious objectives were underwritten by the Arts Council.

The first issue (Summer 1988) announces Belinda Humfrey as editor, Peter Foss as assistant editor, together with Gillian Clarke as the chair of an Editorial Board, aided by a set of distinguished advisers and a group of patrons, including Glyn Jones, Gwyn Jones and Roland Mathias. It would be difficult to imagine a more traditional panoply of supporters. The magazine is based in Lampeter, where the editor has a full-time academic post. The paratext is impressive: the cover in vivid red and white, bearing glossy photographs of contributors. It has a new large format with two columns of print per page and a contents page sub-divided into separate subject areas, in the tradition of London or Dublin reviews. There are advertisements for other magazines including *Planet* and the *Powys Review* as well as for the American-Welsh publication, *Ninnau*. Priced at £12 for an annual subscription, *New Welsh Review* is more expensive than its contemporaries.

Belinda Humfrey's opening editorial accepts that *New Welsh Review* 'is not a pioneer but the inheritor of the modes and achievements of a series of periodicals concerned with Welsh writing in English' (4). This first number will be 'narcissistic by design . . . it is quite healthy "with inbreeding" '.[45] This refusal to be seen as crassly innovative accompanies a list of almost forty names of contributors, most of which could be included in the chapter headings for a history of Welsh writing in English. They also, however, include the Irish and Scottish luminaries, Michael Longley and Norman McCaig. The propitiation of the past continues with Robert Minhinnick's interview with Glyn Jones, dwelling on his articles in earlier Welsh periodicals in English (7–11), a review of a new edition of Caradoc Evans's *My People* by Wynn Thomas (17–22) and, notably, a retrospective on *The Anglo-Welsh Review* by Raymond Garlick (47–9). This deplores the outcome of the Rhodri Williams report and concludes that 'any sense of continuity on the Anglo-Welsh scene remains fragile.' Peter Macdonald Smith contributes the first of his three articles on 'The Making of the Anglo-Welsh Tradition' (61–5) – which, taken together, implicitly deny Garlick's fears about continuity.

Humfrey institutes a practice of presenting poems together in groups of several pages at a time: Minhinnick, Curtis and Christopher Meredith (14–16); MacCaig, Emyr Humphreys, Dannie Abse, J. P. Ward, Mercer Simpson, Michael Longley (30–3).

Duncan Bush has a poem 'In Memory of Raymond Williams, d. 26 January1988':

> Now you're a whole
> shelf of books in my room
> (one's signed) between Williams
> Gwyn A. and Williams
> William Carlos . . . (66)

The knowing insider tone here suggests the audience for which the new magazine has been designed. The key presumption is that there exists in Wales a sizeable set of educated readers, many associated with schools and universities, admirers of the established tradition of Welsh writing in English and enthusiastic about its perpetuation.

The overwhelming presence of the literary is to be the defining feature of Belinda Humphrey's editorship. Subsequent issues pay less regard to the 'narcissistic' celebration of the Anglo-Welsh tradition but they are still closely aligned to the academic blueprint that was originally proffered to the Arts Council. However, destructive tensions quickly arise as the promised audience refuses to appear and sales plateau around the six hundred mark. These strains become apparent in some harsh opinions expressed in the internal review by the Arts Council in 1990, following the first nine issues.[46] This praises the 'balance between creative prose, poetry and critical writing' but finds the overall presentation 'bland and unexciting'. The magazine is said to be 'typographically fussy and self-conscious'. An analysis of the content of these issues actually shows them to be in line with Belinda Humfrey's original prospectus. Compared to some of its predecessors, *New Welsh Review* appears professional and indeed striking in appearance and organisation. However, the decision had already been taken that Belinda Humphrey as editor was to be replaced by Michael Parnell at the end of the initial franchise. There had also been serious problems in the working relationship between Belinda Humfrey and the assistant editor, Peter Foss, leading to Foss's arbitrary dismissal and a subsequent ruling in his favour at an industrial tribunal.[47] While the editorial team had worked well together initially and both had been contributors as well as editors, there had been disagreements about workloads and about financial matters.

Belinda Humfrey's final issue (Spring 1991) has an 'Editor's Endnote' (86–7) which contends that 'Welsh writers can and should be discussed critically in a context of non-Welsh, especially England's, English writers.' This will avoid them being seen as 'marginal or regional'. She has attempted to initiate 'in this glossy successor to a line of Welsh Reviews' a flow of publicity calculated to strengthen their claims. She lists the great variety of material that has appeared in her twelve issues. Her main disappointment has been in the quality of the prose fiction available which has failed to produce any 'extraordinary exploration of, or experiment with form'.

In the editorial for the sole issue (Summer 1991) before his premature death, Michael Parnell concedes the desirability of continuity, although he confirms the need for a wider audience and promises more coverage of non-literary media, such as film, as well as promising to print letters to the editor. Other pieces in this issue follow closely in the manner of his predecessor: there is a selection of poems, letters, stories and criticism by and about Alun Lewis, a review section now extending to nearly thirty pages, and some short fiction that rather bears out the justice of Belinda Humfrey's reservations about the quality of this genre. Parnell presided over the journal's move to Cardiff, the location preferred by some of the board and advisory group. This shift from rural mid-Wales to the south is to be reversed a decade later, when the base shifts again, this time to Aberystwyth.

Robin Reeves takes over from the winter 1991–2 issue. His editorship is to last for a decade and will establish long-term changes. Prior to taking up this role Reeves had been a journalist at the *Financial Times* and a Plaid Cymru activist; he continued to campaign for devolution on a personal basis. The introduction to his archive in the National Library identifies him, along with Raymond Williams, as 'a Welsh European'. He had worked in Brussels in the early years of British membership of the European Union. These experiences have given him a wider international experience than is common in editors of Welsh periodicals in English.[48] The editorial (1) in this first issue introduces Peter Stead's article about *How Green Was My Valley*. Reeves deplores the influence that Richard Llewellyn's novel has had on the image of Wales, while conceding that it has 'a basis in reality'. However, he declares that 'if Wales is not to drown in nostalgia and caricature, it needs a new image based on new realities.' The relationship between the 'Old' and the 'New' is thus once more opened for debate. Some changed priorities are signalled by his conspicuous placement, immediately after the editorial, of 'Plas-y-Parc Notebook' (2–3) containing a range of brief news items such as Swansea's new designation as 'City of Literature' and the announcement of Leonora Brito as the first winner of the Rhys Davies Story Competition.

For the first time in *New Welsh Review* a substantial amount of content lies outside the literary category. Social and political matters take up almost 40 per cent of the issue. Examples include 'Land of Our Mothers' (11–14), a review article by Sian Edwards on Angela John's collection of writings about the role of women in Welsh society (11–14), a sociological article about the transformation of Tiger Bay (26–9) and 'The Fragmented

Image', a piece by Eleri Carey (15–18) exploring the meanings of Welshness. 'Fields of Decline' by Rhys David (22–5) is about the deterioration of Welsh rugby. 'Letters to the Editor' (30–2) include criticisms of the John Tripp Poetry Award, 'an embarrassing and silly spectacle – anti-cultural, anti-intellectual and profoundly anti-poetic'. None of this material would have been likely to appear under earlier editors; Reeves is moving into territory previously reserved for *Planet*. The literary is still well represented, but Reeves introduces subtle changes of critical tone.

This issue also carries an extract from Dannie Abse's autobiography (34–7), Nigel Jenkins's report on a Haiku competition (42–4), and the poems include offerings by relatively unknown practitioners, such as Thomas Kretz (49). Anthony Conran's 'A Welsh Strategy for Literature' (52–8) is given space to challenge the Arts Council establishment again, arguing that 'until they can find themselves as citizens of Wales the Anglo-Welsh constituency will remain a pipe-dream,' and criticising the 'absurd compartmentalisation' practised by the Arts Council. The proportion of women contributors increases, including contributions by Mary Parnell, Sally Roberts Jones, Sheenagh Pugh, Catherine Fisher and Amy Wack. Robin Reeves produces a more contemporary magazine with a radical edge, less in thrall to already established figures in the field of Welsh writing.

In the winter 1992–3 issue, a year later, most of these features have been retained, but the literary content has reasserted itself at around threequarters of the issue. The tone, however, is more pungent. There is a reprint of John Harris's Gwyn Jones lecture: 'The Devil in Eden: Caradoc Evans and his Wales' (10–18) considering the politics of Evans's reception and asking 'How can we reform Wales by demonstrating its faults to the English, whose opinion of Wales is already ridiculously low?' D. Hywel Davies, in 'Literary Voyeurism' (5–9) quotes from letters between Saunders Lewis and Kate Roberts (5–9), with Lewis expressing contempt for 'the serf-like *gwerin*' while Roberts sees audiences in Aberdare as 'simple barbarians'. John Osmond discusses John Barnie's autobiographical novel, *The Confirmation*, about growing up in Abergavenny, and observes that 'he is of course the Editor of *Planet* magazine, whose smallness of circulation is only matched by its largeness of ambition' (24). Some of the poetry is experimental, for instance Mike Jenkins's Merthyr dialect 'Once a Musical Nation' (50) or Chris Torrance's 'Birdcalls' (62). As promised, there is more attention to public media, especially radio and television broadcasts.

The reassertion of the literary element in the magazine is reinforced in summer 1993 when a new subtitle appears: *Wales's leading literary quarterly in English*, perhaps intended to reassure the Arts Council. In the winter 1993–4 issue Reeves emphasises his sense of tradition by establishing a new regular feature, 'By the Forelock', nostalgic reprints of articles from older periodicals, appearing on the first page. The first in this series is a piece (1–3) by Jack Jones, 'Collier Boy of the Gay "Nineties"', taken from *The Welsh Review* of March 1939. The Plas y Parc Notebook' (4–7) opens with an announcement of the annual publication, *Welsh Writing in English: A Yearbook of Critical Essays*, edited by Tony Brown. This is to publish longer, more academic studies than *New Welsh Review* can accommodate. However, the cover of this issue of *New Welsh Review* has a portrait of Shakespeare, highlighting an academic article by Tom Lloyd-Roberts, 'Bard of Lleweni; Shakespeare's Welsh Connection' (11–18), arguing that a Welsh manuscript now housed at Christchurch, Oxford contains previously unknown verse by Shakespeare. A contemporary piece by Meic Stephens (37–42), one of three articles in this issue about Glyn Jones, describes a piece of plagiarism by Hugh MacDiarmid from a story by the Welsh writer, including a firsthand account of an amicable resolution of the problem at a personal meeting between the two writers. Some of the poetry challenges conventional tastes, for example the extract from Gareth Calway's 'Newport Nocturnes':

> Sex, drugs and rock and roll and lapsed non-conformism in the Bristol Channel port/capital of Gwent . . . (60)

or, on the same page, Penny Windsor's 'A Civil Offence', about her experiences in Pucklechurch Prison after refusing to pay her poll tax. The review section (68–84) opens with Ned Thomas's views on *Culture and Imperialism* by Edward Said, followed by Russell Jackson on Terence Hawkes's *Meaning by Shakespeare*, registering his admiration for the writer's lucidity and incisiveness. Peter Finch reviews no fewer than twelve books in all, including Wolfgang Gortschacher's *Little Magazine Profiles*, said to demonstrate 'Aryan thoroughness'. In its return to the literary, *New Welsh Review* displays consistently a sympathetic attitude to 1990s literary theory, which contrasts with the more sceptical reactions of editors of *Poetry Wales* around the same time.

The Arts Council became concerned around this time about maintaining clearer distinctions between the territories of *Poetry Wales*, *Planet* and *New Welsh Review*. The Council's review in 1993 (in the context of considering renewal of the franchise for 1994–7) noted that the 'cultural material' included in *New Welsh Review* was sometimes 'more typical of *Planet*'. The topical notes and letters were seen as having 'contributed to a radical shift in the magazine's tone'. Robin Reeves had acknowledged some personal lack of expertise in poetry and fiction. There were worries about 'the occasional cramming of poetry pages'. Sales had remained static around the six hundred mark. However, the editor's 'sense of urgent engagement with the matter in hand' was welcomed.[49]

A readers' survey in autumn 1993 showed high satisfaction among respondents; a very substantial proportion of the magazine was regularly read, and nearly all regular readers intended to renew subscriptions. The readership appeared, however, to be 'heavily concentrated in education', and the age profile suggested that more than a fifth of subscribers were over sixty-five, while less than two per cent were under the age of twenty-four. Almost half the respondents also read *Planet*. Some readers recorded worries about the magazine's reliance on an elite band of contributors.[50] This self-consciousness in the Anglo-Welsh public sphere is characteristic of its history. Self-congratulatory or aspirational feelings cause people to take comfort in being a part of a group of forward-looking intellectuals, but these positive reactions are balanced by some sensations of guilt about setting oneself apart.

Later issues under Robin Reeves show the extent to which he was prepared to entertain controversy. For example, in winter 1994–5, Reeves feels it necessary to spell out (à propos of a nationalist review by D. Hywel Davies of Dai Smith's book on Aneurin Bevan) that '*The New Welsh Review* is not in the business of censorship or political correctness' (1). In the same issue he publishes K. O. Morgan's urbane commentary on Davies's review, described as 'a bracing and attractive piece' but nevertheless seen as being unjust to Dai Smith's treatment of 'the industrial world which was fast losing its Welsh' (8–11). Perhaps the apex of this readiness to court controversy appears in the autumn 1997 issue, immediately following the successful referendum on devolution. Nigel Jenkins's satiric poem on the death of George Thomas, 'An Execrably Tasteless Farewell to Viscount No', gained the magazine national press coverage. The editorial in this issue deplores Norman Tebbitt's outburst about perpetuating ethnic divisions in the UK, seeing it as a deliberate rebuttal of the democratic decisions to endorse devolution for Scotland and Wales. The overlap with *Planet* is reinforced.

From spring 2000 onwards, Reeves takes on Victor Golightly as assistant editor. The Editorial Board remains in place but the band of advisers disappears from the masthead. The number appears resolutely literary. The editorial's theme is the contribution of adopted Welshmen to their country, examining the careers of Josef Herman, B. L. Coombes, Alexander Cordell and Gerard Manley Hopkins, all seen (in a phrase of Jim Perrin's) as 'implanted-and-now-belonging'. The poetry includes satiric verse by Nigel Wells (5) and a piece of occasional verse by Peter Finch about the opening of the Cardiff Bay barrage (7). Most of the poetry is still massed together, with a dozen poets in as many pages (52–63), many of them well known, such as Tony

Curtis, Jeremy Hooker or Sam Adams. They appear non-heroic, neatly paradoxical, like Neil Wenborn's 'The White Van', ending in mock paranoia:

> There's no way out,
> The van will be back, you see if it isn't
> The Recording Angels have got us taped. (54)

John Gower claims that the Welsh short story has now moved on (23–6) but still finds that a recent Parthian collection lacks 'that zest and flair and vividness that is the hall mark of Wales's earlier craftsmen'. The prevalent tone of the stories in this issue is resolutely miserable, including murder, alienation and suicidal sex. One of them, however, Catherine Merriman's 'Delivery' (27–32), while still a characteristic example of south Wales *noir*, is a powerful piece that maintains suspense right to the end. The issue has nearly twenty pages of reviews, followed by more material on theatre and film than has been the practice in earlier numbers. There is still a section on broadcasting (102–4).

The fiftieth issue in autumn 2000 gives Robin Reeves an opportunity for taking stock. He congratulates regular writers on creating 'Wales's leading literary quarterly in English' and recalls the historic link with *The Anglo-Welsh Review*. However, 'the growth of a discrete audience for Welsh writing in English' has been 'slower and more difficult to achieve than we foresaw.' Following Reeves's sudden illness and death, Victor Golightly took over for just three issues, In the light of the events of 9/11, Golightly's first editorial (autumn 2001) begins:

> These are grave times, and naturally the contents of this issue of *New Welsh Review* are marked by the terrible events and the awareness of what may befall our critically interlinked world in the weeks and months to come. I say 'naturally' because there were no editorial nudges to contributors. (1)

He draws parallels with the situation facing the periodicals of the 1930s and the 'dignity and passion' of their responses.

Golightly's three numbers significantly alter the balance in favour of political and social content. His final 'bumper' issue in summer 2002 runs to 206 pages. Mike Jenkins's interview with Tyrone O'Sullivan, the chairman of Tower Colliery, about his new autobiography (53–6), the accompanying review of that book by Alec Thraves (57–61) followed by a piece on regeneration (62–8) and another about T. E. Nicholas (Nonconformist minister and founder-member of the Communist Party of Great Britain) all reflect Golightly's personal priorities. In the decade under Robin Reeves and Victor Golightly, *New Welsh Review* has shifted priorities away from the primarily literary and cultural material originally proclaimed as its signature ground. It has become more metropolitan; it has challenged *Planet* on its own territory; it has significantly increased the contributions of women writers.

New Welsh Review underwent a key change in style and content under Francesca Rhydderch's editorship between 2002 and 2008. The magazine's base moved again, this time from Cardiff to Aberystwyth, where it has remained ever since. She is careful, however, to avoid presenting this as a retreat from the urban world. In her first two-page editorial (Summer 2002, 2–3) Rhydderch adopts a modernising agenda, emphasising the metropolitan status of Cardiff as the capital of a devolved Wales, advocating a 'new Welsh cosmopolitanism' as a keynote feature and once again concentrating the magazine on literary and cultural content, including covering 'populist genres which have been pretty much snubbed by the literary press in Wales until now'.

A former associate editor of *Planet*, Rhydderch aims to re-establish *New Welsh Review*'s key differences from its rival magazine. Her editorial in the autumn 2003 issue (2–5) notes 'the instability of the fictional landscapes which have traditionally been the preserve of Welsh writing in English' and comments on Tony Bianchi's concept of 'Welsh *noir*', seen as 'an expression of the pathology of national decay' (3). The issue has more high-quality colour illustrations than formerly, reverts to the practice of massing poems together in one fifteen-page section and cites Ed Thomas: 'The Wales I know is bilingual, multi-cultural, pro-European, messed-up, screwed-up and ludicrously represented in the British press . . . New Wales is already a possibility' (84). A new, more compact design appears in winter 2005 (88 pages rather than nearly 120). The emphasis on the cultural has been firmly reasserted – with only twenty pages devoted to political or social topics. Guest editors (Kathryn Gray, Tristan Hughes, Patrick McGuiness and Matthew Jarvis) appear in 1976, maintaining a protracted discussion about the role of poetry in Wales. Rhydderch returns in spring 2007 with an editorial on 'Wales and Film', remarking that

> In most places in the world, after all, poetry is seen as a niche at best, and, at worst, elitist and somewhat esoteric, while film is largely popular and populist . . . [However] Welsh poets are recorders of an ancient culture that refuses to lie down and die despite the steady creep of globalisation. (6–7)

In the Summer 2007 issue Rhydderch's editorial 'Dead Poets' Society' (6–7) continues this key debate:

> I have quite deliberately taken the magazine away from a primarily academic literary criticism towards a far broader, more catholic – but no less serious – approach to literature . . . This magazine is not a wake, a commemoration of death, a dead poets' society; it is a celebration of life, movement, progress . . . It is a single, small magazine which over the years has become over-determined by the various expectations of worthy organisations and individuals. (6–7)

This represents a key attempt to differentiate her editorial approach from the mode in which the magazine has been cast since its origins in *The Anglo-Welsh Review*. This was a moment when it was again appropriate to renegotiate the balance between 'Old' and 'New.' In her final editorial (autumn 2008, 6–7) Francesca Rhydderch remarks that her editorship fell 'at a time when Wales's highly politicised literary culture was able to relax into itself a little following the establishment of a National Assembly for Wales'.

The first editorial by Kathryn Gray – formerly the poetry editor – praises Rhydderch's 'courageous editorship' while promising further innovations (Winter 2008, 4–5). An editor's blog and a Facebook presence signal engagement with new technologies. Gray emphasises 'the creative process' and ends 'themed issues'. She balances 'Old' and 'New' by including a piece by Terry Eagleton marking the twentieth anniversary of Raymond Williams's death (9–16) while adding an opinion column, 'The Last Word', in which Anthony Brockway advocates an adventurous approach to Welsh science fiction and less attention to 'a few "authentic" authors (91–5).' A new design appears in Summer 2009: a plainer cover, blocks of coloured pages and more book reviews. The literary emphasis remains: articles on major Welsh writers (such as Margiad Evans or David Jones) but also fresh talents such as Joe Dunthorne. The magazine avoids politics but engages with controversies such as gay writing or the fate of Palestinian refugees. Most contributors have Welsh affiliations but there are exceptions, such as Tishani Doshi's piece on life between Wales and India (Spring 2010, 9–15). Kathryn Gray seeks to 'inform the culture' during difficult times.

In her first two issues (Summer and Autumn 2011) Gwen Davies also concentrates on literary contributions. The redesigned contents page has a new 'Pulp Kitchen' feature, dealing with lighter themes, such as Wallander films or the role of popular music in film sound-tracks. In spring 2012 this carries a contribution by Dylan Moore, editor of the little magazine *The Raconteur*, on football in Wales. There is also a 'Trade Winds' section on publishing matters, and there is regular commentary on classic texts from the Welsh writing in English pantheon, such as the account of the work of Dorothy Edwards by Claire Flay (Spring 2012, 98–100). There is less self-conscious striving for international material and a higher proportion of creative writing. Some experimental work appears, such as Ciaran O'Rourke's poem, 'For a Garden Slug', creeping in an arc across the page in winter 2011 (21).

Gwen Davies estimates that as much as 85 per cent of the magazine is still produced by writers domiciled in Wales. While avoiding politics in the electoral sense, *New Welsh Review* continues to make cultural interventions that inherently mark out positions on political issues. Examples include the celebration of gay writing, such as the planned article on Amy Dillwyn's novel, *Jill*. She has also achieved a roughly equal gender balance among contributors. Significant numbers among the readership were involved with creative writing schools or came from the senior ranks of academia.

The website has an editor's blog (initiated by Kathryn Gray). Gwen Davies has added additional free content and the site now carries reprints of articles and commentaries, together with interviews with contributors. The planned new digital issue, to be available for purchase online, has been designed to appeal to a younger demographic. This new initiative represents a major investment for *New Welsh Review* and is supported by recent decisions to broaden the income stream by using new distributors (in addition to the Books Council) and by establishing an ISBN for the magazine (in addition to the customary ISSN) – an innovation thought likely to enhance the magazine's appeal to a wider group of UK distributors. *New Welsh Review* continues to concentrate most of its energies in the 'literary, cultural, aesthetic' areas and aims at establishing a consistent stable of contributors, likely to inspire reader loyalty.[51]

The three franchised periodicals, *Poetry Wales*, *Planet* and *New Welsh Review* are distinguished from other periodicals in the same period by their generally superior contents and more sophisticated production values. They are also marked by their unusual longevity, extreme by the standards of most of their contemporaries and their predecessors. Cyril Connolly's famous dictum on *Horizon* that the life of a magazine was similar to that of a dog (maybe ten to eleven years) does not seem to apply to periodicals that have the advantage of generous public funding. The three magazines in question have endured for between twenty-four and forty-seven years. They have consequently acquired a particular character of their own. I have argued elsewhere that *Poetry Wales*, for example, has remained at heart true to the genre of the little poetry magazine whilst still acquiring a kind of institutional status over time.[52] This has also become true in their individual ways in the separate cases of the miscellany productions, *Planet* and *New Welsh Review*. This is not to argue that the periodicals concerned fail to innovate or to change, but it does support the idea that they may be a kind of protected species. They are certainly exposed to different pressures from those affecting a number of independent publications that have appeared in Wales over recent years. I want to finish this review of the later twentieth-century productions with some of these periodicals. The first three have all secured some assistance from the Books Council, albeit relatively minor in character, paid from the funds set aside for grants for small magazines.

blown (2009–)

blown is a biannual glossy magazine in a large format, published since 2009, edited by Ric Bower. Issues are about 160 pages, produced to high production standards. *blown* was originally launched as a response to the Welsh Arts Council's interest in a visual-culture magazine. About half the content is textual; the remainder is visual. Each page of text is accompanied by facing full-page illustrations, photographs or reproductions. The textual material is mostly prose; there is some creative writing, mainly extracts from forthcoming novels. Separate sections of the magazine are devoted to 'fluff', 'music', 'fashion' and 'cultural intelligence'. *blown* appeals to a youthful demographic; it tries hard to be trendy and streetwise. The monosyllabic title, reminiscent of Wyndham Lewis's *Blast,* signals a desire to look different, even revolutionary. Indeed, the first of the Editors Letters (*sic: blown*'s headlines dispense with apostrophes) is headed 'Long Live the Manifesto'; it promises 'crazy provocative statements' and cites Marinetti's *Futurist Manifesto* (Autumn 2009, 7). It suggests that 'Art must not to be enjoyed' (*sic*) and argues that 'post-modernism has failed society.' Ric Bower starts his second editorial by describing his release from prison at age eighteen, a traumatic experience, but, he says, 'more vagrant than *crim*' (2011, 9). He seeks practitioners who are 'so passionate about their work that they exude sparks like a Van der Graaf generator'. *blown* combines strong emphasis on appearances with a palpable desire to shock – the occasional use of swear words, a prevalent edginess and a consistently radical stance. The irreverent phonic titles of the sections (Myoo- sik; kuhl-cher-uhl-in-tel-i- juhns) deflate the magazine's own pretensions. The magazine's appearance and design is shiny enough for coffee-table presentation; it rivals fashion magazines. It has attracted some well-established Welsh writers: Richard Gwyn, Rachel Trezise, Niall Griffiths. It claims a wide distribution network outside Wales, especially in London and North America.

Agenda (1994–)

Agenda could hardly be more different. Published twice a year by the Institute of Welsh Affairs, edited by John Osmond (the editor of *Arcade* in the 1980s), it is essentially the house journal of the Institute but is also available to the general public. It is produced in a large format, with three columns a page, a dense and even intimidating presence. The model is closer to *The Economist* than it is to any other contemporary Welsh magazine. Osmond's one-page editorials usually deal with a current political topic, for example in his summer 2010 issue he discusses David Cameron's visit to the Welsh Assembly and the British government's attitudes to funding mechanisms for the devolved administration (1). The two-page contents list that follows the editorial is divided into segments such as 'opinion', 'politics', 'economy', 'culture', each of which demands several pages. There is no creative writing, but the 'culture' section deals with topics such as visual arts, the role of Cynghanedd in Welsh verse or the place of music in education. The concentrated format allows in-depth coverage of these subjects. The formal reviews section allows more generous space than is given by other magazines. Thus, in winter 2010 Tom Nairn can devote more than two pages (seven columns of print) to a review of Harold Carter's *Against the Odds: The Survival of Welsh Identity*, using the publication in the classic review manner, as an opportunity to develop his own opinions as well as delivering a (generally favourable) verdict on the book (81–3). The institutional membership, spread across many sectors of Welsh public life, gives *Agenda* assured access to an influential part of the Welsh public sphere.

Cambria (1997–)

Yet another variation is offered by *Cambria*, a general-interest periodical which has been published since 1997. Frances Jones-Davies took over the editorship in 2007 from her husband, the founder-editor. Published six times a year, *Cambria* has in the past received financial help from the Books Council in respect of its literary pages, edited by Meic Stephens. There was an interruption in December 2010, following a decision by a major creditor to force it into administration, but it recommenced publication in June/July 2011. However, the Books Council has recently decided to withdraw its support. *Cambria* is a miscellany with a nationalist tone, urging readers to involve themselves in events such as the National Eisteddfod, promoting Welsh products, with articles on topics such as heritage, travel, visual arts, topography, environment, music, education, motoring, food and sport. The tone is designed to appeal to a middle-class and probably middle-aged demographic. The one-page editorials by Frances Jones-Davies are usually personalised and inconsequential in tone. Apologising for the break in production, she asserts in June/July 2011 that 'we had tried to produce a magazine which really did represent the psyche of this country and its people and would also be commercially viable' (5). The 'literary pages' are light on creative writing, usually featuring a single page of poetry and no fiction. There are, however, articles on places associated with Welsh writers, accounts of Welsh publishers and profiles of Welsh authors. Meic Stephens supplies a comprehensive listing of recent Welsh-interest publications and a critique of selected books. In June/July 2011, in a section headed 'Masterpieces that Help to Build the Nation' (51–2), Stephens discusses M. Wynn Thomas's recent study of Nonconformist Wales, Dai Smith's *In the Frame* (both 'essential reading'), together with Ned Thomas's recent autobiography in Welsh. The review section (52–5) deals for example with *The Penguin Book of Irish Poetry*, a book on *The Working Whippet* and Bobi Jones's *Yr Amhortreadwy a Phortreadau Eraill* (The Unportrayable and Other Portraits). The magazine reaches out to a less literary readership who can perhaps be persuaded, in the context of the Welsh national sentiment that is *Cambria*'s hallmark, to interest itself in such literary productions.

These three periodicals, while overlapping to some degree with the traditional audience of the franchised magazines, all appear to have successfully recruited different groups of potential readers. They introduce alternative approaches to the periodical scene in Wales in the twenty-first century. I want to finish by discussing some examples of the many 'little magazines' that still live on in Wales. Some of these are irregular in production; some have moved from print to web-based production. Their ubiquity, however, and their survival for varying periods, usually against the odds, demonstrate a continuing thirst for alternative periodical production within Wales. They serve the countercultures which may feel neglected by more respectable productions.

The poetry magazine *The Yellow Crane* ran for eleven years, from 1995 to 2006. Edited from Cardiff, it published between fifteen and thirty pages of 'interesting new poems from south Wales and beyond'. It was light-hearted in tone though it provided early publishing opportunities for such established writers as Sheenagh Pugh, Chris Torrance and Anna Wigley. The editor, Jonathan Brookes, originally applied to the Arts Council for funding but decided that 'the few pounds I received weren't worth the bother of applying'.[53] *Roundyhouse* has been in production since 1999, edited from Cardiff by Brian Smith and Herbert Williams, and then from Port Talbot by Sally R. Jones. Brian Smith observed feelingly, in an editorial in April 2002, that 'the artist in his garret has become a cliché but stereotypes exist only because they contain a kernel of truth' (8). Poets published in *Roundyhouse* include Gwyneth Hughes, Ruth Bidgood, Richard Poole and Alison Bielski. There is a 'Young Poet's Corner', some pithy reviews and a lively correspondence column.

In Anglesey, *Skald* (edited by Zoë Skoulding and Ian Davison) published poetry and short fiction from 1994 to 2007, aiming at the innovative and experimental, and seeking contributors well beyond Wales. Since 2008 it has changed direction and now produces single-author pamphlets. Malcolm Bradley edits *Quattrocento* from Llandudno, (strap line: 'Subscribe and be Ravished'), a magazine of arts, fiction and poetry produced to very high production standards, again seeking subscribers and contributors outside Wales. A similar function is served by the venerable *Envoi* edited by Jan Fortune Wood in conjunction with her publishing house, Cinnamon Press. Former figures from *Poetry Wales* appear again as editors of speciality magazines. Duncan Bush has produced *The Amsterdam Review* as an online magazine since 1994, seeking to 'encapsulate the cosmopolitan values of a European literary culture', appearing twice annually and publishing work by writers as diverse as Tom Paulin and Robert Minhinnick. Mike Jenkins edits the annual *Red Poets*, concentrating on radical poets from Wales. *Leaf Magazine* (started in 2010) comes from the background of the world of creative writing departments and provides opportunities for early publication. *The Raconteur* appeared as a quarterly for two years (2009–10) with ambitious literary aims, but was later produced as a highly stimulating web magazine, edited by Gary Raymond and Dylan Moore (the former editor of the lively but now defunct 'webzine', *CFUK*). *The Raconteur* attracted contributions from Owen Sheers, Rachel Trezise and Niall Griffiths, as well as well-known contributors from outside Wales, such as Alain de Botton. Early in 2012 *The Raconteur* launched a substantial 'America' issue, under the Parthian imprint, running to more than three hundred pages. This turned out to be a swansong, however, and *The Raconteur* has now ceased production. Dylan Moore has turned again to the web and is the editor of the new site *Wales Arts Review*.

These are only the better-known of the little magazines in modern Wales. I am regularly reminded of others that are new to me. Their uncertain fates, shaky periodicity and regular demises record experiences that have more in common historically with the mass of small magazine productions than they have with the long runs of the franchised periodicals. Their persistent lively presences are evidence of the energy and desire for this form of communication that still exists in Wales. The dedication of their editors is rewarded by the support of many established writers and of enthusiastic coterie readerships. With their different formats, selectively targeted audiences and creative use of the web, they may be seen as in some respects more in tune with the twenty-first century *zeitgeist* than their more sedate, better-funded companions in the field. Successive editors have battled with the fundamental problem of gaining a viable share of a limited audience within Wales. I would now like, in a brief final chapter, to discuss the contemporary situation in the light of the common themes that have emerged from this study.

4
Conclusion

In the 130 years of their history Welsh periodicals in English have created a tradition within which writers in English have had opportunities for publishing within their own country that would otherwise have been scarce. For many younger poets and writers of fiction these productions have made possible their first ventures into print. Reflecting and sometimes leading the social and cultural norms of Welsh society, these publications have celebrated Welsh culture and opened doors to a better understanding of Welsh society for many people living in Wales and for others outside its boundaries. They have helped to establish an Anglophone public sphere that is by now seen as an accepted and valid expression of Welsh nationality. They have deliberately achieved advances in gender equality, so that at least a roughly equivalent balance has been secured over time. Political, economic, social and cultural issues have been explored and the relationships between these topics opened up.

These periodicals have inevitably also had their problems and weaknesses. The audiences they have established have tended to be weak and unstable, relative to their ambitions. Many of them have been over-reliant on public funding and there has been little movement towards financial independence or towards opening up alternative sources of support. The funding bodies have generated and maintained a narrow definition of what is cultural, artistic or creative – and therefore considered deserving of public support. Perhaps because of this, whole areas like film, popular music, theatre, sport, have had less coverage than might have been expected. The magazines have sometimes seemed to

Conclusion

avoid controversy and reviewing has often appeared bland. There have been few successful ventures into humour or satire; seriousness, sometimes verging on solemnity, has been the preferred mode of address.

At the end of the previous chapter I outlined the wide range of periodicals that is still available to the English-speaking public in Wales in 2012. Over the period since 1965 a particular configuration has developed, in which three franchised periodicals have come to dominate the scene, aided by substantial subsidies from the public purse. The Books Council of Wales, which took over responsibility for funding periodicals in 2003, has maintained the Arts Council's practice (established since 1987) of granting three-year franchises to *Poetry Wales*, *Planet* and *New Welsh Review*, while giving more limited support to selected entrants into the field, such as *Cambria*, *Agenda*, *Leaf* or *The Raconteur*. Such assistance is still usually confined to the 'literary pages' of any periodical. These productions, however, form only a part of the picture. Over the last few years at least thirty English-language magazines have managed to find audiences for their work; a few of these also receive aid from the small magazines grants of the Books Council while most others survive, usually precariously, by their own unaided efforts.[1] At the time of writing, the Books Council has mounted an inquiry into its funding process for magazines, to be informed by a panel, led by Tony Bianchi, which is due to report early in 2013 on the future of these arrangements after the current franchises expire in 2015. Implicit in this exercise is a decision to make the best use of available funds in the belief that the numbers of subscribers are decreasing. The inquiry will also consider the interplay between digital material and printed magazines. At the same time the Books Council will invest in a professional market research project.

This is, then, an opportune time to review the main themes that have emerged in the researching of this topic. The magazines published today are the products of complex interactions between their own individual histories, the talents and intentions of their editors, and the unique character of the public sphere that they serve. Mikko Lehtonen, in his work on the analysis of texts, remarks that 'producing texts is never purely or even primarily creating anew, but always exploiting already existing models.'[2] The 'New' still draws on the legacy of 'the Old'. Continuity and tradition have been important, sometimes overriding factors, and the apostles of fundamental change have usually found the going hard. Several editors from Gillian Clarke in 1976 to Jasmine Donahaye in 2012 have felt themselves facing opposition to quite minor shifts in presentation, let alone to proposals for significant changes in content, which are thought likely to alienate existing readerships. Periodicals starting life as exciting, youthful little magazines (such as *Wales* in 1939 or *Dock Leaves* in 1958) have migrated quite rapidly from their radical beginnings into more solemn productions, expanding from primarily creative writing into more critical material, and more social and political commentary. Frequently periodicals have entertained an educative mission, with editors drawn from an educational or academic background, anxious to inform potential readers about recent developments and to undertake a leadership role in matters of taste and opinion.

Since 1882 there has always been an audience within Wales for periodical production in English. But the size and character of that audience has always been a matter of conjecture, with decisions about potential circulation being decided largely by the ambitions of editors. Such judgements have usually been over-optimistic. Whether in the cases of Owen Morgan Edwards misjudging the appetite of the English-speaking population for the kind of instruction and entertainment offered by his 1894 *Wales*, of Keidrych Rhys overestimating the audience for his 1958 series of a very different *Wales* as potentially in the region of thirty-five thousand (a mere 1 per cent of the three and half million Welshmen in the world) or of Gwyn Jones imagining a potential million readers for his *Welsh Review* – a common feature has been an exuberant editorial disregard for the cold facts. It may perhaps be significant that, since the arrival of regular subsidies, there have been fewer published estimations of the size of the audience. At the same time the magazines have mounted their appeals more obviously to the comparatively limited 'counter cultures'. More recently, however, in the light of worries about the growing audience for digital productions, serious anxieties about the whole future of print magazines have surfaced. The extent of the inroads into magazine subscribers likely to arise on this account remains a matter of personal judgement. There is at least one possible scenario within which niche print magazines will be actively promoted through web-based productions.[3] *New Welsh Review* plans to become an 'early adopter' of the concept of a digital version, whilst some other magazines already exist solely on the web and others bide their time.

Concerns over audiences and sales are not, of course, confined to periodicals. In September 2011, the Welsh Assembly Government set up a Task Group on the Future of Media in Wales which has attracted a wide range of commentary from interested individuals and organisations.[4] At the time of writing most attention is given in these consultations to issues regarding broadcasting, newspapers and digital media, and few of the comments relate to periodical culture in Wales. Hugh Lewis, the minister for regeneration, housing and heritage (who has responsibility for the Books Council), does remark that the Council also supports English-language magazines, one of which (presumably *Planet*) is devoted to 'current affairs/culture'.[5] I understand, however, that the Books Council will be drawing attention in more detail to the traditional strengths of periodical literature in serving the public sphere in Wales. It seems important that the segment to which the periodicals belong is not seen as wholly different from or sealed off from the audiences for the rest of the media. There has always been a risk that the appeal of the magazines can be seen as limited to a restricted, intimate part of the public sphere within Wales, dominated by intellectuals, educators and academics. The value of such a specialist 'knowable community', with its deep but narrow pool of contributors and readers, must be offset against the limitations it brings with it – the dangers of 'inbreeding' cheerfully acknowledged by Belinda Humfrey in her first issue of *New Welsh Review* in 1988 or the problems of there being too narrow a critical base that featured in Jasmine Donahaye's final editorial contribution for *Planet* in 2012.

Early editors of English-language magazines in the nineteenth century were conscious of the strength of the older tradition of Welsh-language periodicals (predating the first English magazines by at least forty years). The awareness of the power of the alternative language is strongly present in translations and references throughout Welsh periodicals in English, from early examples such as *The Red Dragon*'s series 'The Shake of the Hand' up to *The Welsh Outlook*'s celebration of Welsh as 'a mighty bulwark' against alien influences. Keidrych Rhys's sponsorship of the debate about Lord Raglan's hostility to Welsh led to sustained controversy. Periodicals such as *Poetry Wales* and *Planet* were supportive of the Welsh-language movement of the 1970s. Ned Thomas's view of English as 'the language of servility' had a wide currency at that time. There have been conscious treatments of the language theme in recent issues of *Planet* and *Poetry Wales*. However, the majority of bilingual magazines (such as *Cymru Fydd* or *Mabon*) have for the most part been short-lived. The current Welsh-language publications appear to have stronger circulations and a more consistent readership than their Anglophone equivalents.

Colm Tóibín has recently developed some thoughts about societies which work in more than one language. He suggests that consideration needs to be given to 'the idea that they are living in a place that does not have full political autonomy or where the public sphere in which they suffer has somehow been damaged'. The idea 'is there in the shadows, as it were by implication'.[6] Tóibín does not specifically mention Wales but writes about Ireland, Catalonia, Bengal and Scotland, where, he suggests, 'two languages were in conflict, or at least there was an older shadow language against the one of substance.' There is a real question, however, in Welsh periodicals in English about which language could be regarded as 'the one of substance'. Relatively few readers will engage with periodicals in both languages. Jasmine Donahaye, in a recent essay, identifies 'a distinct unease with notions of a residual ethnic Welshness' and notes that there is 'a fear of exclusiveness, of the development of hierarchies of belonging'.[7] This explores the 'internal difference' that Wynn Thomas wants to negotiate. The public sphere which Welsh periodicals in English serves may not be 'damaged', as Tóibín suggests, but is certainly divided linguistically and, despite devolution, seems recently to have diminished in power and extent. In the days of *Dock Leaves* and *The Anglo-Welsh Review* the presence of a tangible cause in the promotion of English-language writing in Wales may have been a stronger rallying point than it has since become. Writers who were not publishing in Welsh but not adopting the values of English literature either were seen to have a particular cause to champion and a specific population to serve.

Colm Tóibín draws attention, in the same article, to 'the fetishisation, first by poets and playwrights and painters, then by intellectuals and politicians of the countryside itself . . . This was the primal landscape where the idea of the nation was at its most pure and uncontaminated and uncomplex.' The presence of this phenomenon in Welsh periodicals in English can be recognised in the work of writers such as R. S. Thomas and Gillian Clarke. Matthew Jarvis, writing about Clarke, points out that 'far from being any sort of dead end, a focus on the rural continues to be a significant strand of thought for poets writing from Wales – and . . . aspects of Clarke's work also indicate the ongoing importance of a fairly tough interpretation of Welsh rurality.'[8] Such a focus captures the concept of what Tóibín calls 'a primal landscape' and relates well to concerns about the environment. Too often, however, until very recently, a preference for this kind of topic has been seen as inimical to the development of more experimental writing. Nerys Williams goes so far as to suggest that 'experimentation, or avant-gardism, was never a key characteristic of an emerging Welsh literature in English.'[9] Even modernism, she suggests, was always seen as contributing to 'a British modernist literary project', rather than introducing one to Wales. However, there are exceptions. Keidrych Rhys's ready embrace of modernist writing about Welsh environments in his early issues of *Wales* challenges this analysis, although the tensions between Peter Finch and the Arts Council in the context of *Second Aeon* go some way to support it. Zoë Skoulding's recent inclusion of more experimental work in *Poetry Wales* extends, as we have seen, to new, radical ways of writing about place, but also recognises a need for introductory material to prepare the magazine's readership for such innovative writing.

I would like to end on a comparative note. At the conclusion of my 2008 book about Irish periodical culture, I tried to show how the main genres of the periodical – the review, the miscellany and the little magazine – behaved in Wales, Scotland and Ireland during the first decade of the twenty-first century.[10] Five years later, a few of the magazines discussed then have ceased to exist, but the great majority survive. As in Wales, the established longer-term publications continue to promote excellent writing, despite growing problems linked to economic stringencies and some changing attitudes among funders. I want to discuss just two out of several examples where Irish magazines deal with similar issues to their Welsh equivalents. As I have argued throughout this study, the similarities and differences exposed in the detail of the contents of particular periodicals can be suggestive.

The *Dublin Review*'s spring 2012 issue opens with Philip Ó Ceallaigh's surging account of the turbulence of life in contemporary Cairo during the recent elections (5–24), immediately followed by Tim Robinson's Parnell Lecture (from Magdalene College, Cambridge) pleading the case for relieving the wildness of Connemara from the incursions of wind turbines, and urging the importance of retaining communities with place-names in the Irish language, avoiding the danger of having 'sacrificed them to the technology of short cuts, in a misdirected effort to save the world' (25–44; 44). Two preoccupations that have been noticed in Welsh magazines, the desire to relate to other countries and the need to celebrate the land, immediately present themselves together. There is a taut short story by Anthony Caleshu about a couple discovered in adultery by the woman's husband, followed by Ed O'Loughlin's account of a maverick killer being hunted down by Mounties in the Canadian Arctic in 1931. An essay, 'Ireland on Fire' by Rachel Anderson, deals with the growing problems of forest fires in Ireland, bringing in discussions with farmers and foresters. *Dublin Review*'s editor, Duncan Barrington, claims to enshrine no particular ideology and contributes no editorial material in this issue. He aims to provide a space where excellent writing can be displayed. But the magazine still manages to breathe an individualist, liberal stance, questioning accepted opinions and attitudes.

Chris Agee's *Irish Pages* appears twice a year from Belfast. The spring/summer 2012 issue has 'Sexuality' as its theme and has a substantial section in Irish, including prose and poetry with translations. The opening essay, 'Home from Andalucia' by Gerard McCarthy, is about a return to Cordoba, the plangent details recollected in his home in Streedagh in the west of Ireland, looking out to the now deserted island of Inishmurray: 'How can one see one's heritage unless one steps outside it into that space we share in common with all heritages?' (14). Tony McMahon writes about 'A Café in Tangiers' from the standpoint of a traditional musician, describing a drug-induced, highly erotic experience. Denis Sampson, in 'Reflections on Attachment' describes the ambivalences he experiences in living alternately at Portally Cove near Waterford and in Montreal. Manus Charleton writes a personal memoir set in Landscape Road in suburban Dublin, describing his introduction to existentialism and the cave paintings of Chauvet, as shown in Werner Herzog's film, *The Cave of Forgotten Dreams*. Pieces on bisexuality and on the Oscar Wilde centenary, as celebrated in Paris, justify the issue's subtitle. There are notes of uproar in Rodge Glass's story, '59 Places to Fuck in Arizona' or in Stephen

Dornan's pieces 'In the Habbie Stanza' taken from Scots dialect. Once again the editor, Chris Agee, without ostensibly directing the reader, rehearses some major themes that have also become familiar in Welsh periodicals in English, including the representation of domestic landscapes, their emotional associations and the lessons that emerge from productive contrasts and comparisons with other countries. In a six-monthly periodical of 150 pages he is perhaps better able to indulge himself with idiosyncratic materials.

The mature Irish examples cited here suggest at once some close identity of interests with contemporary Welsh periodicals in English, and at the same time one or two distinct differences. Intensely personal contributions about aspects of the land (especially touching on remote places and extreme conditions) appear juxtaposed against other offerings that reach out from Ireland's secure base in geography and history to encompass different countries and wider patterns of ideas. There is a strong sense of identification with the imagined reader. Both magazines convey an almost carnivalesque enjoyment of the quality of the writing they publish; at the same time they refrain from drawing conclusions or canvassing opinions. There is little straining for effect, little obvious anxiety; the writing is allowed to speak for itself. Both periodicals nevertheless appear to be stamped with a strong personality; they are intensely individual productions. In both cases they sustain considerable print runs and command readerships outside their country of origin.

Welsh periodicals in English started their history in the late nineteenth century, driven by the immense personal energies of individual editors, aiming independently to provide for what was then a new linguistic constituency. Charles Wilkins and Owen Morgan Edwards were examples of dedicated individuals who had to create their audience. Together with the other Anglophone magazines of the century they worked to generate the nucleus of a new public sphere. As a result, since their time, there has never been a period without at least one major English-language periodical in Wales. Their successors in the turbulent early decades of the twentieth century, editors such as Thomas Jones, Keidrych Rhys and Gwyn Jones, established the idea of a Welsh magazine in the English language as a necessity of civilisation for a growing population of aspirants to intellectual life. In the 1960s Roland Mathias and Raymond Garlick between them created *Dock Leaves* and *The Anglo-Welsh Review* and Meic Stephens launched *Poetry Wales*: the first Welsh magazines in English to secure public funding for their efforts, consequently launching the present generation of periodicals, including *Planet* and *New Welsh Review*. At all stages along the way there have been numbers of rival productions, often relatively short-lived little magazines, challenging the hegemony of the long-standing periodicals. This recapitulation of the history underlines the strength, vitality and flexibility of the tradition. The common feature has been the presence of the play of individual minds on the topics of the time. Whatever the changes and challenges in the way ahead for Welsh periodicals in English, it is certain that the abundant energies of editors can find ways of creating new patterns to suit the needs of a new day.

Notes

Introduction

1. Raymond Williams, *Marxism and Literature* (Oxford: Oxford University Press), pp. 122–3.
2. M. Wynn Thomas, *Corresponding Cultures: The Two Literatures of Wales* (Cardiff: University of Wales Press, 1999), p. 46.
3. Gwyn A. Williams, *When Was Wales? A History of the Welsh* (Harmondsworth: Penguin, 1986), p. 140.
4. John Davies, *A History of Wales*, new edn (London: Penguin, 2007 [1993]), pp. 311, 403.
5. Huw Walters, *A Bibliography of Welsh Periodicals: 1851–1900* (Aberystwyth: National Library of Wales, 2003), p. xxv.
6. Ibid., p. xxix.
7. Brynley F. Roberts, *The Welsh Periodical Press, 1735–1900* (Aberystwyth: National Library of Wales, 1989), p. 13.
8. Ibid., p. 15.
9. Jürgen Habermas, *The Structural Transformation of the Public Sphere: An Inquiry into a Category of Bourgeois Society*, trans. Thomas Burger with the assistance of Frederick Lawrence (Cambridge: Polity Press, 1992 [original German, 1962]), p. 59.
10. Oscar Negt and Alexander Kluge, *Public Sphere and Experience: Towards an Analysis of the Bourgeois and Proletarian Sphere*, trans. Peter Labanyi, Jamie Owen Daniel and Assenka Oksilof (Minneapolis and London, University of Minnesota Press, 1993 [orig. German, 1972]), p. xxviii.
11. Nancy Fraser, 'Rethinking the public sphere: a contribution to the critique of actually existing democracy' in Craig Colhoun (ed.), *Habermas and the Public Sphere* (Boston, Massachusetts Institute of Technology, 1997), pp. 109–42 (123).
12. M. Wynn Thomas, *Internal Difference: Twentieth-Century Writing in Wales* (Cardiff: University of Wales Press, 1992), p. xiii.
13. Stefan Collini, *Absent Minds: Intellectuals in Britain* (Oxford: Oxford University Press, 2006), pp. 2, 10.
14. Ibid., p. 434.
15. Stefan Collini, *Common Reading: Critics, Historians, Publics* (Oxford: Oxford University Press, 2008), p. 233.

[16] Malcolm Ballin, 'Welsh Periodicals in English 1880–1965: Literary Form and Cultural Substance', in *Welsh Writing in English: A Yearbook of Critical Essays*, 9 (2004), 1–32.

[17] Clifford Geertz, *The Interpretation of Cultures: Selected Essays* (New York: Basic Books, 1973), p. 6.

[18] Lyn Pykett. 'Reading the periodical press: text and comment', in, Laurel Brake, Aled Jones and Lionel Madden (eds), *Investigating Victorian Journalism* (Basingstoke: Macmillan, 1990), 3–18 (7).

[19] Brynley F. Roberts, *The Welsh Periodical Press, 1735–1900* (Aberystwyth: National Library of Wales, 1989); Huw Walters, *A Bibliography of Welsh Periodicals, 1735–1850* (Aberystwyth: National Library of Wales, 1993).

[20] Arthur Gwynn and/or Idwal Lewis, *Subject Index for Welsh Periodicals, 1931–55*, 7 vols (Cardiff and Swansea: Wales and Monmouthshire Branch of the Libraries Association, 1931–55); David Jenkins and/or R. Geraint Gruffydd, *Subject Index for Welsh Periodicals, 1968–80*, 3 vols (Aberystwyth: National Library of Wales, 1968–80). Further series have since been produced covering the period up to 1984.

[21] See my article, 'Spaces of International Comparison in Welsh Periodicals in English', *Almanac: Yearbook of Welsh Writing in English*, 14 (2009–10), 93–120.

[22] The best current example of such a digitised resource is the Modernist Magazine's Project at Brown University in the United States: *http://dl.lib.brown.edu/mjp/* (accessed 8 June 2010). This developing work provides the full text of a large number of magazines, including, for example, *Blast*, *The New Age* and *The English Review*, but does not at present include any Welsh examples. The National Library of Wales has a project to digitise a selection of Welsh periodicals. This is still in development, however, and at the time of writing the only journal relevant to this study is Keidrych Rhys's *Wales* (1937–60), published on the Library's website since February 2011.

[23] Klaus Krippendorf, *Content Analysis: An Introduction to the Methodology*, second edn (Thousand Oaks, Calif.: Sage Publications, 2004), p. 33.

[24] Alyce von Rothkirch, 'Visions of Wales: *The Welsh Outlook*, 1914–1933', *Almanac: Yearbook of Welsh Writing in English,* 14 (2009–10), 65–92.

[25] Benedict Anderson, *Imagined Communities: Reflections on the Origin and Spread of* Nationalism, revised edn (London and New York: Verso, 2006 [1983]), pp. 7, 154.

[26] Ned Thomas, *The Welsh Extremist* (London: Victor Gollancz, 1971), p. 35.

27 Sian Rhiannon Williams, 'The True "Cymraes": images of women in women's nineteenth-century periodicals', in Angela V. John (ed.), *Our Mothers' Land: Chapters in Welsh Women's History, 1830–1939* (Cardiff: University of Wales Press, 1991), pp 69–91 (p. 80). Also Ceridwen Lloyd Morgan, 'From temperance to suffrage?', ibid., pp. 135–58.

28 Katie Gramich, *Twentieth-Century Women's Writing in Wales: Land, Gender and Belonging* (Cardiff: University of Wales Press, 2007), pp. 4, 196.

I

1 John Wilkins, 'Charles Wilkins, Writer 1830–1913: A Biographical Note by his Great Grandson', *Merthyr Historian*, 13 (2001), 5–13 (6).
2 Gwyn A. Williams, *When Was Wales? A History of the Welsh* (Harmondsworth: Penguin, 1986), p. 210.
3 A. N. Wilson, *The Victorians* (London: Arrow Books, 2003), pp. 440, 444, 475.
4 Kenneth O. Morgan, *Rebirth of a Nation; A History of Modern Wales* (Oxford, Oxford University Press, 1981), pp. 3, 9, 22, 25, 26, 29.
5 Ibid., p. 6.
6 John Davies, *A History of Wales* (London, Penguin, 2007 [1993]), p. 375.
7 See Brynley F. Roberts, 'Charles Wilkins: the historian of Merthyr Tydfil', *Merthyr Historian*, 12 (2001), 1–19 (4, 5).
8 John Davies, *A History of Wales*, p. 293.
9 Richard Altick, *The English Common Reader: A Social History of the Mass Reading Public: 1800–1900* (Chicago: University of Chicago Press, 1957), p. 395.
10 Jürgen Habermas, *The Structural Transformation of the Public Sphere* (Cambridge: Polity Press, 1992 [original in German, 1962]), p. 175.
11 Altick, *The English Common Reader*, p. 380.
12 David Finkelstein, *The House of Blackwood: Author–Publisher Relations in the Victorian Era* (Pennsylvania, Pennsylvania University Press, 2000), p. 91, 101 .
13 T. H. S. Escott, 'Thirty Years of the Periodical Press', *Blackwood's* (October 1894), 532–42 (539, 542).
14 Roland Mathias, *The Lonely Editor: A Glance at Anglo-Welsh Magazines* (Cardiff: University College Cardiff Press) 1984, p. 9.
15 Bound copies of *The Red Dragon* usually exclude the 'wrapper pages' that carry advertisements. However, the May 1883 issue in the Cardiff University Library does display the examples quoted above and they are probably typical.

Notes

16 Daniel G. Williams, *Ethnicity and Cultural Authority: From Arnold to Dubois* (Edinburgh: Edinburgh University Press, 2006), p. 17.
17 Gwyn A. Williams, *When Was Wales?* p. 219.
18 Laurel Brake and John Codell, 'Introduction: Encountering the Press', in Laurel Brake and John F. Codell (eds), *Encounters in the Victorian Press* (Basingstoke: Palgrave Macmillan, 2005), 1–7 (2).
19 Brynley Roberts, 'Welsh Periodicals: A Survey', in Brake, Jones and Madden, *Investigating Victorian Journalism*, pp. 71–84 (pp. 82, 84).
20 See for example: August 1882: (unsigned), 'The Rise and Growth of the Science and Art of Education', 30–4; October 1882: 'A Pendragon', 'Our Red Dragons at Westminster', 372–6.
21 Joseph Bristow (ed.), *The Victorian Poet: Poetics and Persona* (London, Croom Helm, 1987), pp. 2, 9.
22 Kathryn Ledbetter, *British Victorian Women's Periodicals: Beauty, Civilisation and Poetry* (New York: Palgrave Macmillan, 2009), pp. xi, 5–6.
23 Belinda Humphrey, 'Prelude to the twentieth century' in M. Wynn Thomas (ed.), *A Guide to Welsh Literature*, vol. 7: *Welsh Writing in English* (Cardiff: University of Wales Press, 2003), pp. 7–46 (p. 38). Humphrey records the sale of eleven thousand copies of Lewis Morris's *Collected Works* (1891) over five years, pays tribute to his academic success but describes his writing as 'largely unmemorable'. For Morris and Oscar Wilde see Meic Stephens, *The New Companion to the Literature of Wales* (Cardiff: University of Wales Press, 1998), p. 413.
24 Stephens, *New Companion*, p. 323.
25 Brynley F. Roberts, 'Charles Wilkins: The Historian of Merthyr Tydfil', 19.
26 Brynley Roberts, *The Welsh Periodical Press, 1735–1900* (Aberystwyth: National Library of Wales), p. iv.
27 Glanmor Williams, *Religion, Language and Nationality in Wales: Historical Essays* (Cardiff: Cardiff University Press, 1979), pp. 142–3.
28 Kirsti Bohata, 'En-gendering a New Wales: Female Allegories, Home Rule and Imperialism: 1890–1910', in Alyce von Rothkirch and Daniel Williams (eds), *Beyond the Difference: Welsh Literature in Comparative Contexts: Essays for M. Wynn Thomas* (Cardiff: University of Wales Press, 2004), pp. 57–70 (p. 61).
29 Ibid., p. 63.
30 Tom Nairn, *Faces of Nationalism: Janus Revisited* (London and New York: Verso, 1997), pp. 91, 110.
31 Huw Walters, *A Bibliography of Welsh Periodicals: 1851–1900* (Aberystwyth: National Library of Wales, 2003), p. lvii.
32 The cartoon figures are identified by handwritten annotations in the copy of this issue in the Salisbury Collection in Cardiff University's Arts and Social Science Library.

33 Nora Philipps,'The Problem of the Nineteenth Century', February 1892, 348–58 (348); Eliza Orme, 'A Commonplace Correction' (a response to Nora Philipps), March 1892, 467–70; Nora Philipps, 'A Commonplace Correction Corrected', May 1892, 670–80.
34 See Hazel Davies, *O. M. Edwards* (Cardiff: University of Wales Press, 1988), p. 21. Also see *Cymru Fydd* (July1888): 'Llyr', 'Cymru y Colegau: Rhydychen [Oxford]', 459–65.
35 Quoted in Hazel Davies, *O. M. Edwards*, p. 45.
36 See Hazel Davies, 'Divisions: Hazel Davies on the private and public lives of Owen M. Edwards', *Planet* (August/September 1989), 76–81: she attributes the suicide of his wife, Ellen, in 1919 to strains brought about by his continuous work ethic: he 'never saw the need for laying the foundations of family life' (76).
37 Katie Gramich, 'Creating and Destroying 'The Man who does not Exist': The Peasantry and Modernity in Welsh and Irish Writing', *Irish Studies Review*, special issue: *Welsh and Irish Writing* (February 2009), 19–30 (19, 21). Huw Walters remarks that 'the myth of the Welsh *gwerin* or common Welshman [was] created to a large extent by Owen Edwards himself' (*A Bibliography of Welsh Periodicals*, p. lviii).
38 Hazel Davies, *O. M. Edwards*, p. 48.
39 The listings supplied alongside the annual introductions to each volume of *Wales* show that a group of seventeen 'overlapping' writers appear in each of the three volumes: 1894–6. Most of these are academics, clergymen, Justices of the Peace, schoolmasters or local historians. All of them are male. About half a dozen of them have achievements that earn mentions in Stephens, *New Companion* or in the online *Dictionary of Welsh National Biography*.
40 I thank Katie Gramich for pointing out that Owen M. Edwards mentored several women writers, including, for example, Winnie Parrry and Sioned Pryce.
41 I thank M. Wynn Thomas who made this connection in a paper, 'Creating a National Consciousness: Cymru Fydd, Young Ireland and the Pan-Celtic Movement', read to the symposium on 'Cultural Institutions and Creativity in Ireland and Wales', held at Aberystwyth University on 17/18 April 2009 under the auspices of the AHRC Ireland/Wales Research Network.
42 For more examples of women's writing in *Young Wales* see Ursula Masson, 'Gender, Class and Party: Liberal and Labour Movement Writings' in Jane Aaron and Ursula Masson (eds), *The Very Salt of Life: Welsh Women's Political Writing from Chartism to Suffrage* (Dinas Powys, Honno, 2007), pp. 159–71.

[43] Articles on 'Britannic+Hebraic Eschatology' by D. Wynne Evans appeared in *Young Wales* in March, June and August 1901 and April and June 1902. For a full discussion of this phenomenon see Jasmine Donahaye, *Whose People? Wales, Israel, Palestine* (Cardiff: University of Wales Press, 2012), pp. 37–8 and 42–8.

[44] Gwyn A. Williams draws attention to the 'recurrent explosions of the Welsh into English society' that have occurred since Tudor times. He cites the law and education as major examples and the milk and hotel trades as minor ones (*When Was Wales?*, p. 122).

[45] Tomos Owen, 'The London Kelt, 1895–1914: Performing Welshness, Imagining Wales', *Almanac: Yearbook of Welsh Writing in English* (2008–9), 109–25 (116).

[46] Ibid., 109–12.

[47] I thank Tomos Owen for pointing out this occasional usage.

[48] See *New Companion*, p. 470.

[49] Very unusually, no editor is listed in any issue.

[50] Eight out of sixteen are by MPs, including three by J. H. Edwards himself, and one each by E. T. John, W. Llewelyn Williams, Ellis Davies, Tom Richards and W. J. Gruffydd.

[51] W. H. Davies, 'How does it feel to be unemployed?', in R. B. Cunninghame Graham, 'Aspects of the Social Question', *The English Review* (December 1908), 168–71.

[52] See Mark S. Morrisson, *The Public Face of Modernism: Little Magazines, Audiences and Reception: 1905–1920* (Madison, University of Wisconsin Press, 2001), pp 43–51.

[53] Huw Walters, *A Bibliography of Welsh Periodicals: 1851–1900*, p. lxiii.

2

[1] Kenneth O. Morgan, *Rebirth of a Nation: A History of Modern Wales* (Oxford: Oxford University Press, 1981), p. 264.

[2] John Carey, *The Intellectuals and the Masses: Pride and Prejudice among the Literary Intelligentsia, 1880–1939* (London and Boston: Faber and Faber, 1992), p. 16. Also see Janet Lyon, *Manifestoes: Provocations of the Modern* (Ithaca and London: Cornell University Press, 1999), pp. 9–10.

[3] Gwyn Jenkins, 'The Welsh Outlook: 1914–33', *National Library of Wales Journal*, 24 (1986), 463–92, especially 464–5 (471, 483, 492).

[4] Alyce von Rothkirch, 'Visions of Wales: *The Welsh Outlook*, 1914–1933', *Almanac: Yearbook of Welsh Writing in English*, 14 (2010), 65–92. The quotation from Watkin Davies comes from 'Notes of the Month' (January 1926), 4.

5. Gwyn Jenkins, 'The Welsh Outlook', 469.
6. Meic Stephens, *The New Companion to the Literature of Wales* (Cardiff: University of Wales Press, 1998), p. 632.
7. For the response to the war by the *Beirniad* and *Y Geninen* see Morgan, *Rebirth of a Nation*, p. 159.
8. Tecwyn Lewis, 'Welsh Public Opinion and the First World War', *Planet* (February/March 1972), 25–37.
9. Gwyn Jenkins, 'The Welsh Outlook', 472, 474.
10. Ibid., 473–7.
11. Ibid., 479.
12. For 'the miners' stand', see John Davies, *A History of Wales*, new edn (London: Penguin, 2007 [1993]), p. 538.
13. Gwyn Jenkins, 'The Welsh Outlook', 479–81.
14. Alyce von Rothkirch, 'Visions of Wales', 86–7.
15. For more detail on international coverage in *The Welsh Outlook*, see my article, 'Spaces of Comparison in Welsh Periodicals in English: 1882–2008', *Almanac: Yearbook of Welsh Writing in English* (2010), 93–120 (111–12).
16. Kenneth O. Morgan, *Rebirth of a Nation*, p. 265.
17. Samuel Hynes, *The Auden Generation: Literature and Politics in England in the 1930s* (London: Bodley Head, 1976), p. 46.
18. M. Wynn Thomas, *Internal Difference: Twentieth-Century Writing in Wales* (Cardiff: University of Wales Press, 1992), pp. 44, 48.
19. Ibid., pp. 50, 53, 61.
20. Samuel Hynes, *The Auden Generation*, pp. 75–8.
21. Meic Stephens, *New Companion*, p. 637.
22. Chris Hopkins, 'Wales (1937–9); The Welsh Review (1939–40)', in Peter Brooker and Andrew Thacker (eds), *The Oxford History of Modernist Magazines*, vol. 1: *Britain and Ireland 1880–1955* (Oxford: Oxford University Press, 2009), pp. 714–34 (p. 715).
23. Tony Brown, *R. S. Thomas* (Cardiff: University of Wales Press, 2006), p. 29. Brown here draws on two essays from *Wales* (Summer 1943): W. Moelwyn Merchant, 'The Relevance of the Anglo-Welsh' and H. Idris Bell, 'The Welsh Poetic Tradition'.
24. *Life and Letters To-day*, Welsh numbers: March 1940; March 1943, subtitled *Cambria*; March 1946 (shared by Scottish poets); March 1947; and September 1948.
25. Alvin Sullivan (ed.), *British Literary Magazines: The Modern Age, 1914–1984* (Westport, Conn. and London: Greenwood Press, 1986), pp. 222–5.
26. Glyn Jones, *Setting Out: A Memoir of Literary Life in Wales* (Cardiff: Cardiff University College Press, 1982), p. 12.

[27] For a full account of the development of *Life and Letters To-day* see Meic Stephens, 'The Third Man: Robert Herring and *Life and Letters To-day*', *Welsh Writing in English: A Yearbook of Critical Essays*, 3 (1997), 147–69.

[28] For further commentary on 'A Peasant', see Tony Brown, *R. S. Thomas*, p. 16 and Justin Wintle, *Furious Interiors: Wales, R. S. Thomas and God* (London: Flamingo, 1997), pp. 178–86.

[29] Meic Stephens, 'The Third Man', 157, 161, 162.

[30] For Gwyn Jones's career – see Stephens, *New Companion*, pp. 380–1; also see Dai Smith, *In the Frame: Memory in Society, 1910–2010* (Cardigan: Parthian, 2010), p. xiii.

[31] Gwyn Jones, *The First Forty Years: Some Notes on Anglo-Welsh Literature* (Cardiff: University of Wales Press, 1957), pp. 11, 14, 25.

[32] Peter MacDonald Smith, 'Poetry, Politics and the Use of English: The Periodicals and the Anglo-Welsh Tradition (3)', *New Welsh Review* (Winter 1988), 63–7 (63).

[33] For the attribution of 'Mulciber's' article to Gwyn Jones, see Dai Smith, *In the Frame*, pp. xiv–xv.

[34] The Thomas Jones who was Gwyn Jones's collaborator was professor of Welsh at Aberystwyth and not the 'TJ' associated with *The Welsh Outlook*.

[35] Sam Adams, *Roland Mathias* (Cardiff: University of Wales Press, 1995), p. 32.

[36] Don Dale-Jones, *Raymond Garlick* (Cardiff: University of Wales Press, 1996), p. 23.

[37] I am grateful to Matthew Jarvis for drawing my attention to *The Penvro* and supplying me with a copy of the first page of issue 106 (January 1950).

[38] Sam Adams, *Roland Mathias*, p. 45.

[39] Don Dale-Jones, *Raymond Garlick*, p. 25.

[40] Sam Adams, *Roland Mathias*, p. 60.

[41] Raymond Garlick, 'On the Growing of Dock Leaves', *Planet* (December 1971/January 1972), 71–6 (74).

[42] Sam Adams, *Roland Mathias*, pp. 71ff.

[43] See, for example no. 38 (Winter 1967).

[44] Roland Mathias, *The Lonely Editor: A Glance at Anglo-Welsh Magazines* (Cardiff: University College of Cardiff Press, 1984), pp. 4, 17.

[45] Sam Adams, *Roland Mathias*, p. 72.

[46] For a more detailed account of these funding arrangements see my essay, 'Welsh Periodicals in English: 1880–1965', *Welsh Writing in English*, 9 (2004), 1–32 (24–5). For the higher proportion of literature funding in Wales, see David Sawers, *Should the Tax Payer Support the Arts?* (London: IEA, 1993), table 3, p. 19.

[47] John Davies, *A History of Wales*, new edn (London: Penguin, 2007 [1993]), p. 605.

3

[1] Kenneth O. Morgan, *Rebirth of a Nation: A History of Modern Wales* (Oxford: Oxford University Press, 1981), p. 395.
[2] John Davies, *A History of Wales*, new edn (London: Penguin, 2007 [1993]), pp. 625–42.
[3] The Welsh Arts Council Annual Report for 1971 gives a figure of £345.
[4] Wolfgang Gortschacher, *Little Magazine Profiles: The Little Magazine in Great Britain: 1939–1993* (Salzburg: Salzburg University Press, 1993), pp. 20–2.
[5] Roland Mathias, *The Lonely Editor: A Glance at Anglo-Welsh Magazines* (Cardiff: University College Cardiff Press, 1984), p. 14.
[6] Rhodri Williams, 'Review of Subsidised Periodicals' (Welsh Arts Council, 1987), p. 96. See Welsh Arts Council Archive, National Library of Wales, vol. II, DIR/286: Director's Files, 1986/7, quoted with the permission of the chief executive, Arts Council of Wales.
[7] Press release: 'Major Review of Subsidized Periodicals', 18 May 1987, from Welsh Arts Council papers.
[8] More detail on the Welsh content of *Poetry Wales* appears in my article 'Welsh Periodicals in English: *Second Aeon* and *Poetry Wales* (1965–1985)', *Welsh Writing in English*, 11 (2006–7), 147–87 (164–5).
[9] Ned Thomas, 'A letter to the editor', in Cary Archard (ed.), *Poetry Wales: 25 Years* (Bridgend: Seren, 1990), p. 76; Kirsti Bohata, *Postcolonialism Revisited* (Cardiff: University of Wales Press, 2004), p. 13.
[10] David Lloyd, *Writing on the Edge: Interviews with Writers and Editors of Wales* (Amsterdam: Rodopi, 1997), p. 34.
[11] 'Under Two Hats', *Planet* (December 1971–January 1972), 55–63 (61).
[12] Sam Adams, 'Editorial', *Poetry Wales* (Summer 1975), pages not numbered.
[13] Peter MacDonald Smith, 'Poetry, Politics, and the Use of English', *New Welsh Review* (Winter 1988), 63–7 (66).
[14] Cary Archard (ed.), *Poetry Wales: 25 Years*.
[15] Tony Conran, '*Poetry Wales* and the Second Flowering', in M. Wynn Thomas (ed.) *Welsh Writing in English* (Cardiff: University of Wales Press, 2003), 222–53 (226, 234–5, 251–3).
[16] Difficulties with Christopher Davies Ltd were also mentioned by Meic Stephens and Tony Bianchi, as well as by Cary Archard, during interviews in 2003 and 2005.

Notes

[17] Stefan Collini, *Absent Minds: Intellectuals in Britain* (Oxford: Oxford University Press, 2006), p. 10.

[18] In an email to the writer in January 2005 Robert Minhinnick said that 'we are still living in a literary world (in Wales) that Meic Stephens helped to create during his time at the Arts Council'. By 'Byzantine' he wanted to convey something like 'profound' or 'inescapable'.

[19] Examples of overseas 'launches' include: July 2000, Piemonte; October 2001, Manhattan; July 2004, Vilnius.

[20] Matthew Jarvis, *Welsh Environments in Contemporary Poetry* (Cardiff: University of Wales Press, 2008), p. 87.

[21] I have drawn here and in the next two paragraphs on a telephone discussion with Zoë Skoulding, 4 July 2012.

[22] For a more detailed study of *Second Aeon*, see my 'Welsh Periodicals in English: *Second Aeon* and *Poetry Wales* (1965–1985)'.

[23] Letter from Kris Hemensley, *Second Aeon*, 14 (1972), 109.

[24] John Powell Ward, letter to the writer, 15 May 2007.

[25] Martin Booth, *British Poetry 1964–84: Driving Through the Barricades* (London: Routledge and Kegan Paul, 1985), quoted in http://peter finch.co.uk/2ndaeon.htm (accessed 24 August 2011).

[26] See note 16 above.

[27] Roland Mathias, *The Lonely Editor*, p. 16.

[28] Ned Thomas's interview with Daniel Williams at http//www.planet magazine.org.uk/ html/newsite/audio/ (accessed 5 August 2011).

[29] Welsh Arts Council Archive L/1990/10: *Planet* 1969–72.

[30] Christopher Driver in the *Guardian*, 31 August 1970.

[31] In his interview with Daniel Williams, Ned Thomas recalls that his decision to leave the *Times Educational Supplement* to return to Wales on a Welsh Arts Council bursary had received front-page coverage in the *Western Mail*.

[32] Ned Thomas, *The Welsh Extremist: A Culture in Crisis* (London: Victor Gollancz, 1971), pp. 100, 108.

[33] In his interview with Daniel Williams on the *Planet* website (accessed 10 October 2011) Thomas refers to the need for 'some sleight of hand' in order to satisfy the Literature Committee.

[34] See his discussion document 'The Further Development of Planet' in Welsh Arts Council Archive L/1990/263: *Planet* 1977–8.

[35] Raymond Williams, 'Introduction', in Meic Stephens (ed.), *The Arts in Wales 1950–75* (Cardiff: Welsh Arts Council, 1979), pp. 1–4.

[36] *Planet* website (accessed 10 October 2011).

[37] See Clare Morgan, 'John Barnie: rebel with several causes', *New Welsh Review* (Summer 1990), 59–64 (60, 62).

[38] John Barnie, *The King of Ashes* (Llandysul: Gomer Press,1989); *Fire Drill: Notes on the Twenty-First Century* (Bridgend: Seren, 2010).

39 I have relied here on an interview with Jasmine Donahaye, Aberystwyth, 29 June 2012 and on subsequent correspondence.
40 I have relied here and in the next few paragraphs on an interview with Emily Trahair, Aberystwyth, 29 June 2012, and on subsequent correspondence.
41 See Welsh Arts Council Archive L1990/355WAC: 'Rebecca 1979/80', where it is noted that four out of forty pages are to be devoted to 'arts coverage and a further five pages to 'events listings'. However, later in 1979, the Literature Committee registered concerns about 'leaking of confidential information' and took the view that the magazine was 'not sufficiently literary or artistic' (minutes of 66th meeting, Cardiff, 14 December 1979).
42 Discussion with Tony Bianchi, 17 July 2012.
43 John Osmond, *The Divided Kingdom* (London: Constable, 1988), pp. 121, 133.
44 Belinda Humphrey, letter to Meic Stephens, 18 September 1987, from Welsh Arts Council papers.
45 This phrase supplied the title of my retrospective, marking the periodical's twenty-first year of publication: 'Quite Healthy "with Inbreeding"?' *New Welsh Review* (Summer 2009), 9–17.
46 'W.A.C. Appraisal of Clients: Assessment of periodicals: The New Welsh Review', September 1990, Welsh Arts Council Papers.
47 In an interview with Peter Foss in November 2009 he explained that some of these tensions had surfaced in a bad-tempered meeting of the Welsh Academy Committee he had attended with Belinda Humfrey, as early as April 1988, i.e. even before the first issue appeared. Also see the correspondence on Peter Foss's tribunal case (dated 7 March 1991) in Welsh Arts Council Archive L/1996/70: *New Welsh Review*, 1990–1.
48 I am grateful to Rosanne Reeves who discussed her late husband's career with me in an interview on 9 November 2009.
49 Report on *New Welsh Review*, 1993, Arts Council papers, Cardiff.
50 Arts Council paper: 'New Welsh Review – Survey Findings', 26 January 1994.
51 Throughout this paragraph I have drawn on the notes of my interview with Gwen Davies, Aberystwyth, 28 June 2012 and on subsequent correspondence.
52 See my 'Welsh Periodicals in English: *Second Aeon* and *Poetry Wales* (1965–1985)', 179.
53 Letter to the writer, 28 October 2006. The Books Council has, since then, reduced the amount of paperwork required for smaller grants (interview with Kirsti Bohata, publishing grants officer, Welsh Books Council, 6 February 2007).

4

[1] See the following two websites, which carry information (sometimes outdated) about little magazines in Wales: 'The Poetry Kit': *www.poetrykit.org/magslt.oz.htm#l*; 'Welsh Magazines': *www.benybont.co.uk/author/welsh/htm* (both accessed 17 July 2012).

[2] Mikko Lehtonen, *The Cultural Analysis of Texts*, trans. Aija Ahonen and Kris Clarke (London, Thousand Oaks, Calif. and New Delhi: Sage Publications, 2000), p. 127.

[3] See for example: Mark Hooper, 'Who says print is dead? *Guardian*, G2, 4 June 2012, p. 10; also *http://www.guardian.co.uk/media/2012/jun/03/who-says-print-is-dead#start-of-comments* (accessed 17 July 2012). Emily Trahair drew my attention to this article.

[4] 'Inquiry into the Future of Media in Wales': *http://www.senedd.assembly wales.org/mgIssueHistoryHome.aspx?IId=1787* (accessed July 18, 2012). Tony Bianchi drew my attention to this source.

[5] Ibid.: Consultation Response Media 43.

[6] Colm Tóibín, 'Dreamers and Chancers', *Guardian Review*, 16 June 2012, pp. 2–4.

[7] Jasmine Donahaye, 'Identification, rejection and cultural co-option in Welsh poetry in English', in Daniel G. Williams (ed.), *Slanderous Tongues: Essays on Welsh Poetry in English, 1970–2005* (Bridgend: Seren, 2010), pp. 226–45 (p. 226).

[8] Matthew Jarvis, 'Repositioning Wales: poetry after the Second Flowering', in Daniel Williams (ed.), *Slanderous Tongues*, pp. 22–59 (p. 30 and n. 36).

[9] Nerys Williams, 'Peter Finch: recycling the avant-garde in a Welsh wordscape', in Williams (ed.), *Slanderous Tongues*, pp. 112–33 (p. 112).

[10] Malcolm Ballin, *Irish Periodical Culture: Genre in Ireland, Scotland and Wales* (New York: Palgrave Macmillan, 2008), pp. 201–19.

Bibliography

Adams, Sam, *Roland Mathias* (Cardiff: University of Wales Press, 1995).
Altick, Richard, *The English Common Reader: A Social History of the Mass Reading Public, 1800–1900* (Chicago: University of Chicago Press, 1957).
Anderson, Benedict, *Imagined Communities: Reflections on the Origin and Spread of Nationalism*, revised edn (London and New York: Verso, 2006 [1983]).
Archard, Cary (ed.), *Poetry Wales: 25 Years* (Bridgend: Seren, 1990).
Ballin, Malcolm, 'Welsh Periodicals in English 1880–1965: Literary Form and Cultural Substance', *Welsh Writing in English: A Yearbook of Critical Essays*, 9 (2004), 1–32.
——, 'Welsh Periodicals in English: *Second Aeon* and *Poetry Wales* (1965–1985)', *Welsh Writing in English*, 11 (2006–7), 147–87, 164–5.
——, *Irish Periodical Culture: 1937–1972: Genre in Ireland, Scotland and Wales* (New York: Palgrave Macmillan, 2008).
——, 'Spaces of International Comparison in Welsh Periodicals in English', *Almanac: Yearbook of Welsh Writing in English*, 14 (2009–10), 93–120.
Barnie, John, *The King of Ashes* (Llandysul: Gomer Press), 1989.
——, *Fire Drill: Notes on the Twenty-First Century* (Bridgend: Seren, 2010).
Bohata, Kirsti, 'En-gendering a new Wales: female allegories, home rule and imperialism: 1890–1910', in Alyce von Rothkirch and Daniel Williams (eds), *Beyond the Difference: Welsh Literature in Comparative Contexts: Essays for M. Wynn Thomas* (Cardiff: University of Wales Press, 2004), pp. 57–70.
——, *Postcolonialism Revisited* (Cardiff: University of Wales Press, 2004).
Brake, Laurel and John Codell, 'Introduction: Encountering the Press', in Laurel Brake and John F. Codell (eds), *Encounters in the Victorian Press* (Basingstoke: Palgrave Macmillan, 2005).
Bristow, Joseph (ed.), *The Victorian Poet: Poetics and Persona* (London: Croom Helm, 1987).
Brown, Tony, *R. S. Thomas* (Cardiff: University of Wales Press, 2006).
Carey, John, *The Intellectuals and the Masses: Pride and Prejudice among the Literary Intelligentsia: 1880–1939* (London and Boston: Faber and Faber, 1992).

Collini, Stefan, *Absent Minds: Intellectuals in Britain* (Oxford: Oxford University Press, 2006).
——, *Common Reading: Critics, Historians, Publics* (Oxford: Oxford University Press, 2008).
Conran, Tony, '*Poetry Wales* and the Second Flowering', in M. Wynn Thomas (ed.), *Welsh Writing in English* (Cardiff: University of Wales Press, 2003), pp. 222–53.
Dale-Jones, Don, *Raymond Garlick* (Cardiff: University of Wales Press, 1996).
Davies, Hazel, *O. M. Edwards* (Cardiff: University of Wales Press, 1988).
——, 'Divisions: Hazel Davies on the Private and Public Lives of Owen M. Edwards', *Planet* (August/September 1989), 76–81.
Davies, John, *A History of Wales*, new edn (London: Penguin, 2007 [1993]).
Davies, W. H., 'How does it Feel to be Unemployed?' in R. B. Cunninghame Graham, 'Aspects of the Social Question', *The English Review* (December 1908), 168–71.
Donahaye, Jasmine, 'Identification, rejection and cultural co-option in Welsh poetry in English', in Daniel G. Williams (ed.), *Slanderous Tongues: Essays on Welsh Poetry in English: 1970–2005* (Bridgend: Seren, 2010), pp. 226–45.
——, *Whose People? Wales, Israel, Palestine* (Cardiff: University of Wales Press, 2012).
Escott, T. H. S., 'Thirty years of the periodical press', *Blackwood's Magazine* (October 1894), 532–42,
Finkelstein, David, *The House of Blackwood: Author–Publisher Relations in the Victorian Era* (University Park: Pennsylvania University Press, 2000).
Fraser, Nancy, 'Rethinking the public sphere: a contribution to the critique of actually existing democracy', in Craig Colhoun (ed.), *Habermas and the Public Sphere* (Boston: Massachusetts Institute of Technology, 1997), pp. 109–42.
Geertz, Clifford, *The Interpretation of Cultures: Selected Essays* (New York: Basic Books, 1973).
Gortschacher, Wolfgang, *Little Magazine Profiles: The Little Magazine in Great Britain, 1939–1993* (Salzburg: Salzburg University Press, 1993).
Gramich, Katie, *Twentieth-Century Women's Writing in Wales: Land, Gender and Belonging* (Cardiff: University of Wales Press, 2007).
——, 'Creating and Destroying 'The Man who does not Exist': The Peasantry and Modernity in Welsh and Irish Writing', *Irish Studies Review*, special issue: *Welsh and Irish Writing* (February 2009), 19–30 (19 and 21).
Gwynn, Arthur and/or Idwal Lewis, *Subject Index for Welsh Periodicals: 1931–55*, 7 vols (Cardiff and Swansea: Wales and Monmouthshire Branch of the Libraries Association, 1931–55).

Habermas, Jürgen, *The Structural Transformation of the Public Sphere: An Inquiry into a Category of Bourgeois Society*, trans. Thomas Burger with the assistance of Frederick Lawrence (Cambridge: Polity Press, 1992 [original in German, 1962]).

Hopkins, Chris, '*Wales* (1937–9); *The Welsh Review* (1939–40)', in Peter Brooker and Andrew Thacker (eds), *The Oxford History of Modernist Magazines*, vol. 1: *Britain and Ireland 1880–1955* (Oxford: Oxford University Press, 2009), pp. 714–34.

Humphrey, Belinda, 'Prelude to the twentieth century', in M. Wynn Thomas (ed.), *A Guide to Welsh Literature*, vol. 7: *Welsh Writing in English* (Cardiff: University of Wales Press, 2003), pp. 7–46.

Hynes, Samuel, *The Auden Generation: Literature and Politics in England in the 1930s* (London: Bodley Head, 1976).

Jarvis, Matthew, *Welsh Environments in Contemporary Poetry* (Cardiff: University of Wales Press, 2008.

——, 'Repositioning Wales: Poetry after the Second Flowering', in Daniel G Williams (ed.), *Slanderous Tongues: Essays on Welsh Poetry in English: 1970–2005* (Bridgend: Seren, 2010), pp. 22–59.

Jenkins, David and/or R. Geraint Gruffydd, *Subject Index for Welsh Periodicals 1968–80*, 3 vols (Aberystwyth: National Library of Wales, 1968–80).

Jenkins, Gwyn, 'The Welsh Outlook: 1914–33', *The National Library of Wales Journal*, 24 (1986), 463–92.

Jones, Glyn, *Setting Out: A Memoir of Literary Life in Wales* (Cardiff: University College Cardiff Press, 1982).

Jones, Gwyn, *The First Forty Years: Some Notes on Anglo-Welsh Literature* (Cardiff: University of Wales Press, 1957).

Krippendorf, Klaus, *Content Analysis: An Introduction to the Methodology*, second edn, (Thousand Oaks, Calif.: Sage Publications, 2004).

Ledbetter, Kathryn, *British Victorian Women's Periodicals: Beauty, Civilisation and Poetry* (New York: Palgrave Macmillan, 2009).

Lehtonen, Mikko, *The Cultural Analysis of Texts*, trans. Aija Ahonen and Kris Clarke (London, Thousand Oaks, Calif. and New Delhi: Sage Publications, 2000).

Lloyd, David, *Writing on the Edge: Interviews with Writers and Editors of Wales* (Amsterdam: Rodopi, 1997).

Lloyd Morgan, Ceridwen, 'From Temperance to Suffrage?' in Angela V. John (ed.), *Our Mothers' Land: Chapters in Welsh Women's History 1830–1939* (Cardiff: University of Wales Press), pp. 135–58.

Lyon, Janet, *Manifestoes: Provocations of the Modern* (Ithaca and London: Cornell University Press, 1999).

Masson, Ursula, 'Gender, class and party: Liberal and Labour movement writings', in Jane Aaron and Ursula Masson (eds), *The Very*

Salt of Life: Welsh Women's Political Writing from Chartism to Suffrage (Dinas Powys: Honno, 2007), pp. 159–71.

Mathias, Roland, *The Lonely Editor: A Glance at Anglo-Welsh Magazines* (Cardiff: University College Cardiff Press, 1984).

Morgan, Clare, 'John Barnie: rebel with several causes', *New Welsh Review* (Summer 1990), 59–64,

Morgan, Kenneth O., *Rebirth of a Nation: A History of Modern Wales* (Oxford: Oxford University Press, 1981).

Morrisson, Mark S., *The Public Face of Modernism: Little Magazines, Audiences and Reception: 1905–1920* (Madison: University of Wisconsin Press, 2001).

Nairn, Tom, *Faces of Nationalism: Janus Revisited* (London and New York: Verso, 1997).

Negt, Oscar and Alexander Kluge, *Public Sphere and Experience: Towards an Analysis of the Bourgeois and Proletarian Sphere*, trans. Peter Labanyi, Jamie Owen Daniel and Assenka Oksilof (Minneapolis and London: University of Minnesota Press, 1993 [original in German, 1972]).

Owen, Tomos, '*The London Kelt*, 1895–1914: Performing Welshness, Imagining Wales', *Almanac: Yearbook of Welsh Writing in English* (2008–9), 109–25.

Pykett, Lyn, 'Reading the periodical press: text and comment', in Laurel Brake, Aled Jones and Lionel Madden (eds), *Investigating Victorian Journalism* (Basingstoke: Macmillan, 1990), pp. 3–18.

Roberts, Brynley F., *The Welsh Periodical Press, 1735–1900* (Aberystwyth: National Library of Wales, 1989).

——, 'Welsh Periodicals: A Survey', in Laurel Brake, Aled Jones and Lionel Madden (eds), *Investigating Victorian Journalism* (Basingstoke, Macmillan, 1990), pp. 71–84

——, 'Charles Wilkins: The Historian of Merthyr Tydfil', *Merthyr Historian*, 12 (2001), 1–19.

Rothkirch, Alyce von, 'Visions of Wales: *The Welsh Outlook*, 1914–1933', *Almanac: Yearbook of Welsh Writing in English*, 14 (2009–10), 65–92.

Smith, Dai, *In the Frame: Memory in Society, 1910–2010* (Cardigan: Parthian, 2010).

Smith, Peter MacDonald, 'Poetry, Politics and the Use of English: The Periodicals and the Anglo-Welsh Tradition (3)', *New Welsh Review* (Winter 1988), 63–7.

Stephens, Meic, 'The Third Man: Robert Herring and *Life and Letters Today*', *Welsh Writing in English: A Yearbook of Critical Essays*, 3 (1997), 147–69.

——, *The New Companion to the Literature of Wales* (Cardiff: University of Wales Press, 1998).

Sullivan, Alvin (ed.), *British Literary Magazines: The Modern Age, 1914–1984* (Westport, Conn. and London: Greenwood Press, 1986).
Thomas, Ned, *The Welsh Extremist* (London: Victor Gollancz, 1971).
Thomas, M. Wynn, *Internal Difference: Twentieth-Century Writing in Wales* (Cardiff: University of Wales Press, 1992).
——, *Corresponding Cultures: The Two Literatures of Wales* (Cardiff: University of Wales Press, 1999).
Tóibín, Colm, 'Dreamers and Chancers', *Guardian Review*, 16 June 2012, pp. 2–4.
Walters, Huw, *A Bibliography of Welsh Periodicals: 1851–1900* (Aberystwyth: National Library of Wales, 2003).
Wilkins, John, 'Charles Wilkins, Writer 1830–1913: A Biographical Note by his Great Grandson', *Merthyr Historian*, 13 (2001), 5–13.
Williams, Daniel G., *Ethnicity and Cultural Authority: From Arnold to Dubois* (Edinburgh: Edinburgh University Press, 2006).
——, *Slanderous Tongues: Essays on Welsh Poetry in English, 1970–2005* (Bridgend: Seren, 2010).
Williams, Glanmor, *Religion, Language and Nationality in Wales: Historical Essays* (Cardiff: Cardiff University Press, 1979).
Williams, Gwyn A., *When Was Wales? A History of the Welsh* (Harmondsworth: Penguin, 1986).
Williams, Nerys, 'Peter Finch: recycling the avant-garde in a Welsh wordscape', in Daniel G. Williams (ed.), *Slanderous Tongues: Essays on Welsh Poetry in English: 1970–2005* (Bridgend: Seren, 2010), pp. 112–33.
Williams, Raymond, *Marxism and Literature* (Oxford: Oxford University Press, 1997).
——, 'Introduction', in Meic Stephens (ed.), *The Arts in Wales 1950–75* (Cardiff: Welsh Arts Council, 1979), pp. 1–4.
Williams, Rhodri, 'Review of Subsidised Periodicals' (Welsh Arts Council, 1987), p. 96 (Welsh Arts Council Archive, National Library of Wales, vol. 2, DIR/286: Director's Files, 1986/7).
Williams, Sian Rhiannon, 'The true "Cymraes": images of women in women's nineteenth-century periodicals', in Angela V. John (ed.), *Our Mothers' Land: Chapters in Welsh Women's History 1830–1939* (Cardiff: University of Wales Press, 1991), pp. 69–91.
Wilson, A. N., *The Victorians* (London: Arrow Books, 2003).
Wintle, Justin, *Furious Interiors: Wales, R. S. Thomas and God* (London: Flamingo, 1997).

Index

Aberystwyth 17, 19 43, 74, 110, 158, 164, 188, 191, 194
Abse, Dannie 130, 132, 156, 159
Abse, Leo 140, 152
Academi Gymreig, Y [The Welsh Academy] 106, 120, 154, 194
Adams, Sam (ed. *Poetry Wales*, 1973–5) xii, 98, 103, 104, 118, 120, 127, 163, 191, 192, 196
Adcock, Fleur 122
'Adfyfyr' [pseud. Thomas John Hughes] (ed. *Cymru Fydd*, 1888–9) 22–3
Agee, Chris (ed. *Irish Pages*, 2002–) 181–2
Agenda (1994–) 107, 169–70, 175
Almanac: Yearbook of Welsh Writing in English 185, 189, 190, 196, 199
Altick, Richard 186, 196
Amis, Kingsley 99
Amsterdam Review, The (1994–) 172
Anderson, Benedict 7, 185, 196
Anglo-Welsh 60, 71, 72, 75, 81–3, 84–6, 90–5, 97, 98, 100–5, 106, 109, 110, 112, 116–18, 121–2, 129, 133, 137–9, 141, 153, 159, 161, 186, 190, 191, 192, 198, 199
Anglo-Welsh Review, The (1949–58) xi, 5, 99–113, 117, 132, 152, 156, 163, 165, 179, 183
Arcade (1980–2) 151–3, 154
Archard, Cary (ed. *Poetry Wales*, 1980–86; guest ed. July 1996) xi, xii, 119, 120, 124, 127, 192, 196
Aspden, Brian (guest ed. *Poetry Wales*, April 1997) 121, 124
Auden, W. H. 71, 190, 198
audience 3, 5, 9, 11, 21, 22, 23, 26, 27, 28, 31, 33, 35, 40, 45, 47, 57, 62, 82, 88, 93, 100, 105, 107, 111, 113, 151, 156, 157, 159, 163, 171, 173–7, 182, 189, 199

Ballin, Malcolm 185, 195, 196
Baner ac Amserau Cymru 47, 80
Bangor 35, 36, 78, 129
Barddas [Bardic Lore] (1862, 1874) 122
Barnie, John (co-ed. *Planet*, 1988–92; ed. 1992–2006) 141–7, 159, 193, 196, 199
Barrington, Duncan (ed. *The Dublin Review*, 2000–) 181
Bates, H. E. 92
Beach, Sylvia 85
Beirniad, Y [The Critic] (1911–20) 65, 190
Bell, H. Idris 75, 92, 93, 190
Benjamin, Walter 119, 150
Berry, Ron 139
Bevan, Aneurin 60, 91, 162
Bianchi, Tony xi, 102, 111, 152, 164, 175, 192, 194, 195
Bidgood, Ruth 109, 113, 122, 172
Bielski, Alison xii, 109, 113, 117, 132, 154, 172
Bilton, Allan 150
Bishop, Elizabeth 120
Blackwood's Magazine (1817–1980) 3, 12, 15, 186, 197
Blast (1914–15) 56, 168, 185
Bloomsbury 72, 77
blown (2009–) 168–69
Bohata, Kirsti xi, 24, 116, 187, 192, 194, 196
Booth, Martin 132, 193
Botterill, Denis 85
Bowen-Rowlands, Ernest (ed. *The Welsh Review*, 1891–2) 26, 28, 30, 33
Bowen-Rowlands, Lilian 46

Bower, Ric (ed. *blown*, 2009–) 168
Bradley, Malcolm (ed. *Quattrocento*) 172
Brake, Laura 15, 185, 187, 196, 199
Bristow, Joseph 17, 187, 196
Brito, Leonora 158
Brockway, Anthony 166
Brooker, Peter 190, 198
Brookes, Jonathan (ed. *The Yellow Crane*, 1995–2006) 172
Brookes, Simon 150
Brown, Tony xi, 82, 160, 190, 196
Bush, Duncan (ed. *The Amsterdam Review*, 1994–; guest ed. *Poetry Wales*, January 1997) xii, 124, 126, 156, 172
Butt, Oliver 83

Calway, Gareth xii, 160
Cambrensis (1988–2006) 107, 151–4
Cambria (1997–) 107, 170–1, 175
Cambrian Register, The (1795–1818) 3
Cambrian Visitor, The (1813) 3
Cardiff 12, 14, 15, 16, 30, 45, 46, 47, 48, 49, 50, 54, 62, 63, 67, 86, 120, 133, 138, 144, 158, 162, 164, 171
Cardiff-Barry Circle, The 61, 67
Carey, Eleri 159
Carey, John 60, 189, 196
Carter, Harold 169
CFUK (*c*.2006–10) 172
Chamberlain, Brenda 90, 113, 135
Chamberlain, Neville 73, 74
Chappell, Edgar L. (ed. *The Welsh Outlook*, 1917–21) 66
Christopher Davies Ltd. 120, 192
Cinnamon Press 172
circulation 2, 26, 37, 38, 56, 61, 70, 95, 107, 110, 111, 146, 160, 176
Clancy, Joseph P. 143
Clarke, Austin 97
Clarke, Gillian (co-ed. *The Anglo-Welsh Review*, 1974–6; ed. 1976–84) 102, 105, 109–10, 152, 155, 176, 179
Codell, John 187, 196
Coleg Harlech 68, 122, 147
Colhoun, Craig 184, 197
Collini, Stefan 4, 45, 93, 124, 145, 184, 193, 197
Connolly, Cyril 80, 167

Conran, Anthony 117, 118, 120, 133, 135, 159, 192, 197
Coombes, B. L. 109, 162
Cooper, Kenneth 97
Cordell, Alexander 162
'Cranogwen' [Sarah Jane Rees] (ed. *Y Frythones* [The Female Brython], 1839–1916) 8
Cymmrodorion 11, 18
Curtis, Tony 118, 156, 163
Cymdeithas yr Iaith Gymraeg [The Welsh Language Society] 116, 138
Cymru [Wales] (1891–1920) 26, 31, 32, 37, 64
Cymru Fydd [Future Wales, magazine] (1888–91) 5, 22–6, 27, 29, 31, 40, 44, 178, 188
Cymru Fydd [organisation] 22, 39, 41, 45, 46, 48, 188
Cymru Llundain a'r Celt [The London Welshman and Celt] 48
Cymru'r Plant [The Children's Wales] (1892–1920) 31

Dafydd ap Gwilym 18, 118, 130
Dafydd ap Gwilym Society 131
Dale-Jones, Don 191, 197
Davies, Aneirin Talfan 98
Davies, Brian xii, 140
Davies, D. Hywel 159, 162
Davies, David (prop. *The Welsh Outlook*, 1914–33) 61, 66–8, 104
Davies, Gwen (assoc. ed. *Planet*, 1988–92; ed. *New Welsh Review*, 2011–) xi, xii, 143, 166–7, 194
Davies, Gwilym 69, 87, 88, 90
Davies, Hazel 31, 38, 188, 197
Davies, Idris xii, 70, 71, 73, 74, 89, 90, 101, 135
Davies, John (reviews ed. *The Anglo-Welsh Review*, 1976–88) 102, 110, 121
Davies John (historian) 12, 106, 184, 186, 190, 192
Davies, Lyndon 130
Davies, Margaret 139
Davies, Pennar 117
Davies, Rhys 70, 71, 73, 80, 92, 158
Davies, T. Huws (ed. *The Welsh Outlook*, 1921–5) 67, 70

Davies, W. H. 46, 55, 56, 87, 90, 189
Davies, William Watkin (ed. *The Welsh Outlook*, 1925–7) 61, 68–9
Davison, Ian (joint ed. *Skald*, 1994–2007) 172
Ddau Wynne, Y (pseudonym Mallt and Gwenfreda Williams) 39, 42, 43
Ddinas, Y 48
Ddolen, Y 48
design 5, 32, 36, 39, 53, 56, 62, 71, 80, 83, 86, 95, 110, 112, 137, 147, 155, 157, 160, 165, 166, 167, 169, 182
Dillwyn, Amy 14–15, 22, 166
Dock Leaves (1949–58) xi, xii, 4, 5, 60, 95–100, 101, 103, 108, 110, 112, 117, 176, 179, 183, 191
Donahaye, Jasmine (ed. *Planet*, 2011–12) xi, xii, 147–49, 176, 178, 179, 189, 194, 195, 197
Dorion, Hélène 129
Doshi, Tishani 166
Dowding, Walter 84, 97
Driver, Christopher 193
Drysorfa, Y [The Treasury] (1831–) 2
Dublin Magazine, The (1921–78) 82, 90, 101
Dublin Review, The (2000–) 180–1
Dunthorne, Joe 166

Eagleton, Terry 119, 166
Earle, Jean 119
Edwards, Dorothy 166
Edwards, John Hugh (ed. *Young Wales*, 1895–1904; *Wales: The Magazine for the Welsh People*, 1911–14) 39, 52–6, 62, 64, 189
Edwards, Lewis 3
Edwards, Owen Dudley 133
Edwards, Owen Morgan (joint ed. *Cymru Fydd*, 1889–91; *Wales*, 1894–7; *Cymru*, 1891–1920; *Cymru'r Plant* 1892–1920; *Y Llenor* [The Man of Letters] 1895–8; 1897–8) 5, 23, 31–39, 57, 148, 176, 182
Edwards, Siân 158
Elfyn, Menna 125
Eliot, T. S. 71, 72, 90, 101
Ellerman, Winifrid Annie (pseudonym 'Bryher') 83

Ellis, Tom 23, 28, 30, 41, 45, 140
English Review, The (1908–10) 56, 185, 189, 197
Envoi (1959–) 172
Erfyl, Gwyn 140
Escott, T. H. S. 12, 186, 197
Evans, Caradoc 46, 72, 85, 91, 101, 137, 155, 159
Evans, Christine, 119
Evans, D. Wynne 44 189
Evans, George Ewart 73, 77, 99
Evans, Iestyn 109
Evans, Margiad 70, 72, 85, 90, 93, 166

Faner, Y [The Flag] (1843–1992) 113
Feld, Val 144
Feldner, Heiko 150
feminism (*see also* women's issues) 3, 122, 124
Finch, Peter (ed. *Second Aeon*, 1960–74) xi, 107, 121, 131–32, 143, 154, 161, 162, 180, 193, 195, 200
Finkelstein, David 186, 197
Fire Drill 146, 193, 196
First Forty Years, The 86, 101, 191, 198
Fisher, Catherine 122, 159
Flay, Claire 166
Fortune Wood, Jan (ed. *Envoi*, 2007–) 172
Foss, Peter (asst. ed. *New Welsh Review*, 1988–90) xi, 155, 157, 194
franchise(s) 107, 112, 113, 122, 131, 151, 154, 157, 161, 167, 171, 173, 175
Fraser, Nancy 3, 184, 197
French, Paddy (ed. *Rebecca*, 1973–93) 151–2
Frythones Y [The Female Brython] (1878–91) 8
funds, funding (of periodicals) 99, 104, 106–8, 111–12, 117, 149, 152, 153, 154, 167–8, 169, 171–3, 174, 175, 180, 183, 191
Futurist Manifesto, The 168

Garlick, Raymond (ed. *Dock Leaves*, 1949–58; *The Anglo–Welsh Review*, 1958–60) xi, xii, 5, 95–9, 100–2, 103, 112, 116, 117, 127, 133, 135, 137, 139, 156, 183, 191, 197
Geertz, Clifford 5, 185, 197

Geninen, Y [The Leek] (1888–1928) 64, 190
genres of periodicals 4, 5, 39, 57, 97, 151, 154, 158, 164, 167, 180, 195, 196
Giardelli, Arthur 97, 102
Gilonis, Harry 130
Glen, Duncan 117
Golightly, Victor (ed. *New Welsh Review*, 2001–2) 162–4
Goodby, John 125, 130
Gortschacher, Wolfgang 107, 161, 192, 197
Gower, John 163
Gramich, Katie xi, 8, 33, 186, 188, 197
Graves, Robert 78
Gray, Kathryn (ed. *New Welsh Review*, 2008–11) xi, 1, 2, 8, 165, 166–7
Griffith, Wyn 75, 85, 90
Griffiths, Bryn 115
Griffiths, Jim 75, 91
Griffiths, John 19
Griffiths, Niall 169, 172
Griffiths, Steve 121
Gruffydd, Peter xii, 113, 132
Gruffydd, R. Geraint 185, 198
Gruffydd, W. J. 54, 77, 94, 189
Guardian, The [Manchester] 44, 77, 137, 193, 195, 200
Guild of Graduates of the University of Wales 35, 94, 104
Gwerinaethwr, Y [Welsh Republican] (1950–7) 104
Gwyn, Richard 129, 169
Gwynn, Arthur 185
Gymraes, Y [The Welshwoman] 8

Habermas, Jürgen 3, 12, 33, 184, 186, 197, 198
Hailsham, Lord 139
Hamilton, Ian 123
Hardy, Barbara 123
Harris, James (ed. *The Red Dragon*, 1885–8) 19, 20–1
Harris, John 159
Hawkes, Terence 161
Heaney, Seamus 119
Heatherington, H. J. W. (ed. *The Welsh Outlook*, 1917) 66
Heddiw [Today] 32

Hemensley, Chris 193
Henry, Paul (guest ed. *Poetry Wales*, July 1997) xii, 124
Herbert, Joyce 119
Herman, Josef 162
Herring, Robert (ed. *Life and Letters To-day*, 1935–50) 73, 83–105, 191, 199
Heseltine, Nigel (ed. *Wales*, 1939) 71, 73–4
Hill, Greg (ed. *The Anglo-Welsh Review*, 1984–8) 102, 110, 112
Hitchins, Steven 129
Hodges, Cyril 109, 131
Hodgkiss, Peter 107
Hollindrake, Sybil 113
Hooker, Jeremy 117, 118, 121, 139, 163
Hopkins. Chris 190, 198
Hopkins, Gerard Manley 18, 162
Horizon (1940–9) 167
Howells, Kim 141
How Green Was My Valley 90, 158
Hughes, Cledwyn 85
Hughes, Gwilym Rees (Welsh ed. *Poetry Wales*, 1967–74) 116
Hughes, Gwyneth 172
Hughes, Ted 99–100
Hughes, Thomas John ['Adfyfyr'] (ed. *Cymru Fydd*, 1888–9) 22–3
Hughes, Tristan 165
Humfrey, Belinda (ed. *New Welsh Review*, 1988–9) xi, 154–8, 178, 194
Humphreys, Emyr 73, 133, 151, 156

Independent Labour Party 43
Institute of Welsh Affairs 169
intellectuals 4, 26, 31, 45, 47, 50, 58, 60, 68, 74, 87, 93, 105, 120, 123–4, 142, 145, 147, 151, 159, 162, 177, 179, 183, 184, 189, 193, 196, 197
international 6, 13, 27, 64, 66, 69, 72, 73, 80, 85, 87, 119, 125, 127–9, 139, 140, 142, 144, 145, 147, 148, 149–50, 158, 166, 185, 190, 196
Iorwerth, Dylan 140
Iwan, Dafydd 135

Jackson, Russell 161
Jarvis, Matthew xi, 128, 129, 165, 179, 191, 193, 195, 198

Jenkins, David 185, 198
Jenkins, Gwyn 61, 62, 189, 190, 198
Jenkins, Islwyn 101, 135
Jenkins, Mike (ed. *Poetry Wales*, 1986–92; ed. *Red Poets*, 1997) xii, 121, 123, 125, 154, 160, 164, 172
Jenkins, Nigel 118, 121, 122, 125, 153, 159, 162
John, Angela V. 158, 186, 198, 200
John, Augustus 62, 93
John, Ieuan E. 94
Johnson B. S. 117
Jones, Alun R. (ed. *Mabon*, 1972) 134–5
Jones, Aled 185, 199
Jones, Bobi xii, 98, 122, 123, 171
Jones, David 97, 109, 118, 135, 166
Jones, Elias Henry (ed. *The Welsh Outlook*, 1927–33) 68–70
Jones, Glyn xii, 70, 71, 73, 78, 82, 83, 84, 85, 90, 94, 117, 125, 155, 160, 190, 198
Jones, Gwyn (ed. *The Welsh Review*, 1939, 1944–8) 60, 77, 86–95, 101, 102, 116, 135, 155, 159, 176, 183, 191
Jones, Harry Pritchard 133
Jones, Huw (co-editor *The Anglo-Welsh Review*, 1988) 102, 112
Jones, Jack 91, 135, 160
Jones, Kathryn 145
Jones, Sally Roberts (ed. *Roundyhouse*, 1999–) 159, 171
Jones, T. Gwynn 63, 68, 70
Jones, T. H. 126
Jones, Thomas [TJ] (ed. *The Welsh Outlook*, 1914–16) 61, 64–6, 68, 70, 77, 92, 93, 183
Jones-Davies, Frances (ed. *Cambria*, 2007–) 170
Jones-Davis, Henry (ed. *Cambria*, 1997–2007) 170

Kilbrandon Report (1973)106
King of Ashes, The 142, 146, 193, 196
Kluge, Alexander 184, 199
Kretz, Thomas 159
Krippendorf, Klaus 7, 185, 188

Labour Party; Labour Government 59, 69, 104, 188, 198
language issues 2, 4, 7, 8, 10, 21, 23, 24, 31 44, 47, 48, 62, 69, 79–81, 86, 87, 98, 103, 104, 106, 110, 116, 122, 123, 124, 130, 138, 139, 140, 142, 145, 150, 178–9, 183
Lampeter 17, 155
Lawrence, D. H. 83
Leaf Magazine (2010–) 172, 175
Leavis, F. R. 102
Ledbetter, Katherine 17, 187, 198
Lehmann, John 72
Lehtonen, Mikko 176, 198
Lewis, Alun 72, 75, 84, 89, 157
Lewis, E. Glyn 91–2, 93
Lewis, Idwal 185, 197
Lewis, Saunders 60, 75, 79, 92, 98, 135, 138, 159
Lewis, Tecwyn 64, 190
Lewis, Wyndham (ed. *Blast*, 1914–15), 168
Liberal; Liberalism; Liberal Party 5, 7, 10, 11, 23, 25, 26, 27, 29, 31, 35, 39, 41, 42, 43, 46,48, 49, 52, 56, 57, 59, 61,63, 64, 66, 78, 87, 88, 89, 94, 105, 141, 181, 188, 198
Library of Wales 128, 150
Life and Letters To-day (1935–50) xii, 60, 82, 83–5, 86, 88, 90, 190, 191, 199
Literature Committee (Welsh Arts Council) 100, 104, 107, 111, 131, 133, 152, 193, 194
Liverpool 50, 89
Liverpool Echo 77
Llenor, Y [The Man of Letters] (1895–8) 31, 37
Llewelyn-Williams, W. 40, 53, 56, 189
Llewellyn Williams, Alun 72
Llewellyn, Richard 158
Lloyd, David 123, 192
Llwyd, Iwan 125
London Kelt, The (1895–1917) 45–8, 189, 199
London Magazine, The (1732–) 137
London Mercury, The (1919–39) 87
London Welsh 11, 43, 46, 56, 67, 81, 82, 9, 105, 106
London Welshman, The (1959–) 116

Lonely Editor, The 103, 186, 191, 192, 193, 199
Longley, Michael 155, 156
Lucas, John 126
Lyon, Janet 189, 198

Mabon (1969–76) 107, 131, 132, 133–5, 178
McCaig, Norman 155
MacCarthy, Desmond 83
MacDiarmid, Hugh xii, 73, 90, 160
Macdonald Smith, Peter 88, 119, 156, 191, 192, 199
McGuinness, Patrick 129, 165
MacNeice, Louis 98
Machen, Arthur 46, 91, 92
Madden, Lionel 185, 187, 199
Marinetti, Filippo Tomasso 168
Masson, Ursula 188, 198
Mathias, Roland (ed. *The Anglo-Welsh Review*, 1960–76) xi, 12, 79, 94–102, 103–104, 108, 109, 110, 112, 118, 120,125, 127, 135, 155, 183, 186, 191, 192, 193, 196, 199
Menai, Hugh 80, 87
Merchant, W. Moelwyn 75, 118, 190
Meredith, Christopher 156
Merriman, Catherine 163
Merthyr 10, 11, 14, 19, 20, 72, 125, 160, 186, 199, 200
Merthyr Historian, The 186, 199, 200
Michelsen, Helle (asst. ed. *Planet*, 1998–2006; ed. 2006–11) 147
Mills, Christopher xii, 121
Mills, Ida M. 113
Minhinnick, Robert (ed. *Poetry Wales*, 1997–2008) xi, xii, 118, 121, 123, 124, 125–8, 155, 156, 172, 193
Modernist Magazines Project, Brown's University 190, 198
modernism 18, 56, 60, 71, 72, 82, 83, 145, 180, 189, 199
Moore, Dylan (ed. *CFUK*, 2006–10; co-ed. *The Raconteur*, 2009–12; ed. *Wales Arts Review*, 2012) 166, 172, 173
Morgan, Clare 143, 193
Morgan, Gerald (ed. *Poetry Wales*, 1967–9) 116–17

Morgan, Kenneth O. 11, 60, 71, 86, 189, 190, 192
Morgan, Richard Humphreys (joint ed. *Cymru Fydd*, 1889–91) 123
Morris, Delyth 145
Morris, Lewis 18, 27, 41, 46, 50, 187
Morrisson, Mark 189, 199

Nairn, Tom 26, 169, 187, 199
National Assembly for Wales 106, 165
nationalist/nationalism 3, 7, 22, 24–6, 33, 40, 41, 50, 54, 60, 72, 78, 84, 119, 127, 138, 139, 141, 142, 162, 170, 185, 187, 196, 199
National Library of Wales 6, 158, 184, 185, 187, 189, 192, 198, 199, 200
Negt, Oscar 184, 199
New Age, The (1894–1938) 185
New Signatures (1931) 72
New Welsh Review (1988–) xii, 1, 7, 8, 107, 112, 113, 151, 154–68, 175, 177, 178, 183, 191, 192, 193, 194, 199
Nicholas, T. E. 164
Ninnau 155
Nonconformity, Nonconformist 2, 10, 28, 44, 60, 71, 79, 140, 160, 164, 171
Norris, Leslie 117, 139
North, Christopher (pseudonym John Wilson) 3

Orme, Eliza 29, 188
Ormond, John 91, 131, 139
O'Rourke, Ciaran 166
Osborne, John 99
Osmond, John (ed. *Arcade*, 1980–2; ed. *Agenda*, 1994–) 140–1, 144, 152–3, 159, 169, 194
O'Sullivan, Seumas (ed. *The Dublin Magazine*, 1923–78) 90
O'Sullivan, Tyrone 164
Owen, Tomos xi, 66, 189, 199

Page, Rev. Alun L. 96
Parnell, Mary 159
Parnell, Michael (ed. *New Welsh Review*, Summer 1991) 157–8
Parry, Winnie, 39, 188
Parry-Williams, T. H. 118
Paulin, Tom 172

Index

Penvro, The 96, 191
Perie-Williams, Gwladys 67
Perrin, Jim 162
Petit, Pascal 127
Peyman, Eric 97
Phillips, Elspeth 42
Phillips, Nora 42
Pikoulis, John 120, 123
Pinsent, Arthur 94
Plaid Cymru 59, 104, 106, 113, 158
Planet (1970–80; 1985–) xii, 7, 8, 64, 100, 101, 107, 111, 112, 117, 120, 131, 135–51, 152, 155, 159, 160, 161, 162, 164, 167, 175, 177, 178, 183, 188, 190, 191, 192, 193, 197
Plebs or *The Rhondda Socialist* (1909) 59
Poetry Wales (1965–) xii, 100, 107, 112, 113–31, 132, 153, 161, 167, 175, 177, 178, 183, 191, 192, 193,194, 196, 197
Poole, Richard (ed. *Poetry Wales*, 1992–6) xii, 122–4, 127, 139, 145, 147, 172
Popham, Mrs Cecil 55
Powys Review, The 155
post-modern 143, 168
Powys, John Cowper 139
Pryce, Sioned 39, 188
Prys-Jones, A. G. 97
Pugh, Sheenagh 119, 120, 122, 127, 159, 172
Pykett, Lynn 185, 199

Quattrocento 172

Raconteur, The (2009–12) 166, 172–3, 175
Raglan, Lord 79–82, 178
Raine, Allen 38, 39, 54, 55
Raymond, Gary (co-ed. *The Raconteur*, 2009–12) 172
readers, readership 1, 2, 3, 4, 5, 8, 11, 13, 14, 16, 18, 19, 21, 23, 25, 33, 37, 39, 41, 44, 53, 58, 59, 61, 80, 88, 93, 103, 110, 111, 118, 119, 129, 130, 132, 139, 141, 145, 149, 154, 156, 161, 167, 171, 173, 176, 178, 179, 180, 181, 182
Rebecca (1973–93, with breaks) 107, 111, 141, 151–2, 153, 194

Red Dragon, The (1882–7) 3, 7, 10–22, 23, 25, 27, 29, 31, 40, 49, 61, 178, 186
Red Poets (1997–) 172
Rees, Alwyn D. (ed. *The Welsh Anvil*, 1949–58) 94–5
Rees, Ioan Bowen 94
Rees, Olwen 96
Rees, Sarah Jane ['Cranogwen'] (ed. *Y Frythones* [The Female Brython], 1839–1916) 8
Rees-Jones, Deryn (guest ed. *Poetry Wales*, October 1996) 124
Reeves, Robin (ed. *New Welsh Review*, 1991–2001) xii, 152, 158–63, 164
Reeves, Roseanne xi, xii, 194
religion 3, 6, 24, 33, 36, 37, 41, 44, 47, 50, 60, 61, 62, 63, 70, 78, 93, 187, 200
reviews 15, 21, 24, 29, 63, 64, 68, 69, 71, 72, 85, 87, 90, 92, 93, 97, 98, 99, 101, 103, 108, 109, 111, 115, 117, 120, 123, 125, 127, 130–1, 132, 133, 135, 137, 139, 140, 142, 143, 147, 148, 150, 153, 154, 155, 157, 158, 161, 162, 171, 172, 175
Rendell, Stuart 23, 30, 45
Rhydderch, Francesca (ed. *New Welsh Review*, 2002–2008) xi, 164–5, 166
Rhydderch, Samantha Wynne 126, 127
Rhys, Ernest 33, 43, 46
Rhys, Eva xi, xii
Rhys, Keidrych (ed. *Wales*, 1937–9; 1943–8; 1958–9) xi, xii, 5, 60, 71–3, 84, 85, 86, 03, 94, 101, 102, 105, 117, 176, 178, 180, 183, 185
Rhys, Morgan John (ed. *Y Cylchgrawn Cymraeg*, 1793) 2
Richards, Alun xii, xi, 81, 82, 137
Roberts, Brynley F. 6, 15, 23, 184, 185, 186, 187, 199
Roberts, Kate 90, 92, 142, 159
Roberts, Lynette 73, 78, 110, 120
Roberts, Michael 72
Roberts, Richard Glyn 150
Roberts, Silyn 68
Rothkirch, Alyce von xi, 7, 61, 69, 185, 187, 189, 190, 196, 199
Roundyhouse (1999–) 171–2
Rowe, Dilys 79

Said, Edward 161
Sassoon, Siegfried 126
Scannell, Vernon 126
Second Aeon (1966–74) 107, 112, 131–2, 180, 192, 193, 194, 196
'Second Flowering, The' (Meic Stephens, 1967) 116, 122, 192, 195, 197, 198
Seren y Mynydd [The Mountain Star] 32
Sheers, Owen 126, 127, 172
Simpson, Mercer 156
Skald (1994–2008) 172
Skoulding, Zoe (co-editor *Skald*, 1994–2007; ed. *Poetry Wales*, 2008–) xi, xii, 128–31, 172, 181, 193
Smith, Arthur (ed. *Cambrensis*, 1988–2006) 154
Smith, Brian (co-ed. *Roundyhouse*, 1999–) 171–2
Smith, Dai 86, 142, 144, 162, 171, 191
Smith, Peter MacDonald 89, 119, 156, 191, 192, 199
South Wales Worker, The (1911) 59
Stead, Peter 158
Stephens, Meic (ed. *Poetry Wales*, 1965–7; 1969–73) xi, xii, 64, 85, 105, 107, 113–18, 10, 125, 127, 128, 135, 137, 152, 153, 160, 170, 171, 183, 187, 188, 190, 191, 192, 193, 194, 199, 200
Stephens, Thomas 10, 11
Stevenson, Anne 123, 147
subsidy, subsidise 79, 103–4, 107–08, 111, 112, 117, 120, 122, 133, 141, 152, 175, 177, 192, 200
Sullivan, Alvin 83, 190, 200
Swansea 3, 14, 15, 48, 139, 150

Thacker, Andrew 190, 198
Thomas, Ben Bowen 99
Thomas, Dafydd Elis 118
Thomas, Dylan 71, 73, 81, 84, 85, 92, 93, 98, 118, 133
Thomas, Ed 145, 165
Thomas, Edward 67, 102
Thomas, George 135, 137, 162
Thomas, Gwyn 92, 94
Thomas, Gwyn (co-editor *Mabon*, 1972) 135

Thomas, John Ormond 91
Thomas, M. Wynn 2, 4, 71, 125, 156, 171, 179, 184, 187, 188, 190, 192, 196, 197, 198, 200
Thomas, Ned (ed. *Planet*, 1970–80; 1985–90) 7, 111, 116, 135–42, 143, 147, 152, 161, 171, 178, 185, 192, 193, 200
Thomas, R. S. xii, 77, 84, 85, 94, 109, 111, 115, 117, 118, 122, 123, 13, 135, 142, 143, 179, 190, 191, 196, 200
Times Literary Supplement, The 77
Tóibín, Colm 178–80, 195, 200
Torrance, Chris 160, 172
Traethodydd, Y [The Essayist] (1845–) 3
Trahair, Emily (assoc. ed. *Planet*, 2006–12; ed. 2012–) xi, 149–51, 194, 195
Trezise, Rachel 150, 169, 172
Tripp, John 117, 137, 138, 139, 140
Tripp, John, Poetry Award 159
Triskel Press 113

University of Wales 32, 35, 37, 41, 42, 56
University of Wales Association for Welsh Literature in English 155
University of Wales, Guild of Graduates of 94

Wain, John 99
Wainwright, Eddie 134
Wales (1894–97) 5, 31–9, 40, 48, 49, 51, 176, 188
Wales (1911–14) 52–7, 62, 64
Wales (1937–9, 1943–8, 1958–9) xi, xii, 5, 72–83, 85, 93, 94, 101, 102, 117, 176, 180, 190, 198
Wales Arts Review (2012–) 171
Walters, Huw 2, 3, 6, 57, 184, 185, 187, 188, 189, 200
Walters H. G. 100, 110
Ward, John Powell (ed. *Poetry Wales*, 1975–80) xii, 118, 127, 132, 156, 193
Wack, Amy 159
Watkins, Vernon xii, 71, 73, 75, 84
Webb, Harri (ed. *The Welsh Republican*, 1950–7) 104, 133
Wells, Nigel 162

Welsh Academy, The [Yr Academi Gymreig] 106, 120, 154, 194
Welsh Anvil, The [*Yr Einion*] (1949–58) 60, 94–5
Welsh Arts Council xii, 100, 102, 103, 104, 106, 107, 108, 110, 111, 112, 115, 116, 117, 120, 12, 131, 132, 133, 135, 137, 140, 141, 152, 153, 154, 155, 156, 159, 160, 161, 168, 171, 175, 180, 192, 193, 194, 200
Welsh Books Council 106, 149, 154, 167, 168, 170, 175, 177
Welsh Extremist, The 138, 185, 193, 200
Welsh-language periodicals 3, 6, 8, 29, 31, 45, 64, 112, 178, 194
Welsh Language Society 116, 138
'Welsh noir' 163, 164
Welsh Outlook, The (1914–33) 5, 7, 47, 60–70, 86, 87, 102, 178, 185, 189, 190, 191, 198, 199
Welsh Republican, The [*Y Gwerinaethwr*] (1950–7) 104
Welsh Review, The (1891–2) 26–31, 40, 47
Welsh Review, The (1906–07) 109–52
Welsh Review, The (1939; 1944–8) xii, 60, 77, 82, 86–94, 95, 102, 117, 157, 160, 176, 190, 198
Welsh writing in English 2, 116, 123, 154, 155, 156, 163, 164, 166
Welsh Writing in English: A Guide to Welsh Literature 17 (ed. M. Wynn Thomas) 187, 196, 197, 198
Welsh Writing in English: A Yearbook of Welsh Writing [see also *Almanac*] 191, 192, 196, 199
Wenborn, Neil 163
Western Mail, The 78, 80, 144, 145, 147, 193

Wigley, Anna 172
Wilkins, Charles (ed. *The Red Dragon*, 1882–5) 3, 20, 21, 33, 36, 57, 182, 186, 187, 193, 195, 197, 198, 200
Williams, Daniel G. 141, 144, 187, 193, 195, 196, 197, 198, 200
William, Emlyn 80
Williams, Frances 126
Williams, Glanmor 23, 187, 200
Williams, Gwenfreda 93
Williams, Gwyn A. 10, 156, 184, 186, 187, 189, 200.
Williams, Herbert Lloyd (ed. *Roundyhouse*, 1997–) 115, 154, 172
Williams, Kyffin 135
Williams, Alis Mallt 42, 43
Williams, Nerys 179, 195, 200
Williams, Raymond 1, 8, 141, 147, 150, 156, 159, 166, 193, 200
Williams, Rhodri 107, 111, 112, 120, 121, 142, 154, 156, 159, 193, 200
Williams, Siân Rhiannon 196, 200
Wilson, A. N. 186, 200
Wilson, John 3
Windsor, Penny 161
Wintle, Justin 191, 200
women's issues, women's writing 8, 12, 18, 22, 24, 29, 36, 39, 40, 42, 43, 53, 55, 57, 59, 63, 66, 67, 69, 85, 90, 105, 10, 113, 119, 122, 124, 144, 158, 159, 164
Woolf, Virginia 83
Writers of Wales series 106
Wynne-Rhydderch, Samantha 126

Yellow Crane, The (1995–2006) 171–2
Young Wales (1895–1904) 39–45, 48, 49, 52, 188, 189

Zobole, Ernie 144